P9-DBN-540

UNDERSTANDING SOCIAL EXCLUSION

Understanding Social Exclusion

Phil Agulnik
Brian Barry
Tania Burchardt
Simon Burgess
Martin Evans
Howard Glennerster
John Hills (editor)
John Hobcraft
Kathleen Kiernan
Julian Le Grand (editor)
Ruth Lupton
Abigail McKnight
Katharine Mumford
David Piachaud (editor)
Anne Power
Carol Propper
Liz Richardson
Jo Sparkes
Holly Sutherland

HN
400
.M26
U53
2002

WITHDRAWN

OXFORD
UNIVERSITY PRESS

OXFORD
UNIVERSITY PRESS

Great Clarendon Street, Oxford OX2 6DP

Oxford University Press is a department of the University of Oxford.
It furthers the University's objective of excellence in research, scholarship,
and education by publishing worldwide in

Oxford New York

Auckland Bangkok Buenos Aires Cape Town Chennai
Dar es Salaam Delhi Hong Kong Istanbul Karachi Kolkata
Kuala Lumpur Madrid Melbourne Mexico City Mumbai Nairobi
São Paulo Shanghai Taipei Tokyo Toronto

Oxford is a registered trade mark of Oxford University Press
in the UK and in certain other countries

Published in the United States
by Oxford University Press Inc., New York

© the several contributors, 2002
editorial matter © John Hills, Julian Le Grand, and
David Piachaud, 2002

The moral rights of the author have been asserted

Database right Oxford University Press (maker)

First published 2002

All rights reserved. No part of this publication may be reproduced,
stored in a retrieval system, or transmitted, in any form or by any means,
without the prior permission in writing of Oxford University Press,
or as expressly permitted by law, or under terms agreed with the appropriate
reprographics rights organization. Enquiries concerning reproduction
outside the scope of the above should be sent to the Rights Department,
Oxford University Press, at the address above.

You must not circulate this book in any other binding or cover
and you must impose this same condition on any acquirer.

British Library Cataloguing in Publication Data
Data available

Library of Congress Cataloguing in Publication Data
Data available

ISBN 0–19–925107-X (hbk.)
ISBN 0–19–925194-0 (pbk.)

5 7 9 10 8 6 4

Typeset by Newgen Imaging Systems (P) Ltd., Chennai, India
Printed in Great Britain
on acid-free paper by
Biddles Ltd, *www.biddles.co.uk*

IPFW
WITHDRAWN
AUG 2 2006
HELMKE LIBRARY

Acknowledgements

This book brings together some parts of the recent research from the ESRC Research Centre for Analysis of Social Exclusion (CASE) at the London School of Economics. The Centre started work in October 1997 and is supported by core funding from the Economic and Social Research Council, whose support made possible much of the work reported here. The authors and editors are very grateful to ESRC for this support and to others who have supported parts of the research, including the Suntory and Toyota International Centres for Economics and Related Disciplines, the Joseph Rowntree Foundation, the Nuffield Foundation, the UNICEF Innocenti Research Centre, and the Gatsby Charitable Foundation. We should also like to thank warmly all those working in local authorities and the NHS, local community groups, and residents who gave their time so generously in answering Ruth Lupton's and others' questions for the areas study. We are also grateful to the Data Archive at Essex University for access to various datasets used in this book, including the National Child Development Study, the 1970 Birth Cohort Study, the British Household Panel Survey, the Family Expenditure Survey, and the General Household Survey; to the Office for National Statistics, for access to data from the New Earnings Survey; and to the Department of Social Security for the Family Resources Survey and Households Below Average Income dataset. Data from the Family Expenditure Survey are Crown Copyright. They have been made available by the Office for National Statistics (ONS) through the Data Archive and are used by permission. Neither the ONS nor the Data Archive bears any responsibility for the analysis or interpretation of the data reported here.

The chapters of the book have benefited greatly from comments and suggestions from other members of CASE. We are most grateful for this and for support from Jane Dickson, Nic Warner, and Charles Affor. But our greatest debt is to Rebecca Morris who assembled the whole typescript and consolidated the separate chapters into a form suitable for publication. We are very grateful for this and for all her other efficient assistance during her time at CASE.

John Hills
Julian Le Grand
David Piachaud

London
June 2001

Contents

Contents

List of Figures

List of Tables

Notes on Contributors

Phil Agulnik is currently working on pension policy for the Department for Work and Pensions. He has recently completed a Ph.D. in the Department of Social Policy at the London School of Economics (LSE) on 'Pension Reform in the UK'. He has also written on the dynamics of tax benefit reform, and the basic income proposal.

Brian Barry is Arnold A. Saltzman Professor in Philosophy and Political Science at Columbia University, New York, and Emeritus Professor of Political Science at the LSE. He is the author of *Theories of Justice, Justice as Impartiality*, and *Culture and Equality: An Egalitarian Critique of Multiculturalism*. His most recent book is *Why Justice Matters*.

Tania Burchardt is a Research Fellow at the ESRC Research Centre for Analysis of Social Exclusion (CASE) at the LSE. She recently published *Enduring Economic Exclusion: Disabled people, income and work* for the Joseph Rowntree Foundation, and is continuing her research on disabled people and operationalization of Sen's capabilities framework.

Simon Burgess is a Professor of Economics in the Department of Economics at the University of Bristol. His main research interests lie in labour economics, analysis of poverty and household income dynamics, incentives in organizations, and unemployment dynamics.

Martin Evans is a senior Research Fellow in the Department of Social and Policy Studies at the University of Bath. He was previously a Research Fellow at CASE. His research includes cross-national comparisons of social security systems, examination of 'welfare to work' policies in the UK and other countries, the geographical distribution of public spending, and trends in area polarization and disadvantage.

Howard Glennerster is Professor Emeritus of Social Policy at the LSE and Co-Director of CASE. He has written widely on many aspects of social policy although he has specialized in the economics and finance of social policy. His recent books include: *British Social Policy Since 1945* (2nd edn.); *Paying for Welfare* (3rd edn.); and *The State of Welfare: The Economics of Social Spending*.

John Hills is Director of CASE and Professor of Social Policy at the LSE. His research interests include the distributional effects of tax and welfare systems, income distribution, social security, and housing finance. Recent publications include *Paying for Health, Education and Housing: How does the Centre Pull the Purse Strings?*, and *Public Policy for the 21st Century: Social and Economic Essays in Memory of Henry Neuburger*.

John Hobcraft is Professor of Population Studies in the Department of Social Policy at the LSE. His research interests span both developed and developing countries and he has worked extensively on child mortality and fertility. His recent research within CASE is concerned with the emergence of social exclusion through the life-course from childhood to adulthood. He is a member of *Academia Europaea* and of the Committee on Population of the US National Academy of Sciences.

Kathleen Kiernan is Professor of Social Policy and Demography at the LSE, and Co-Director of CASE. She has published on a wide range of aspects of family life, including teenage parenthood, divorce, cohabitation, non-marital childbearing, lone-motherhood, and the demography of disadvantage. Much of her research uses longitudinal data from the British birth cohort studies and more recently comparative data from a range of European countries. Publications include *Lone-Motherhood in the Twentieth Century*.

Julian Le Grand is the Richard Titmuss Professor of Social Policy at the London School of Economics and Co-Director of CASE. His research interests include health and welfare policy. Recent publications include *Health Care and Cost Containment in the European Union*.

Ruth Lupton is a Research Officer at CASE, working on the Centre's study of disadvantaged areas and neighbourhoods. *Places Apart?*, the first report of that study, was published by CASE in 2001. She has a particular interest in the performance of public service organizations in disadvantaged areas, and is currently conducting doctoral research into the organization and processes of secondary schools in challenging circumstances.

Abigail McKnight is the Toyota Research Fellow at CASE. She is a labour economist and her research interests include: low wage employment, inequality, evaluation of welfare to work programmes, and education. Her recent publications include findings from the evaluation of *Earnings Top-up* and the *New Deal for Lone Parents*, carried out for the Department of Social Security.

Katharine Mumford is a Research Officer at CASE, working on a study involving families in East London. Other research interests include the problem of low demand for housing and area abandonment. Recent publications include *Talking to Families in East London: A Report on the First Stage of the Research*, and *The Slow Death of Great Cities? Urban Abandonment or Urban Renaissance?*

David Piachaud is Professor of Social Policy at the LSE. He was Social Policy Adviser in the Prime Minister's Unit (1974–9) and has been Consultant to the European Commission, ILO, OECD, and WHO. He has written extensively on poverty, social security, and social policy.

Anne Power is Professor of Social Policy at LSE, and Deputy Director of CASE. Her research interests cover housing and urban policy, including housing management, urban regeneration, and community involvement and race relations. She was a member of the Urban Task Force and is a member of the Sustainable Development Commission. She advises the government on urban, housing, and social exclusion issues. Recent publications include *Cities for a Small Country* and *Estates on the Edge*.

Carol Propper is Professor of Economics in the Department of Economics at the University of Bristol, and a Co-Director of CASE. Her research interests include the role of household formation in income and poverty dynamics, the impact of incentives on the behaviour of suppliers of education and health care services, and fairness in the delivery of health care. Recent publications include articles on 'The Demand for Private Insurance in the UK', 'Expenditure on Health Care in the UK', and 'Do Doctors Respond to Financial Incentives? UK Family Doctors and the GP Fundholder Scheme'.

Liz Richardson is a Research Officer at CASE. She has particular interest in community self-help, and has been developing and evaluating a training and small-scale grants programme financed by the Gatsby Charitable Foundation at the National Tenant Resource Centre, Trafford Hall, Chester. Her report *Barefoot Basic Skills Work and Intensive Learning: Two Experimental Basic Skills Projects*, was recently published by CASE.

Jo Sparkes is now working in the Women and Equality Unit at the Cabinet Office. She was formerly a Research Officer at LSE, London and the Centre for Educational Research at LSE, where the chapter included here was written.

Holly Sutherland directs the Microsimulation Unit in the Department of Applied Economics at Cambridge University. Her particular interests include the incorporation of gender effects in microsimulation analysis and the development of comparable methods across countries. She recently co-edited *Microsimulation Modelling for Policy Analysis: Challenges and Innovations*.

1

Introduction

TANIA BURCHARDT, JULIAN LE GRAND,
AND DAVID PIACHAUD

Social exclusion has attracted much attention in recent years in Britain and elsewhere. Although the concept originated in continental Europe it is now part of the common currency of British social policy debates. The Lisbon Summit committed EU member states to adopt the promotion of social cohesion and inclusion as a strategic goal, and the concept had already directly entered the British Government's policy process with the setting up of the interdepartmental Social Exclusion Unit by the Labour Government of Tony Blair in 1997.

The Economic and Social Research Council was a pioneer in encouraging British exploration of the concept, picking social exclusion as one of its nine central themes for focusing social science research in 1995. One consequence of this was the establishment at the London School of Economics of the ESRC's Centre for Analysis of Social Exclusion (CASE) in 1997, of which this book is one product. All the authors of this book are associated with CASE, and it represents an attempt to pull together some of the many strands of the Centre's work over its first three years, together with related work conducted elsewhere, to gain some understanding of the phenomenon of social exclusion in Britain at the beginning of the twenty-first century.

This chapter begins with a discussion of possible answers to the question, what exactly does social exclusion mean? It then discusses different approaches to the analysis and understanding of social exclusion and its causes, some of which are illustrated in subsequent chapters. Finally, it explains the structure of the rest of the book.

CONCEPTS OF SOCIAL EXCLUSION[1]

Social exclusion is a contested term.[2] The concept can be traced to Weber, who identified exclusion as one form of social closure (Parkin 1979). He saw exclusionary

---

[1] Earlier versions of some parts of this chapter were previously included in Burchardt, Le Grand, and Piachaud (1999) and Burchardt (2000a).

[2] As Weinberg and Ruano-Borbalan (1993) note, 'reading numerous enquiries and reports on exclusion reveals a profound confusion among experts' (quoted by Atkinson 1998: 7). Some reject the term entirely on the grounds that it is 'highly problematic' (Peters 1996: 35)

closure as the attempt of one group to secure for itself a privileged position at the expense of some other group through a process of subordination. Taking a similar line, Jordan (1996) draws attention to the active exclusion of one group by another. An extreme example is gated communities, with private provision of high-quality services, and security to prevent 'outsiders' benefiting from the same services (see Brian Barry in Chapter 2). Less extreme examples, but more generally applicable, might include conscious or unconscious racial discrimination, restricted access to higher education, and use of 'old boy networks' for the distribution of top jobs.

Modern usage of the term 'social exclusion' appears to have originated in France, where it was used to refer primarily to those who slipped through the Bismarckian social insurance system; the socially excluded were those who were administratively excluded by the state (Lenoir 1974; Duffy 1997). 'Les exclus' (the excluded) were those who fell through the net of social protection: in the 1970s, disabled people, lone parents, and the uninsured unemployed, especially young adults (Evans 1998). Later, the increasing intensity of social problems on peripheral estates in large cities led to a broadening of the definition to include disaffected youth and isolated individuals. The concept has particular resonance in countries which share with France a republican tradition, in which social cohesion is thought to be essential to maintaining the contract on which society is founded (Silver 1995). Where solidarity is championed, the existence of groups who feel excluded threatens to undermine the unity of the state.

Later French thinking has emphasized the importance of unemployment (Paugam 1993). This concern with unemployment, especially long-term unemployment, was picked up by other continental European countries, and, together with an increasing recognition of the impact of globalization on national and regional economic structure, this led to the establishment of the European Observatory on social exclusion, and to the adoption of various 'social inclusion' resolutions at EU level.

The idea that social exclusion is 'a necessary and inherent characteristic of unequal post-industrial capitalism founded around a flexible labour market' is most fully explored by Byrne (1999: 128). The socially excluded are characterized by him not as a permanent underclass, but rather as a reserve army of labour, continually changing places with those in low-status employment, and serving to keep the power of the working class in check. An analysis of this kind leaves solutions in short supply, but the underlying cause is clear.

Americans tend to use terms such as 'ghettoization', 'marginalization', and 'the underclass', rather than social exclusion, but the concepts are not unrelated. The 'underclass' is usually taken to consist of several generations of people from ethnic minorities, living in ghettos and in receipt of welfare, cut off from the mainstream of society, and representing a threat to it (Murray 1999). Responsibility for the plight of the underclass tends to be placed primarily on the individuals themselves—their perceived antisocial behaviour (drug-taking and crime) and lack of willingness to seek employment—but also on a benefit system which encourages dependency and penalizes work. Although there are many critics of the emphasis on behavioural factors and personality traits, research on 'the underclass' has drawn attention to the ways that geographical concentration may play a part in mechanisms of social exclusion (W. Wilson 1987).

The United Nations Development Programme has been at the forefront of attempts to conceptualize social exclusion across the developed and developing world (Gore and Figueiredo 1997). A series of within-country studies revealed the significance of enforceable civil and social rights—for example, to adequate health care, basic education, and material well-being. Social exclusion was therefore conceptualized as lack of recognition of basic rights, or where that recognition existed, lack of access to political and legal systems necessary to make those rights a reality. Although this approach is less common in the UK, several studies have pursued the theme of discrimination and lack of enforceable rights (Sayce 2000; Leslie 1997).

In the UK, use of the term 'social exclusion' began in a political climate in which the existence of 'poverty' was not recognized by Conservative politicians. The adoption of social exclusion terminology allowed debates about social policy to continue at a European level without offending their sensibilities (Berghman 1995). By the late 1990s, its use was commonplace by Labour politicians, although in some cases the meaning appeared to have shifted to a narrower focus on exclusion as lack of paid work (Levitas 1998).

For some outside these groups it is simply a currently fashionable way of talking about poverty (Levitas 1996, 1997) or even about simply a subset of the poor.[3] For others, it is a broader conception, not focusing primarily on low income (as most conceptions of poverty do), but including polarization, differentiation, and inequality.[4] Some reject any identification of social exclusion with class or inequality, arguing that the latter concerns people's positions on a vertical axis ('up' or 'down') whereas the former is about a quite different geometrical shape: about being 'in' or 'out' of a circle (Touraine 1991).

AGENCY AND FUNDAMENTAL CAUSES

It is partly as a result of the broad compass of social exclusion that views as to its fundamental causes differ so markedly. Three schools of thought are represented in the literature: (1) placing individuals' behaviour and moral values at centre stage (as in the 'underclass' debate); (2) highlighting the role of institutions and systems—from the welfare state to late capitalism and globalization; and (3) emphasizing issues of discrimination and lack of enforced rights.

---

[3] For instance, in Scandinavia the socially excluded are taken to be the 'poorest of the poor' (Abrahamson and Hansen 1996).

[4] The ESRC's social exclusion 'thematic priority' is stated as: 'understanding the processes by which individuals and their communities become polarised, socially differentiated and unequal' (ESRC 1997).

Differing views as to the fundamental causes of social exclusion correspond to differing views about agency; different answers to the question, 'Who is doing the excluding?' A concern with agency is identified by Atkinson (1998) as a key feature of the social exclusion debate. An emphasis on moral values and behavioural explanations is associated with blaming the socially excluded for their own plight.[5] At the opposite extreme, an assertion that civil and economic institutions constrain opportunities for some individuals and groups, suggests a lack of agency on both sides: exclusion is the outcome of the system (unintended or at least beyond the control of any individual or organization), while the socially excluded lack the opportunity to remedy their situation. Indeed a lack of autonomy or decision-making power is sometimes suggested as a definition of exclusion (Askonas and Stewart 2000). Jordan's analysis, according to which the excluded are at the mercy of the powerful, places responsibility firmly with the elite. The exercise of agency by some, acting to protect their own interests, excludes others.

All conceptions of social exclusion have to contend with the possibility of voluntary or self-exclusion. Brain Barry (Chapter 2, this volume) discusses whether the apparently voluntary exclusion of some minority groups from wider society should really be considered as such. The theme is taken up again in Chapter 3, in the search for an empirical measure of social exclusion, although in practice it is found to be difficult to separate voluntary from involuntary non-participation empirically. The collective exercise of agency to counteract exclusion is explored by Liz Richardson and Katharine Mumford in Chapter 12, through an evaluation of the work of self-help community groups.

EMPIRICAL APPROACHES TO SOCIAL EXCLUSION

Those who have sought to operationalize the concept of social exclusion have tended to adopt one of two approaches. The first is to concentrate on specific (and often extreme) problems, which are taken to be instances of social exclusion. The Social Exclusion Unit, set up in the Cabinet Office in Britain after the 1997 General Election, avoided becoming enmeshed in definitional issues, focusing instead on particular manifestations such as teenage pregnancy and street homelessness (SEU 1998a, 1999a). Other studies have focused on long-term unemployment (for example, Clasen, Gould, and Vincent 1997), area abandonment (Power and Mumford 1999), and social networks (DEMOS 1997).

Detailed studies are often revealing but tend not to develop a general conception of social exclusion. The second approach is to characterize social exclusion as lack of participation in key aspects of society. For example, Robinson and Oppenheim (1998) propose four lead indicators of the level of social exclusion

---

[5] Within this school of thought, a sub-group argues that the welfare system has eroded personal responsibility, in which case it is presumably the state which is the agent of exclusion.

in Britain: the proportion of the population falling below 50 per cent of average household income; the ILO unemployment rate; the proportion of 16-year-olds failing to get at least 20 GCSE points; and the Standard Mortality Ratio in Social Class IV/V in relation to other social classes. Paugam (1996), Edwards and Flatley (1996), and Howarth *et al.* (1998) also use a range of indicators across income, labour market engagement, social interaction, and health.

These approaches build on the tradition of measuring poverty and deprivation. Room (1995) makes this development explicit, arguing that the move from poverty to social exclusion involves three steps: (1) from income or expenditure to multidimensional disadvantage; (2) from static to dynamic analysis; and (3) from resources at the individual or household level to local community. This is a neat formulation, but it is oversimplified to suggest that this is a new focus. For instance, Townsend's classic study of poverty implemented both a multidimensional definition of disadvantage and a multilevel definition of resources:

… relative deprivation—by which I mean the absence or inadequacy of those diets, amenities, standards, services and activities which are common or customary in society. People are deprived of the conditions of life which ordinarily define membership of society. If they lack or are denied resources to obtain access to these conditions of life and so fulfil membership of society, they are in poverty.   (Townsend 1979: 915)

In measuring and explaining poverty in a society it is necessary first to describe the ownership and use made by individuals and by social groups of different types of resources which govern their standards of living. … [We] have identified five types: cash income, capital assets, value of employment benefits, value of public social services other than cash, and private income in kind.   (Ibid. 177).

Since the time at which Townsend was writing, new data capable of being disaggregated to small geographical areas have become available, facilitating the classification of areas which lack resources as well as individuals. The identification of multiple deprivation has also become more sophisticated: Townsend was criticized for the apparently arbitrary nature of his list of basic requirements, but later studies (Mack and Lansley 1985; Gordon *et al.* 2000) have endeavoured to establish the general public's view on which goods and services are necessities.

So neither the widening of the range of indicators relevant to identifying a lack of resources, nor the broadening of the focus from an individual- or household-level to include the community and locality should be seen as entirely new. Expanding the time horizon to facilitate dynamic analysis can be seen, at least in part, as the product of improvements in information technology and the availability of longitudinal data. Dynamic analysis has been part of the economist's toolkit for some time, especially in the USA where longitudinal datasets are more mature (see, for example, Bane and Ellwood 1994).

However there is one respect in which the concept of social exclusion can be seen as a genuine extension of its predecessors in social policy: it allows the phenomenon of interest to extend beyond non-participation due to lack of material resources. Poverty research seeks to identify those whose participation in society is constrained by lack of resources and concentrates on low income as an indicator. Research on multiple deprivation broadens the range of indicators but the objective remains an accurate identification of individuals who lack the resources to participate (see Nolan and Whelan 1996).[6] Measures of social exclusion attempt to identify not only those who lack resources, but also those whose non-participation arises in different ways: through discrimination, chronic ill health, geographical location, or cultural identification, for example. Lack of material resources remains a central and important cause of non-participation, but it does not exhaust the possibilities.

This more comprehensive concept of disadvantage is reflected in the Poverty and Social Exclusion survey (Gordon *et al.* 2000). In the section of the survey dealing with issues of social exclusion, respondents are asked not simply whether their use of services is constrained by not being able to afford it, but also whether physical accessibility, childcare, transport, time, fear, or cultural appropriateness act as constraints. Experiencing these constraints may be correlated with low income, but there are individuals who are unable to participate despite having adequate income.

So what can social exclusion add to analyses based on the concepts of poverty and deprivation? The rhetoric of social exclusion emphasizes agency and process but measurable outcomes seem similar to those used for poverty and deprivation. In this respect, social exclusion has some common ground with Sen's idea of capability poverty (Sen 1992).[7] All three reflect forms of non-participation in society, arising from constraint rather than choice. As Atkinson (1998) has argued, it may be that analysis of social exclusion constitutes a change in emphasis rather than a change in direction (see also John Hills in Chapter 13 of this volume). Existing definitions of disadvantage are sufficiently broad to incorporate attention to a range of dimensions, including non-material deprivation, to take a longitudinal view, and to allow for causes of deprivation other than low income, but in fact most research has not reflected all these elements.[8] Social exclusion reminds us of the wider field—and it is this wider approach that characterizes the rest of this book.

A FRAMEWORK FOR UNDERSTANDING SOCIAL EXCLUSION

Most academic analysis of social phenomena reflects the demarcation lines of the social sciences: sociologists have emphasized differences in behaviour

---

[6] Townsend (1979) reserved the term 'poverty' for deprivation due to a lack of resources, while allowing the scope of deprivation itself to be broader. However later commentators have not adhered to this distinction.

[7] Sen himself argues the scope of the term social exclusion should be restricted to instances where lack of participation arises through a failure of social relations (Sen 2000). How broadly 'social relations' are to be defined is another matter.

[8] Exceptions include Walker (1998) and Nolan and Whelan (1996).

between groups or between social classes; economists have concentrated on the market sector in relation to poverty, particularly the labour market; social policy analysts have concentrated on government policies and their impact. All these emphases may be valid but they each present only a partial picture. Some bolder, less boxed-in, analysts have investigated interactions but cross-boundary working has rarely been a route to academic advancement.

In thinking about social exclusion, the demarcated approach is clearly inadequate, whatever theoretical position one adopts with respect to fundamental causes. Ideally a framework for understanding social exclusion should:

1. combine the most relevant causes in a simple and clear way;
2. recognize the interaction between different types of cause or influence;
3. facilitate dynamic analysis;
4. be capable of embracing different aspects of social exclusion;
5. be applicable at different levels—individuals and communities;
6. preferably, be applicable in societies at different levels of economic and social development.

A framework is inevitably abstract, and what one person finds illuminating another may see as ramshackle and confusing. The reader must judge. One alternative is shown in Figure 1.1: an 'onion' diagram. Any level is influenced by many other levels and there is no one cause of any outcome or behaviour, whether at individual or community level.

The individual is influenced by immediate family, by community, by national forces, and ultimately by the global context. The community is influenced not

Individual: e.g. age, gender, race, disability; preferences, beliefs, and values

Family: e.g. partnership, children, caring responsibilities

Community: e.g. social and physical environment, schools, health, and social services

Local: e.g. labour market, transport

National: e.g. cultural influences, social security, legislative framework

Global: e.g. international trade, migration, climate change

Figure 1.1. *An integrated approach*

only by broader levels—national and global influences—but also by the families and individuals who constitute it. This may seem obvious, but it contrasts with much existing analysis which treats personal, family, and community influences as essentially separate factors with their independent effects.

Given the complexity of influences on individuals, it is hard to make sense of the term 'cause' in the context of social exclusion at all. If defined as some philosophers would have us believe, as an event that precedes an outcome, without which the outcome would not have happened, then it is clearly impossible to speak of a single cause of social exclusion. What may be useful is to distinguish between past and present influences on outcomes.

The influence of the past is represented by the amount of capital accrued, whether of the individual or the community. As far as social exclusion is concerned, bygones are not bygones but represent the starting point for the present. Capital may be divided into three components:

Human capital: This depends on: genetic inheritance; childhood circumstances—family, health, housing, poverty, social environment, etc.; education and training
Physical capital: Ownership of housing, land, equipment, etc.
Financial capital: Ownership of financial assets or liabilities

Physical and financial capital may be related if, say, housing is acquired by taking out a mortgage liability. So too human capital may be linked to financial capital if it is paid for by taking out a loan. For many of those facing social exclusion financial capital may be negative.

In a sense all present influences are products of the past. But if today a person makes a decision that affects some outcome, then that is more usefully thought of as a present influence, however much the tendency to make such decisions in a particular way may be a product of the past. Similarly, if there is a change in government policy, that happens in the present rather than the past. (This remains true even though the passage of time means that what is now present will soon be past.) Present influences can be separated into:

External influences: Current constraints facing an individual or community
Internal influences: Choices individuals or communities make

Figure 1.2 brings this together. The rings are the same as those shown in Figure 1.1, with the individual at the centre and spanning out to the global level. Past and present influences may operate at any of these levels, and are shown in the figure feeding in from the top. The levels themselves interact—families with schools, schools with labour markets, for example—producing outcomes, which in turn can be analysed at a range of levels. The outcomes themselves become present influences, affecting the constraints and opportunities available.

The framework outlined is not one which has been systematically applied in all the chapters of this book, but it may serve to clarify some of the complexity

Past influences (human, physical, and financial capital)

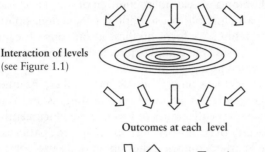

Present influences (constraints and choices)

Interaction of levels
(see Figure 1.1)

Outcomes at each level

Feedback into
influences

Figure 1.2. *Framework for analyzing social exclusion*

involved in the analysis of social exclusion. The 'onion' can be sliced in a number of different ways. Slicing 'vertically' gives the dynamic analysis which is characteristic of research on social exclusion. Slicing horizontally brings to the fore the interaction between individual and family, families and community, and so on. Concentrating on past influences draws attention to the success or failure of preventive strategies, while analysing outcomes may produce insights into the sorts of responsive policies which are required.

OUTLINE OF THE BOOK

Against this background—and with authors putting varying emphasis on different aspects of the concept—the rest of this book is organized as follows. The following two chapters explore further the meaning of 'social exclusion'. Chapters 3 and 4 attempt to quantify the extent of exclusion in various respects. The next four chapters (5 to 8) analyse some of the causes of exclusion, and the relationship between them, while Chapters 9 to 12 examine the policy and practice of attempts to tackle exclusion. The concluding chapter reflects on whether the shift towards analysing social exclusion takes us further in terms of understanding the problems or formulating effective policies.

In Chapter 2, Brian Barry explores some of the ways in which the notion of 'social exclusion' relates to the various layers in Figure 1.1. For instance, an individual may be 'included' within a community, but that community—perhaps differentiated by religion or by wealth—can itself be separated, sometimes by choice, from the rest of the society. He develops a distinction between 'social isolation', where separation may be in some respects voluntary, and exclusion, where it is not. This does not make isolation unproblematic, and he goes on to discuss the issues around the isolation of wealthy groups from the rest of society as the income distribution widens.

In Chapter 3 we develop a measurable definition of social exclusion based on four dimensions of participation: consumption, production, political engagement, and social interaction. We focus on these as outcomes for individuals in their own right, leaving aside the complex interaction of past and present constraints and choices which produced them.

The next three chapters focus on individuals and families, the innermost rings of the 'onion' of Figure 1.1. In Chapter 4, Simon Burgess and Carol Propper review recent evidence on the dynamics of low income, documenting individuals' experience of poverty over time. As well as comparing patterns of mobility in Britain with those in other countries, they go on to discuss some of the challenges in moving to a better understanding of the factors which underlie the patterns observed.

In Chapter 5, John Hobcraft takes a longer perspective, looking at the routes into social exclusion, especially during young adulthood. His focus is, in the terms discussed above, primarily on the influence of 'human capital' on later development. He assesses the evidence on the effect on adult social exclusion of parental endowments (both genetic and environmental), of childhood circumstances, attributes, and behaviour. He uses evidence from the National Child Development Study (NCDS)—which follows a cohort of people born in 1958. This shows the pervasive associations between certain key childhood circumstances such as educational test scores, indications of childhood poverty, contact with the police or family structure, and a range of adverse adult outcomes. He goes on to explore the complexity of some of the links involved across generations and people's lives. Kathleen Kiernan develops this further in Chapter 6, concentrating on the interplay between the two inner rings of Figure 1.1, the relationship between the individual and family circumstances. Also using evidence from the NCDS, she looks in particular at the impact of demographic events such as youthful parenthood, cohabitation, and parental separation and divorce. This shows, for instance, the powerful association between early parenthood or the partnership context within which a child is born and later socio-economic vulnerability.

Abigail McKnight in Chapter 7 widens the focus to examine the impact of the labour market, looking at how low-wage employment is linked with social exclusion and poverty over different time horizons. She shows how the overlap between low pay and poverty at a single point of time understates the extent to which they are related within a longer perspective: childhood poverty is associated with adult low pay; persistence in low pay with greater poverty; and low pay in someone's working life with poverty in old age. She concludes by reviewing the recent development of key policies affecting the low paid.

Chapter 8, by Ruth Lupton and Anne Power, also looks at part of the wider context, examining the relationship between neighbourhood and exclusion.

They argue that the spatial concentration of exclusion is not coincidental: the nature of neighbourhoods contributes to the social exclusion of their residents. This occurs through the intrinsic characteristics of neighbourhoods, such as location and economic structure, and through acquired characteristics such as crime and neighbourhood environment, which are affected by the population mix, particularly when the most disadvantaged are concentrated in the least advantaged locations. They draw on evidence from a continuing study of twelve of the most deprived neighbourhoods in England and Wales, examining these links and the influence of both local and national policy interventions.

The next four chapters examine further aspects of the policy and community-level response to particular aspects of poverty and exclusion. In Chapter 9, David Piachaud and Holly Sutherland analyse evidence on the extent of child poverty—a recurring theme in earlier chapters—in Britain and on the impact of recent policies designed to tackle it. Child poverty remains much higher in Britain than it was twenty years ago, and in relative terms much higher than in most other industrialized countries. They use the results of simulation modelling to suggest that recent tax and benefit changes by the Labour Government since May 1997 should reduce the number of children in poverty by more than a million by 2002, but argue that more needs to be done. By itself, further promotion of opportunities for paid work would help, but their analysis suggests that, even on the most optimistic scenario, it cannot by itself eliminate child poverty: an adequate minimum income for those not in paid work is required as well.

In the following chapter, Phil Agulnik, Tania Burchardt, and Martin Evans look at wider patterns of response and prevention in the welfare state in relation to three risks: unemployment, disability, and loss of income in retirement. They examine the extent to which policies are successful in preventing or responding to social exclusion resulting from each kind of event. Three common themes emerge. First, there has been a tendency for policy-makers to redefine a problem rather than solve it, shifting responsibility elsewhere. Second, benefit and employment policy have not been coordinated. Finally, the common perception of 'responsive' policies as failure and 'preventive' policies as success, is counter-productive: the relationship between the two approaches is complementary.

Jo Sparkes and Howard Glennerster look in more detail in Chapter 11 at another of the recurring themes of earlier chapters: the relationship between education and social exclusion. The evidence is growing that this association is causal, rather than, say, the product simply of qualifications being used as a sorting mechanism. They review evidence on the impact of school-level qualifications and 'soft skills' on later outcomes, on the prior associations between educational outcomes and other background characteristics, and on the impact of schools. The last of these focuses attention on the impact of recent changes in education policy.

In Chapter 12, Liz Richardson and Katharine Mumford look at a different kind of response, that at the community level. They discuss the meaning of 'community', describe processes of community breakdown, and examine the role of community participation in regenerating low-income neighbourhoods. They draw on two studies, one looking at four neighbourhoods facing problems of incipient abandonment in two Northern English cities, the other involving a community training and small grants programme. They argue that community groups on their own cannot combat wider exclusionary forces. But they can play a crucial role in enabling statutory provision to work effectively, adding to services and facilities, and enhancing social organization through informal networks and bolstering shared norms and values.

These chapters present new evidence on the extent of social exclusion defined in various ways, and on the dynamics of incomes, disadvantage, and area deprivation. In the final chapter John Hills draws on this to discuss the policy implications of this kind of evidence. Does focusing on 'social exclusion' rather than, say, poverty by itself in fact change the policy response? Does focusing on groups liable to persistent or recurrent poverty change the focus of action, compared to the groups which would be indicated by a snapshot? Extending the analysis of earlier chapters, does allowing for dynamics change the content of policy—for instance, through more emphasis on early intervention or on an 'active welfare state'—or do the bulk of the activities of the welfare state remain the same? What does a focus on inclusion mean for the structure of social programmes, particularly their delivery systems, and for issues around universalism and targeting? Finally, what has been the impact of using the term been in practice in UK policy-making since 1997?

2

Social Exclusion, Social Isolation, and the Distribution of Income

BRIAN BARRY

INTRODUCTION: WHAT IS SOCIAL EXCLUSION?

As discussed in the first chapter, the thought is often expressed that 'social exclusion' is no more than a relabelling of what used to be called 'poverty'. However, although there is no doubt a close association between economic stratification and the phenomenon of exclusion within a society, it seems clear that in principle social exclusion can occur between groups that are not significantly distinguished from one another economically. Thus, while the Jewish immigrants who came to Britain from eastern Europe were poor to begin with, their descendants moved in large numbers over a few generations into the professions and commerce. When I was growing up in the west London suburbs in the nineteen forties, the local Jewish minority was neither perceptibly better nor worse off than the average. Even so, the prevailing view in the rest of the community was that Jews were 'clannish', and if they were this was no doubt a response to the casual anti-Semitism to whose existence I can attest from knowledge of the attitudes of my own relatives and neighbours.

The continuation of the story, however, suggests that social exclusion tends to become attenuated and eventually disappear in the absence of group economic inequality—unless a distinctive way of life maintains social barriers. Unquestionably, Adolf Hitler made a grim contribution (though this did not, I judge, really occur until after 1945) by making the overt expression of anti-Semitic sentiments unfashionable. But this could scarcely explain why the out-marriage rate among the two-thirds of British Jews who are not Orthodox is currently running at about 50 per cent, thus raising fears in some quarters for the disappearance over a few more generations of a non-Orthodox Jewish identity. At the same time, the Orthodox out-marriage rate is much lower and this reflects the more general tendency for Orthodox Jews to form distinct communities, including in some cases the maintenance of separate religious schools.

Should this count as social exclusion? A parallel question can be asked at the level of the individual. Is a recluse in good mental and physical health with an average income to be regarded as socially excluded? Let me approach this question by suggesting that we should always look at apparently voluntary self-exclusion with some scepticism. The evaluation of any voluntary act depends on the quality of the choices on offer: that the action chosen appeared to the agent preferable to the alternatives available at the time does not tell us much. Thus, an individual or the members of a group may withdraw from participation in the wider society in response to experience of hostility and discrimination. Here, the actual withdrawal is voluntary but the context within which it occurs still makes it a case of social exclusion, understanding by this a process by which individuals or groups are excluded against their will. Taken in context, the exclusion is no more voluntary than is the departure from a job of somebody who resigns one step ahead of the sack.

Suppose, however, that we are satisfied that we have a case of genuine self-exclusion by an individual or a group. Shall we call this social exclusion or not? The answer depends, I take it, on what we want to do with the concept. I believe that many people want the concept of social exclusion to be defined in such a way that social exclusion is always going to be a bad thing. But the idea of social exclusion as a bad thing is itself one that is capable of bearing more than one interpretation. Is the point supposed to be that social exclusion is necessarily bad *for the people excluded* or would it be sufficient if it were bad in some other way—for example, as a threat to social stability?[1]

I suspect that this question is rarely pressed because there is a tendency to assume too readily that anything counting as social exclusion under one conception will do so under the other as well. Genuine self-exclusion challenges that identification if one believes that it might in some circumstances be a good for the people who exclude themselves but a bad from some more comprehensive viewpoint. For instance, the ESRC's statement of the 'thematic priority' under which CASE is funded appears to lean to the broader conception[2] with the agenda being defined as polarization, social differentiation, and inequality of individuals and communities. While the third item in this triad could imply focus only on the 'poor', this kind of definition would make a wealthy socially differentiated group whose members were quite happy to exclude themselves into a case of social exclusion.

It should be said, however, that such a broad conception of social exclusion would not find support among the members of CASE. For instance, a recent article by CASE members on the extent of social exclusion in Britain used the following definition: 'An individual is socially excluded if (a) he or she is geographically resident in a society but (b) for reasons beyond his or her control, he or she cannot participate in the normal activities of citizens in that society, and

---

[1] In certain cases, of course, it may be agreed that being excluded is bad for those excluded but nevertheless that their exclusion is justifiable. An obvious example would be those properly sentenced to a term in gaol.

[2] 'Understanding the processes by which individuals and their communities become polarised, socially differentiated and unequal...forms an urgent research agenda' (ESRC 1997).

(c) he or she would like to so participate' (Burchardt, Le Grand, and Piachaud 1999: 229).

I want to postpone until later the question of what is wrong with social exclusion. However, it is possible to say here that, whatever the answer to that question may be, voluntary and involuntary social exclusion are at any rate sufficiently different to be worth distinguishing conceptually. We may wish to conclude that there is nothing wrong with voluntary social exclusion. But even if we do not do that, we may very well still conclude that the cause for concern about the self-exclusion of individuals or groups is not the same as the cause for concern about exclusion that arises from processes over which the individual or group has no control. I shall therefore follow the CASE formulation and define social exclusion so that only involuntary exclusion counts. However, the ESRC also said that 'the rapid social changes that disrupt traditional forms of social cohesion are of great concern'.[3] I shall use the term 'social isolation' for the absence of social cohesion, on the understanding that groups can be isolated from the rest of society as well as individuals.

Social isolation is thus defined so that it may be either voluntary or involuntary. In other words, social isolation encompasses social exclusion but is not confined to it. Needless to say, social isolation (in both of its forms) is to be conceived of as a variable: an individual or group is not simply socially isolated or not, but is rather more or less socially isolated. Parallel to the dimensions of social exclusion that have been developed elsewhere in this volume (see Chapter 3), we can think of dimensions of social isolation.

There is one unresolved conceptual question left by what has been said so far. Although it may seem at first sight a rather fine-drawn issue, it actually goes to the heart of what is wrong with social exclusion. Let us imagine a group whose members choose to be socially isolated, but now add that they would be unable to break out of social isolation (for whatever reason) even if they wanted to. Clearly, the social isolation of this group is overdetermined. But does this entail that it does not suffer from social exclusion? Recall the definition quoted above. According to this, a British individual would count as socially excluded on the basis of inability to 'participate in the normal activities of United Kingdom citizens', but only with the proviso that 'he/she would like to so participate'. This definition has the implication that our group cannot be said to be socially excluded, even though it meets the condition that its members are unable to participate for reasons beyond their control. I am not happy about this, for reasons that I shall explain.

One reason for having qualms about the result has already been raised: the difficulty in determining that the self-exclusion is truly voluntary where it is apparent that attempts to integrate would be rebuffed. But I think the objection would survive the satisfactory resolution of that difficulty. If you would be refused

---

[3] This clause fills in the ellipsis in the sentence quoted in fn. 2.

membership in a club on the basis of your religion, race, ethnicity, or sex, common sense suggests that you are excluded, in the sense that you are subject to an exclusionary policy. Even if you claim—turning (Groucho) Marx on his head—that you would not want to belong to any club that would not let you in, that does not alter the fact of exclusion.

From the most narrowly conceived utilitarian point of view, being prevented by forces beyond your control from doing something you do not want to do anyway has no moral significance. (The only reason why it might be thought to matter is that you could change your mind later.) But this fails to recognize the legitimate complaint that, say, blacks have when confronted with a 'whites only' restaurant or hotel even if they have no wish to avail themselves of their services. I therefore posit that individuals or groups are socially excluded if they are denied the opportunity of participation, whether they actually desire to participate or not.

Of the three elements in the ESRC's conception of social exclusion (which I have now relabelled social isolation), I have pulled out polarization and social differentiation. The omission of the third, inequality, is deliberate. For inequality is, as I have argued, a conceptually distinct phenomenon. The relation between social isolation and inequality should be a possible topic for investigation, but it cannot be if the concept of social isolation is defined so that inequality is an aspect of it. Two groups in the same country—for example Flemings and Walloons in Belgium—can be roughly equal in power, status, and material resources while at the same time being polarized and socially differentiated. But how far can social cohesion be combined with great inequalities? We should not assume that the answer will be the same for all societies. To give an obvious but important example, inexpensive and reliable public transport that runs long hours will enable poor people to travel for economic, social, and political purposes. In its absence, the participation of those who cannot afford to run a car or hire a taxi will be severely limited. Thus, the same disparity in incomes may have widely different implications for personal mobility.

STRATIFIED SOCIAL EXCLUSION: THE TWO THRESHOLDS

It is clear, as this example illustrates, that under some conditions low incomes can inhibit or prevent participation in mainstream institutions. But high incomes may also under some conditions lead to social isolation. If the wealthiest fraction of a society feel that they can afford to insulate themselves from the common fate and buy their way out of the common institutions, that is also a form of social isolation. Is it also a form of social exclusion? It seems to me that it is. While it may be said that the very rich have the opportunity to exclude themselves from common institutions, what has to be added is that their wealth enables them to erect barriers that keep out their fellow citizens. Hence, the situation is one in which a minority is in a position to exclude the majority.

It must be admitted that social exclusion is conventionally thought of as something that happens to a minority. But I can see no good reason for limiting its scope in this way. Surely, the South African *apartheid* regime could be described as (among other things) one in which a 20 per cent minority of whites excluded the rest of the population from access to the most significant educational, occupational, and political positions.

Everyday linguistic usage supports the claim that social exclusion can be the lot of a substantial majority. An exclusive club is one that is highly selective in admitting members, an exclusive resort is one that few can afford to stay in, an exclusive neighbourhood is one that few people can aspire to live in, an exclusive school or clinic is one that few can attend, and so on. Indeed, the social exclusion of the majority might be seen as acquiring physical shape in the so-called gated communities that have multiplied in the United States during the past twenty years.

Neighbourhoods have always been able to exclude some potential residents through discrimination and housing costs. With gates and walls, they can exclude not only undesirable new residents, but even casual passers-by and the people from the neighbourhood next door. Gates are a visible sign of exclusion, an even stronger signal to those who already see themselves as excluded from the larger mainstream milieu. (Blakely and Snyder 1997: 153)

What all this suggests is that a society marked by a combination of a market economy and liberal democratic institutions is liable to have two thresholds of social exclusion. The lower one divides those who habitually participate in the mainstream institutions from those who are outside them. The upper threshold is the one that divides those in the middle from those who can detach themselves from the mainstream institutions. Looking to the USA, where both thresholds are more sharply defined than in Britain, we see that in a curious way those below the lower threshold and those above the upper one are a mirror image of one another. Thus, the inhabitants of the inner-city ghettoes receive little police protection; the inhabitants of gated communities need little because they employ their own security guards. As in Britain, there are those who make little contact with the publicly funded schools as a result of truancy and early dropping out; there are also those who make little contact because they attend private schools. Those at the bottom do not take part in ordinary democratic politics (even to the extent of voting); those at the top do not need to because they can gain direct access to decision-makers by contributing financially to Political Action Committees and other lobbying organizations. Health care in the USA has a lower threshold that excludes about 20 per cent of the population from the sort of treatment available to others, but there is no clear upper threshold because the rest get whatever they (or their insurers) are willing to pay for. Conversely, Britain has no lower threshold but an upper one defined by possession of private insurance.

The United States is further along the road of social exclusion than Britain, to a large extent because its system of financing public services results in their quality in each area reflecting far more directly the level of prosperity in that area. The effect is that, even when the wealthy do use public services, this is still a form of social exclusion because these services are for their exclusive use and thus create no sense of common fate with those living in less wealthy areas. For example, Henry Huntington arranged for a small municipality to be carved out in the area surrounding his estate in a then undeveloped part of what is now Greater Los Angeles. This area, the City of San Marino, has from the start contained only large and expensive houses. This enables the city to provide excellent services, including high quality public education.[4] But this kind of collective provision among the rich—what has been called 'the secession of the successful' (Blakely and Snyder 1995: 24)—is a phenomenon that connects with the 'theory of clubs' rather than with any conception of the universal entitlement of the citizens of a country to share in a common system of public services.[5]

Nevertheless, neither Britain nor the United States is, in geographical or historical perspective, an extreme example. Every country in Latin America (to mention only one part of the world) has both lower and upper thresholds that create far more differentiation in life chances (including life expectancy), in actual ways of life, and in relation to the major institutions. Similarly, when Disraeli (1845) wrote of 'two nations', it was certainly more true than it is now that there was 'no intercourse and no sympathy' between the rich and the poor and that they enjoyed, as he claimed, different breeding, different food, different manners, and different laws. (Disraeli, incidentally, omitted for his own political purposes those in the middle: in my terms, 'the rich and the poor' who made up his 'two nations' were those above the upper threshold and those below the lower.) However, if we focus on the subset of societies that are liberal democracies, the United States and Britain will appear as being marked by a relatively large amount of stratified social exclusion. This matters because, when we ask what is wrong with social exclusion, we may conclude that in some respects it depends on the nature of the society within which it occurs.

WHAT'S WRONG WITH SOCIAL EXCLUSION? (1): SOCIAL EXCLUSION AND SOCIAL JUSTICE

As the last remark suggests, there are two possible ways of tackling the question: 'What's wrong with social exclusion?' One is to ask what is wrong with it in

---

[4] The process continues and has accelerated in recent years. 'In California, Florida and other states with permissive government formation laws, developers are working with residents to create cities that are separate from the existing jurisdiction—city or county.' This enables residents to 'direct publicly collected taxes to locally specific goals rather than allowing them to be used over a larger area'. (Blakely and Snyder 1997: 25)
[5] For a discussion of the relation between the 'theory of clubs' and social exclusion see Jordan (1996), especially pp. 62–9.

general terms and the other is to ask what is wrong with it in Britain, or in countries similar to Britain in the relevant respects. (That, of course, entails a determination of the respects that are relevant.) Many of the things that are wrong with social exclusion are wrong with it everywhere. Most of the forms taken by social exclusion in contemporary Brazil or early Victorian Britain are simply bad in a more egregious way than the forms taken by it in contemporary Britain. However, we should be prepared to consider ways in which social exclusion (and perhaps also voluntary social isolation) run into special objections in market-orientated liberal democratic societies.

I shall set out the case against social exclusion under two main heads, discussing in passing how far the case extends to voluntary social isolation. The first count against social exclusion is that it violates the value of social justice. The second is that it violates the value of social solidarity. I shall take up the first in this section and the other in the next.

Let me begin, then, with the argument from social justice. It need hardly be said that the concept of social justice is controversial. I shall resist the temptation to articulate the main grounds of dispute and develop my own theory. Instead, I shall put forward a minimal conception of social justice that is nevertheless sufficiently rich to explain why social exclusion is unjust. This is a conception of social justice as equality of opportunity. It is not, of course, wholly uncontroversial. But it is one to which all three major political parties in Britain at least pay lip service, even if they are not prepared to endorse its practical implications. It has, moreover, a good deal of intuitive plausibility, because it makes room for individual human agency to make a difference to legitimate claims, while at the same time maintaining that brute bad luck—disadvantages for which people cannot reasonably be held responsible—should give rise to legitimate claims for aid, redress, or compensation (as appropriate).

One of the reasons for persistent disagreement about the implications of equal opportunity is that it is not straightforward where the boundaries lie between on the one hand the things for which people can properly claim the credit (and hence the associated rewards) or be assigned the onus (and hence the associated losses or penalties), and on the other hand those that are to count as a matter of good or bad fortune. One particular bone of contention is on which side of the boundary natural endowments fall. I myself believe that the only coherent answer is that they are a matter of good or bad luck. However, in order to move forward on as narrow a front as possible, I shall not press that claim. The upshot if we drop natural endowments from the sphere of luck is, roughly speaking, as follows: the principle of justice as equal opportunity holds that people who are equally able (in terms of native talent) should do equally well, unless they make voluntary choices that result in their faring differently. To illustrate the force of the second clause, imagine two people who graduate with a qualification in law of exactly equal quality. If one opts for a high-pressure career while the other prefers a job that leaves a lot of time for playing golf and gardening, it is not unfair according to the principle of justice as equal opportunity if one makes more money than the other, because both faced the same set of options.[6]

It is apparent that no contemporary society comes very close to implementing fully the principle of justice as equal opportunity. At the same time, it can be said that, while there is some variation among them, all contemporary liberal democracies do quite well by historical and contemporary standards. This is scarcely accidental, since only a tiny minority of societies in the history of the world have ever accepted equality of opportunity as an aspiration. So long as the notion of justice as equal opportunity functions as a touchstone for public policy, there is at least some chance that a demonstration of failure to achieve it in a certain area will have some long-term political impact.

Social exclusion conflicts with equal opportunity in at least the following two ways: first, social exclusion leads to unequal educational and occupational opportunities; and second, social exclusion actually constitutes a denial of equal opportunity in relation to politics. I shall take these points up in turn. Both thresholds of social exclusion come into play in creating unequal educational and occupational opportunity. Below the lower threshold, there are socially isolated areas in the inner cities (especially in the USA) and large housing estates that are geographically as well as socially isolated (especially in Britain). In some of these areas, very few people are engaged in full-time permanent legal employment, and the result is that the usual word-of-mouth flow of information about job opportunities is almost entirely lacking. What William Julius Wilson says of the American inner city applies to all such situations:

Inner-city social isolation makes it much more difficult for those who are looking for jobs to be tied into the job network. Even...where job vacancies become available in an industry near or within an inner-city neighbourhood, workers who live outside the inner city may find out about these vacancies sooner than those who live near the industry because the latter are not tied into the job network.   (1987: 60)

Lack of job opportunities among the adults in an area tends to depress scholastic motivation and thus contributes to poor educational outcomes that condemn the next generation to extremely limited job opportunities in their turn. Even if it were said that truancy or lack of effort are 'chosen' by children, the environment in which such choices are made is far too compromised for them to be assimilated to the choice of the leisure-loving lawyer. Rather, they are themselves part of a self-reproducing process of unequal opportunity.

Of course, poverty is in itself a barrier to equal educational opportunity. A hungry or malnourished child is unlikely to be good at concentrating on school work. The lack of a quiet room in which to study at home (and, increasingly, a computer) makes homework unattractive and difficult. Also, to repeat a point

---

[6] Julian Le Grand (1991: 87) expresses the same idea in terms of the concept of equity. Thus, he writes that 'a distribution is equitable if it is the outcome of informed individuals choosing over equal choice sets.' (Emphasis suppressed.)

made earlier, the more closely the resources of a school district reflect its tax base, the more underfunded schools in poor areas will be. However, the concern here is not with unequal educational opportunity in general but specifically with the role played by social exclusion in it. And here it is the social homogeneity of schools created by social exclusion that is significant. An abundance of research suggests that children with middle-class attitudes and aspirations constitute a resource for the rest. A school without a critical mass of such children therefore fails to provide equality of educational opportunity to its pupils.

The social homogenization of schools is greatly increased by the withdrawal of wealthy parents from the state system. Above the upper threshold of social exclusion, the same people live, work, play, and marry together, and the perpetuation of privilege is smoothed by the public school/Oxbridge connection. In stark contrast to the lack of a network providing access to ordinary jobs that afflicts those at the bottom, those at the top are automatically enrolled in a network that offers inside information about and access to the most desirable and lucrative jobs that the society has to offer. Thus, equality of opportunity is eroded from both ends: some have too few opportunities, others too many.

So far I have been looking at ways in which social exclusion leads to a violation of the demands of social justice as equal opportunity. I now want to suggest that social exclusion can in some circumstances actually constitute a denial of social justice. The line of argument here starts from the familiar idea that there are some rights whose enjoyment is unconditional, for example the right to a fair trial. Others, like the right to vote, are dependent on status (generally, it is necessary to be an adult citizen), but it is not necessary to have done anything especially meritorious to enjoy them. The right to vote can be lost as a result of being convicted of a sufficiently serious crime but is in other respects universal. So is, in principle, the right to participate more broadly in politics.

As before, it can be pointed out that inequality may have a direct effect on the ability to exercise such rights. The opportunity to get a fair trial is closed to those who cannot afford high-quality legal representation in the absence of a well-funded system of legal aid. Similarly, it is scarcely necessary to point out the many ways in which opportunities for disproportionate political influence flow directly from the ability to make large financial contributions and from possession of other resources such as ownership of media of mass communication. Once again, however, my concern here is with the more limited question of the relation of social exclusion to social justice.

Let me pursue this question by focusing on political participation. It is surely not controversial that liberal democracies can fulfil the promises that they hold out to their citizens only if the opportunity to engage in political activity extends beyond the mere right to vote once every four or five years. This must include the ability (not formally but really) to take part in the work of political parties and other organizations concerned with public policy, to take part in lobbying and consult with local councillors or MPs, and so on. The inability to engage in these activities is an aspect of social exclusion, so here social exclusion is in itself a form of social injustice in that it is a denial of opportunities that should be open to all. Clearly, genuine opportunity to engage in politics on equal terms has certain material preconditions. Such preconditions are not met, for example, in the case of an unemployed single mother on an out-of-town housing estate who cannot afford costs of political activity such as babysitting, transport, and meals out.

There is a link between exclusion from politics and other kinds of social exclusion in that political networks tend to grow out of social networks. This is especially important for the workings of block associations and community associations or the kind of informal organization that forms to obtain, say, a controlled crossing between a school and a housing estate. To the extent that the interests of the socially excluded are congruent with those of the socially active in relation to these matters, the outcomes may not be any different from those that would have come about if they had participated. But we cannot safely assume that the interests of the socially excluded are not distinct, even in neighbourhood politics. And in any case, the point is that de facto first- and second-class citizenship is in itself objectionable, even if it does not affect outcomes.

The best study I know of the relation between social networks and political efficacy is that carried out by Jane Mansbridge (1980: 103) in a Vermont town that she called Selby. 'Town' is a political designation : the town of Selby consisted of a village and outlying areas. The town administration (elected at a meeting once a year) is not in the habit of sending out written communications to residents, and individual candidates (there are no parties) are equally unforthcoming. This creates a systemic division between insiders and outsiders.

Itinerant town criers like the mailman and the garbageman bring the news to the people back in the hills only sporadically, while villagers hear it every day ... Villagers say of a local political question that they 'discussed it down at the store'. Villagers do not make appointments with town officials; they just 'run into them down at the store'. [Thus,] a part-time farmer who holds a small town office [and lives up a back road] complains that: 'There's too much that goes on before town meeting that we don't know about unless we're part of it. They're slack in presenting all the information you need to function properly.'   (Mansbridge 1980: 103)

Although New England 'town' politics are not exactly like the politics of neighbourhood organizations and the like, because the 'town' decides on issues such as schools and roads, the phenomenon of insiders and outsiders is a familiar one. Indeed, party politics at local level is often an outgrowth of social networks. The main difference is that in Selby a good deal could be done to foster wider participation without any change in social relations. (The problem is that those who run the existing system have no incentive to introduce more formal and open procedures.) In more inherently informal politics, by contrast, there is less scope for weakening the link between location on a social network and political efficacy. Preventing social exclusion is therefore the only route to the prevention of political exclusion.

WHAT'S WRONG WITH SOCIAL EXCLUSION? (2): SOCIAL EXCLUSION AND SOCIAL SOLIDARITY

The conception of social justice utilized in this chapter is sensitive to individual choices. Because of this, social injustice is connected to social exclusion as against the broader phenomenon of social isolation. Even where voluntary separation from the wider society leads to diminished job opportunities, this still does not involve a denial of social justice, because the restricted opportunities themselves arise from a situation that itself came about as a result of choice.[7] Similarly, voluntary withdrawal from political participation (arising, for example, from religious beliefs) does not constitute social injustice, because all that is required is an opportunity to participate.

In this respect, social justice and social solidarity are differently related to social exclusion. For social solidarity is, as we shall see, undermined by social isolation, whether it takes a voluntary or an involuntary form, though (as I shall suggest below) its ill-effects may well be more serious when the social isolation takes the form of social exclusion. By social solidarity I mean a sense of fellow-feeling that extends beyond people with whom one is in personal contact. At the minimum, it is the acceptance that strangers are still human beings, with the same basic needs and rights; at the maximum, it is (in Benedict Anderson's terms) an 'imagined community'.

It is undeniable that social solidarity exists, and also that it is more or less strong in different times and places. This suggests that it has social causes, and the connection that I want to make with the absence of social isolation is that a significant factor in strengthening solidarity is the experience of common institutions and more generally shared experiences. Thus, anyone who lived through the Second World War will be able to attest to the immense increase in social solidarity that occurred in that period. The most plausible explanation is that the shared risks created by the Blitz gave large parts of the civilian population a sense of shared vulnerability to random events, while the army and the evacuation of children from the cities brought together people who would not otherwise ever have been on intimate terms. The universalization of social provision also originated in response to wartime conditions. 'Thus it was believed in 1939 for example, that only the poor would need government aid if their homes were bombed, and the rest could look after themselves; the responsibility for the bombed-out was therefore laid on the Assistance Committees. Naturally the belief and the arrangements both disintegrated with the first heavy raid on London' (Crosland 1965: 98).

---

[7] Left unresolved by the assertion in the text are cases in which the choices of adults (e.g. to send their children to a separate school that provides a poor education or gives instruction in a minority language) restrict the subsequent opportunities of the children. I deal with this difficult question in *Culture and Equality* (Barry 2001, ch. 6).

An alternative explanation that might be offered is the unifying effect of a common enemy. But there are reasons for thinking that the importance of this can easily be exaggerated. The First World War also provided a common enemy, and indeed far greater hysteria about the 'Hun' was whipped up in the press and the politicians than against the real evils of Nazism. Yet there was very little discernible development of a sense of social solidarity. The elections following each war are instructive in this regard: in 1918, the coalition that had fought the war was rewarded with victory, largely on an externally orientated platform of vindictiveness towards the defeated powers; in 1945, the Conservatives who had had a majority were thrown out, and a Labour government elected on an almost entirely domestic platform of social and economic reforms. The reason for the difference is, I suggest, that in the First World War, the lives of the civilian population were very little affected (zeppelin raids were an insignificant threat) while the experience of the soldiers in the trenches was so far out of line with the propaganda fed to civilians that it actually opened up an unbridgeable gulf between them.

There is another reason for thinking that the heightened sense of social solidarity during the Second World War was not solely (or even mainly) created by a common enemy. If that were so, we would expect the sense of solidarity to disappear when the enemy was defeated. But (as the point about the 1945 election illustrates), it survived in a gradually attenuating form. We would, of course, expect such an attenuation as those who were exposed to the experience of the Second World War died and were replaced by others who were not.

Conversely, the whole course of public policy in Britain in the past twenty years (and I see no sign of it changing) has tended to undermine solidarity. Competition for shares of fixed and inadequate resources has been deliberately imposed on institutions such as schools and universities whose lifeblood should be cooperation. The decline of standards in public health care and education have led to an increased desire to opt out, while a phenomenal increase in the ratio of the incomes of the top 10 per cent of the population to the median has made it possible. Private provision of security has been a growth industry.

Why should we care about social solidarity? I shall offer two answers, one of which makes it intrinsically valuable while the other makes it instrumentally valuable. In saying that social solidarity is intrinsically valuable, I do not wish to be taken to mean that we are dealing with something whose value somehow transcends its value to individual human beings. Rather, all that is intended is that human lives tend to go better in a society whose members share some kind of existence. Aristotle said that to live outside society one would have to be either a beast or a god, and we would not altogether missing the spirit of that remark if we were to identify those below the lower threshold with the beasts and those above the upper threshold with the gods: one group lacks the capacity to participate in the common institutions while the other group has no need to. This, it may be argued, is not good for the characters of those in either group.

The theme could clearly be developed much further, but I hope I have sketched in the way in which that development might be carried through. Let me now then turn to the alternative, instrumental argument for the significance of social solidarity. In essence, the argument is that—especially in liberal democratic societies—social justice is more likely to be realized through politics the higher the level of social solidarity that there is in the society. The connection suggested here between social exclusion (or more broadly social isolation) and the denial of social justice is different from that discussed in the previous section.

Nevertheless, there is an interaction between them. Thus, I argued that an aspect of social exclusion is inability to participate as equals in politics. This obviously reduces the relative political influence of groups below the lower threshold of social exclusion. Suppose, however, that lack of resources did not prevent them from punching below their weight, in relation to their numbers. Their distinctive interests would still tend to be neglected as a result of social isolation.

The reason for this is that, even if everybody in a polity had equal power, there would still be winners and losers. Who wins and who loses depends on the alignment of interests. It must be emphasized that there is nothing whatever in the structure of liberal democratic politics that has any built-in tendency to ensure that the interests of all will be taken into account or that the demands of social justice will be met. If anything, the opposite is true: the surest way for a politician to maintain power in a democracy is to find some way of dividing the electorate into two unequally sized parts and identify with the majority. In the longer term, this process is liable to become one of self-reinforcing antagonism that leads to resistance and to repression in response, and ultimately threatens the survival of democratic institutions. This is why liberal democracy is such a rare phenomenon.[8]

The significance of social isolation in all this is simply that the lack of empathy between the majority and socially isolated minorities makes it easier for ambitious politicians to advance their careers by demonizing and ultimately dehumanizing these minorities. The lethal potential of this process has been illustrated only too many times in the twentieth century. The social isolation of any group makes the incorporation of its interests into political programmes more problematic. This is true for voluntary isolation as well as for isolation that is forced on a group. However, social exclusion is more dangerous, simply because the processes that underlie social exclusion are frequently the same as those that lead to stigmatization.

I am especially concerned in this chapter with stratified social exclusion. The application of what has been said so far to this is straightforward. The dynamics of electoral competition in a society that is stratified along socio-economic lines (rather than being divided primarily along lines of ethnic or other communalistic

---

[8] 'What is ordinarily thought of as ordinary democracy is inadequate in societies in which Group *A*, with 60 per cent of the seats, can, under most democratic systems, shut out Group *B*, with 40 per cent. In such conditions, democracy is more the problem than the answer to a problem.' (Horowitz 1997: 450–1)

conflict) drive political parties to compete for the 'middle ground'. This means that the perceived interests—or, more broadly, concerns—of the median voter will be close to the position of the majority party, if there is one. In a multiparty system, it will be close to the position of the median party, which will have a very strong position in any process of coalition formation, because it will have to be included in any majority of ideologically contiguous parties. Everything therefore turns on the concerns of the median voter.

What has been said so far suggests that the more attenuated the bonds of social solidarity become, the less inclusive the concerns of the median voter will be. The socially excluded will thus be failed by democratic politics. To the extent that the median voter pays attention to those below the lower threshold of social exclusion it is liable to be in their capacity as threats to his or her prosperity and personal safety. The result—most clearly evident in the USA but with Britain tagging along—is an increasing resort to coercion, in the forms of 'workfare' and a more and more extensive use of the criminal law as an instrument of social control.[9]

CONCLUSION: SOCIAL EXCLUSION AND THE DISTRIBUTION OF INCOME

The argument of this chapter has been that social exclusion is a phenomenon distinct from poverty and also distinct from economic inequality. Nevertheless, there is an association between the dispersion of incomes and social exclusion, but it is not a straightforward one because the relationship is mediated by the experience of common fate, through the sharing of common institutions. The significance of personal income for the capacity to share in common institutions depends on the accessibility of those institutions to all on a free or heavily subsidized basis. Thus, to take a simple but often overlooked illustration, in a society in which much of life is lived in outdoor public spaces—squares and parks, for example—social isolation will be less than it would be if everything else were the same but the climate and social mores were not conducive to outdoor living.

Schools and health services that are free to all users similarly make personal income levels less important, provided their quality is uniform and high enough to make the free institutions the ones that are used by the vast majority of the population. The importance of public transport in this context can scarcely be exaggerated. As a way of making it true that there is 'no such thing as society' (in the sense of solidarity) the promotion of the private car at the expense of public transport could scarcely be improved upon. The private car is an enemy of solidarity as much as public transport is its friend. The private car isolates people and puts them in a condition of competition with other road users (including pedestrians) at any rate where traffic is congested, as in almost all urban areas. As congestion gets worse, standards of civility decline: it is noticeable, for example,

---

[9] See Jordan (1996), ch. 6 (pp. 189–221) on 'The politics of enforcement'.

how much more reluctant car drivers now are to stop for pedestrians in London, in comparison with only ten years ago. 'Road rage' has become a recognized pathology of drivers and it is impossible to believe that the deterioration of social relations on the road does not have any spillover into the rest of life.

Conversely public transport is the most effective way there is of creating conditions of common fate. (It is no accident that the standard metaphor for common fate is 'all in the same boat'.) Most public services allow some room for manœuvre: the 'sharp elbows of the middle classes', their knowhow and self-confidence in dealing with bureaucracies, may be able to come into play to secure advantages within a public system of health care and education, for example. But public transport is the great leveller. Even where (as with some trains and planes) those who can afford it can travel first class, they still have to go on the same vehicle as the hoi polloi. If the service is unreliable, they suffer along with everybody else.

All this means that there is no universally valid generalization to be sought: the relation of social exclusion to the distribution of income will depend on the way in which institutions are set up. However, there are, in societies such as our own, obvious material conditions that have to be satisfied to avoid social exclusion. The most basic is a place to live: those with 'no fixed abode' (whether sleeping rough or moving between shelters and hostels) are excluded from most forms of participation, including all those elementary social processes that require a mailing address. For many purposes, a mailing address needs to be supplemented by a telephone, as Tony Atkinson (1998: 14) has emphasized:

A person unable to afford a telephone finds it difficult to participate in a society where a majority do have telephones. Children are not invited out to play because neighbours no longer call round—they call up. Letters do not allow the same contact with relatives who have moved away. A person applying for a job may not be called for an interview since he or she cannot be contacted directly.

But much more is required as the material basis for full participation in the life of one's society. To go out in public so as to take part in social and political events, it is necessary to be respectably clothed, by the prevailing standards in one's society; to have access to good public transport, and otherwise (as on some isolated housing estates) the price of a taxi or the money to run a car; to be able to return hospitality, buy a round of drinks or a meal out, and so on. Similarly, to be able to get and hold a job, it is necessary to be respectably clothed and to have access to some reliable means of transport to the place of work.[10] Widely used indexes of 'poverty' take it as being represented by an income half or 60 per cent of that of the median. It seems plausible that something like this income is also necessary for full participation.

What about the upper threshold of social exclusion? If we assume that a liberal society cannot actually prohibit people from opting out of common services such

---

[10] Atkinson points out (1998: 15) that 'to compete for a job, it is today not enough "to avoid being shabby", which was the criterion applied by Seebohm Rowntree in 1899'.

as the state school system or the national health service, the upper bound on incomes is whatever level makes it financially feasible and (in relation to alternative uses of the money) attractive to opt out. This depends on two factors, both of which can be manipulated by a government determined to ensure the conditions of social solidarity. The first is the quality of the public services. Obviously, the higher the quality (and therefore the more expensive) the public provision, the more it will cost to improve on it by going into the private sector. A wider disparity of incomes can therefore be tolerated (other things being equal), the higher the quality of public services. But in practice, of course, the high rates of taxation necessary to finance high-quality public services are themselves unlikely (as in Scandinavia) to leave many people with enough disposable income to enable them to do better privately.

This is the demand side of the equation. Public policy can also influence the supply side. So, for any given quality of the service provided publicly, it is possible to make it more or less expensive to obtain a significantly superior quality privately. For example, private schools may or may not be given charitable status: if they are, that is in effect a gift from everybody else to those who opt out of the state system, and a society committed to the pursuit of solidarity would not make such a gift. This is not a question of discriminating against the private sector, but merely not discriminating in favour of it. Again, consider the stipulation in the Canadian health-care system that employees have to be either entirely in or entirely out of it. Since this would rule out the British practice of moonlighting by consultants who are already in receipt of an almost full-time salary from the National Health Service, it would make it more expensive to run a private system of health care along with the public one. The Canadian experience suggests that a high-quality health-care system with this proviso built into it can virtually drive out private alternatives.

Despite all these complexities, let me hazard a guess that, provided the quality of public service reaches at least tolerable levels, those with incomes up to three times the median will give priority to the purchase of superior versions of the private goods that are within reach of those with an income around the median: a bigger house in a more desirable neighbourhood, a fancier car, longer or more frequent holidays in more exotic locations, and so on. Unless public services are so deplorable that anybody who could possibly afford it would escape them, it is only at some level above three times the median income that opting out of the common institutions will begin to look attractive. If this is so, it follows that social solidarity can be maintained (so long as the quality of public services meet the minimum conditions I have stated) provided that the ratio of the top income to the bottom income in the society does not exceed six to one.[11] We are not, however, dealing here with an all-or-nothing phenomenon.

[11] David Miller (1997: 97) has speculated that a spread of eight to one is the maximum compatible with what he calls social equality, a concept which is in essentials the same as what I have called social solidarity.

Social solidarity may be able to survive a small minority rich enough to opt out of common institutions. Thus, Swedish social solidarity during the most egalitarian period was not apparently undermined by the existence of a few very wealthy families which owned a large part of Swedish industry.

The upshot of this chapter is that a government professing itself concerned with social exclusion but indifferent to inequality is, to put it charitably, suffering from a certain amount of confusion. It is true, as I have emphasized, that public policy can make a difference to the impact that any given degree of inequality has on the extent and severity of social exclusion. Nevertheless, in any society in which the great bulk of goods and services are allocated through the market, and in which even those provided publicly can also be bought privately, there must be a close connection between inequality and social exclusion.

3

Degrees of Exclusion: Developing a Dynamic, Multidimensional Measure

TANIA BURCHARDT, JULIAN LE GRAND, AND
DAVID PIACHAUD

Interpretations of the term 'social exclusion' are legion—as outlined in the Introduction to this volume—but empirical treatments are scarcer. Some analysis has been framed in terms of social exclusion, while focusing on a particular symptom or aspect (for example, crime or long-term unemployment: Jones Finer and Nellis 1998; Lawless *et al.* 1998). Others have produced summaries of a wide range of indicators (Rahman *et al.* 2000), or supplemented research on poverty with evidence on access to services and social support (Gordon *et al.* 2000). In this chapter, we explore a dynamic, multidimensional measure of social exclusion in Britain. The analysis builds on our earlier work (Burchardt, Le Grand, and Piachaud 1999; Burchardt 2000*a*), by refining the longitudinal indicators we use and extending the period covered through the 1990s.[1]

This chapter begins by offering a working definition of social exclusion, and showing how such a definition can be operationalized using existing nationally representative data—in this case, from the British Household Panel Survey for the years 1991 to 1998. The two middle sections present results: firstly, looking across different dimensions of social exclusion at a single point in time, and secondly, tracing the course individuals follow over time. In the concluding section, we reflect on the relationship between concepts and measurement, and between measurement and policy.

A WORKING DEFINITION OF SOCIAL EXCLUSION

The working definition of social exclusion which we attempt to operationalize, is as follows:

An individual is socially excluded if he or she does not participate in key activities of the society in which he or she lives.

---

[1] The variables used here are in some cases different from those used in earlier publications, so results are not directly comparable. See Appendix for details of variable construction.

The definition has a number of features. Firstly, it restricts our attention to those living in a particular society, in recognition of the fact that social exclusion is generally agreed to be a *relative* concept—relative, that is, to the time and place in question. It is not restricted to citizens of a particular state, however, since denial of citizenship rights to residents is an important form of exclusion.

Secondly, the definition refers to *participation*, widely regarded as central to the concept of social exclusion. The definition leaves open which activities are regarded as 'key'. For Britain in the 1990s, we identified four dimensions:

Consumption: the capacity to purchase goods and services[2]
Production: participation in economically or socially valuable activities
Political engagement: involvement in local or national decision-making
Social interaction: integration with family, friends, and community

Each of these dimensions represents an outcome considered important in its own right. This is not to deny that there are interactions between the outcomes, but rather to emphasize that participation in every dimension is regarded as necessary for social inclusion; conversely, lack of participation in any one dimension is sufficient for social exclusion. So, for instance, lack of participation in production is problematic even if the individual has a reasonable level of consumption, and is politically and socially involved. In terms of the 'onion' diagrams in the Introduction to this volume (Figure 1.1), participation in consumption, production, political activity, and social activity would appear as outcomes for the innermost (individual) layer. Many of them are examined in more detail individually elsewhere in this book: Chapter 4 looks at changes over time in individuals' consumption capacity (income); Chapters 7, 9, and 11 consider different aspects of opportunities for productive activity, Chapter 12 discusses involvement in community-based organizations, and Chapter 6 touches on the availability of social and familial support.

Many of the indicators of social exclusion typically discussed in the literature—for example, being a member of an ethnic minority, suffering partnership breakdown, or living in a deprived area—would feature as causes or risk factors (at the top of Figure 1.2 in the Introduction), rather than as outcomes. Our argument is that none of these characteristics would be regarded as constituting social exclusion if the individual was able—perhaps against the odds—to participate in the four dimensions we have identified. This criterion can be used as a test for proposed additions to the list of dimensions.

Inclusion or exclusion on each of these dimensions is clearly a matter of degree. Strictly speaking, the definition should refer to being 'socially excluded to a greater degree' and 'the less the extent of participation'. Participation may be more or less at a point in time, and it may be sustained for a longer or shorter

---

[2] In Burchardt, Le Grand, and Piachaud (1999) we included a fifth dimension, *savings activity*, measured by housing tenure, savings, and pension entitlements. We later came to regard this as a subset of the consumption dimension, although our consumption measure remains income-based.

period. For convenience, we choose an inclusion/exclusion threshold for each dimension at a point in time (detailed below), and analyse degree of participation by number of dimensions and by duration. This concern with the *dynamics* is a key feature of the social exclusion literature (Hills, Chapter 13 in this volume).

Setting relevant thresholds involves answering the question, 'Exclusion relative to whom?' For example, should the adequacy of levels of consumption be gauged relative to your neighbour, your locality, or to the country as a whole? The approach we have taken is to determine the relevant standard by the level at which policy is most likely to be implemented. Thus for consumption and production dimensions, the most obvious policy tools are social security and employment policy; hence a national standard is adopted. For political engagement, in so far as policy is ever addressed in this area, it is to encourage local participation, in community forums, and so on. Promoting social interaction is rarely an explicit policy objective, though support for families, befriending schemes and cultural projects can be seen in this light. These operate at the most immediate individual level. It has been argued that breadth and diversity of social networks are necessary for social inclusion, for example, by providing links between the unemployed and the employed which increase the former's chance of re-employment (DEMOS 1997). However this is an argument about the instrumental value of social networks in promoting economic integration (inclusion on the consumption and production dimensions) rather than their intrinsic worth.

The definition of social exclusion proposed does not address the question of *agency*: who is doing the excluding, and whether the excluded individual would like to be included. Brian Barry's previous chapter in this volume explores the issue in depth; it is also highlighted by Tony Atkinson (1998) as a key feature of the social exclusion concept. The original version of our own definition incorporated two further clauses:

1. the individual is not participating for reasons beyond his/her control, and
2. he or she would like to participate.

These clauses proved too difficult to operationalize at the first attempt, although in further work we are pursuing a number of ways of estimating the extent of voluntary non-participation. In defence of the simpler definition used here, one can argue that voluntary non-participation is unlikely where the thresholds for participation are set very low. For example, few would choose to live on incomes less than half the average, to be long-term sick, or to be without emotional support at times of crisis. However, while this may be plausible for the consumption, production, and social dimensions, it is less convincing for political engagement: there are no doubt many who do not vote and are not involved in a campaigning organization who are quite happy with that state of affairs. For the political dimension, an alternative defence is that while exclusion may be voluntary for the individual, it may still be problematic for the state. Democratic legitimacy is questionable if a majority declines to vote.

DATA AND INDICATORS

The data used are from the British Household Panel Survey (BHPS), for the years 1991 to 1998.[3] The main advantage of this survey is its panel structure: the initial sample of around 10,000 adults was designed to be nationally representative, and the same individuals have been re-interviewed year on year. This allows us to construct a dynamic measure of social exclusion. The main limitation of the survey—common to all household surveys—is the omission of the institutional and homeless populations. A high proportion of the non-private household population might be expected to be socially excluded. However they form a small proportion of the population as a whole.[4] We focus on adults of working age (16 to 59 for women, 16 to 64 for men), since somewhat different indicators would be needed to reflect the same dimensions of inclusion for children and those over pension age.

Table 3.1 summarizes the operationalization of the four dimensions of social inclusion into indicators available in BHPS, and the thresholds used to define exclusion at a point in time. Further details can be found in the Appendix.

The match between dimensions and indicators is imperfect. Since expenditure data are not collected in BHPS, we rely on income as a measure of consumption capability, rather than measuring consumption directly. The threshold, half mean income, is one commonly used in the UK, in the absence of an official poverty line. The production dimension would ideally include voluntary work as an economically or socially valuable activity, in addition to the standard categories, but that information was not available. The indicators of involvement in decision-making we include stand only as proxies for the wide variety of ways in which people may exercise influence over their environment or the future of some institution or policy they care about. Finally, on the social interaction dimension, we have good indicators of availability of support from family and friends, but lack an indicator of wider cultural participation.

Not all the questions needed to construct these indicators were asked at every wave. (Each year of data collection is referred to as a wave). For example, the questions on social support occur only in odd-numbered waves, and questions on voting in General Elections occur only in election years. Net income variables

---

[3] Data from the Derived Current and Annual Net Household Income Variables BHPS Waves 1–7 dataset, deposited by Bardasi, Jenkins, and Rigg, were also used. Both the derived dataset and the main BHPS were supplied by the Data Archive; neither the Archive nor the depositors of the data are responsible for the analyses and interpretations reported here.

[4] M. Evans (1995) estimated that the non-household population was around 2 per cent of the total UK population in 1989, and that they had disproportionately low incomes. However, he found that including them in the distribution added only about half of one per cent to the percentage of the population estimated to have incomes below half average.

Table 3.1. *Indicators of social exclusion*

Dimension	Indicator and threshold
Consumption	Equivalized household net income is under half mean income
Production	Not employed or self-employed, in education or training, or looking after family (i.e. unemployed, long-term sick or disabled, early-retired or 'other')
Political engagement	Did not vote in general election and not a member of a campaigning organization (political party, trade union, parents association, or tenants/residents association)
Social interaction	In any one of five respects, lacks someone who will offer support (listen, comfort, help in crisis, relax with, really appreciates you)

were not available at the time of writing for Wave 8. This creates complications in constructing longitudinal measures; details are given in the Appendix and the implications are discussed with the results below.

A further issue which arises in using panel data is attrition. Some of those interviewed at the first wave cannot be traced, or decline to participate, in later years. Because those who drop out are not a random selection, the remaining respondents are no longer representative of the population as a whole. In the BHPS, there are 8,075 respondents of working age at Wave 1, of whom 65 per cent respond at every wave up to and including Wave 8. Weights can be applied to the remaining sample, based on their characteristics and the characteristics of those who have dropped out, to attempt to counteract attrition bias. Both cross-sectional and longitudinal weights are supplied with the BHPS and are applied as appropriate in the analyses reported below.[5]

EXCLUSION ON ONE OR MORE DIMENSIONS AT A POINT IN TIME

Table 3.2 shows that through the 1990s, the proportion of the working-age population who fell below the threshold on the consumption (income) dimension fluctuated around 16 per cent. On the production dimension, the percentage excluded was around 13 per cent, while for social interaction it fell from 12 per cent in 1991 to 9 per cent in 1998. The rise in political disengagement between 1992 and 1997 was due to lower turnout at the later election.

The proportion of the population counted as 'excluded' is sensitive to the particular threshold chosen: the higher the threshold, the more people will be

[5] The weighted sample may not be representative in respects other than those characteristics used to calculate the weights. See Freed Taylor (2000) for details of weights in the BHPS.

Table 3.2. *Exclusion at a point in time, by year, and by dimension*
(% of working-age population)

Year	Consumption	Production	Political engagement	Social interaction	Unweighted base*
1991	16	13	n/a	12	7799
1992	17	14	17	n/a	7801
1993	17	14	n/a	10	7644
1994	17	14	n/a	n/a	7548
1995	15	13	n/a	9	7354
1996	15	13	n/a	n/a	7562
1997	16	12	21	9	7502
1998	n/a	12	n/a	n/a	7259

*Cross-sectional sample at each Wave, excluding cases from ECHP. Base for 'Consumption' slightly lower, due to higher item non-response.

Source: Authors' calculations using BHPS Waves 1–8.

Table 3.3. *Exclusion on multiple dimensions, Wave 7*

Number of dimensions on which excluded	Percentage of working-age population
0	57.5
1	30.1
2	10.0
3	2.3
4	0.1
0–4	100.0

Note: Cross-sectional sample at Wave 7, excluding cases from ECHP.

Source: Authors' calculations using BHPS Wave 7.

appear under it. So possibly of more interest than the levels of exclusion on each dimension is the relationship between them.

In Table 3.3, we look across dimensions of exclusion at a single point in time (1997).[6] Calculating the number of different dimensions on which individuals are excluded is not meant to imply that exclusion on each dimension is equally serious, nor even that exclusion on two dimensions is twice as bad as exclusion

---

[6] Wave 7 is selected because it contains full information on all dimensions.

on one dimension. Rather, the multiple dimension score is an indication of the extent to which 'excluded' groups overlap.

Over half the sample are not excluded on any dimension at Wave 7, while just under one in three are excluded on a single dimension. Very few—less than 1 per cent of the sample—fall below the threshold on all four dimensions. The distribution indicates that inclusion–exclusion is a continuum in terms of numbers of dimensions of exclusion. There is no evidence of a concentration of individuals who are excluded in all four respects—who might be called an underclass.

This is confirmed if we examine the overlap between each pair of dimensions (Table 3.4). The largest overlaps are between the consumption and production dimensions, and between the consumption and political engagement dimensions—but even these account for only 1 in 20 of the overall sample. The overlaps are also small relative to the levels of exclusion on each dimension shown in Table 3.2. This suggests each dimension is picking up different kinds of people.

Of particular interest is the relationship between extent to exclusion and income. This is shown in Table 3.5. The overlap between consumption exclusion

Table 3.4. *Overlap between dimensions of exclusion, Wave 7*
(% of whole sample excluded on both dimensions in the pair)

	Consumption	Production	Political engagement
Production	5		
Political engagement	5	3	
Social interaction	2	1	2

Note: Cross-sectional sample at Wave 7, excluding cases from ECHP.
Source: Authors' calculations using BHPS Wave 7.

Table 3.5. *Low income and exclusion on different dimensions, Wave 7* (%)

Income quintile group	Production	Political engagement	Social interaction
Bottom	46	28	28
2nd	24	23	21
3rd	15	18	19
4th	9	17	17
Top	6	14	16
All	100	100	100

Note: Income quintiles defined over equivalized net household incomes of the working-age population.
Source: Authors' calculations using BHPS Wave 7.

and income cannot be measured here because our proxy for consumption is income; the issue has been explored in detail by Nolan and Whelan (1996) amongst others.

Just under half of those in the bottom income quintile group are not engaged in a socially valued activity, falling to only 6 per cent of the top income group. A particularly large difference is observed between those in the bottom and one-but-bottom income groups. The gradients for political and social dimensions are much less steep, but also smoother. Between 1 in 5 and 1 in 6 of top income quintile group are socially isolated or politically disengaged.

EXCLUSION OVER TIME

Connections over time in exclusion on a particular dimension are much stronger than the associations between different dimensions at a single point in time. Table 3.6 shows, for each dimension, the correlation between exclusion at this wave and exclusion at previous waves or observations. As is to be expected, correlations between current exclusion and exclusion at the previous observation are stronger than correlations over longer time periods, but they are all positive and statistically significant. The production and consumption dimensions show higher correlations over time than the political and social dimensions, but this could be an artefact of the frequency with which information on those variables is collected.

Table 3.7 takes the full eight waves of data (for those responding at every wave), and shows the total duration of exclusion on each dimension.[7] Nearly two-thirds of the sample never experience exclusion on the consumption dimension. On each of the production, political, and social dimensions, around three-quarters of the sample are never excluded. Between 10 and 20 per cent are excluded at just one wave out of the eight, and decreasing proportions are excluded for two and more waves. The decreasing frequency from 0 to 8 waves suggests that inclusion–exclusion is a continuum over time. If there were two distinct groups, the 'included' and the 'excluded', one would expect to find a distribution clustered at the extremes.

Although the long-stayers are a small group overall, they represent a relatively high proportion of total observations of exclusion—as is always the case in dynamic analysis. Just under half (45 per cent) of all observations of consumption exclusion are accounted for by those who remain excluded for five or more waves; 58 per cent of total observations of production exclusion are accounted for by a similar group. Long-stayers are a small but important constituency in policy terms.

---

[7] The experience of exclusion need not be consecutive, so three waves might be 1, 2, 3 or 1, 3, 7, etc. Also, since the status of individuals between interviews is unknown, duration is approximated by number of waves (interviews) at which they reported an excluded status.

Table 3.6. *Correlation between exclusion on each dimension over time* (correlation coefficients for working-age population)

This wave (=t)	Last observation (t−1)	One but last observation (t−2)
Consumption	0.521*	0.430*
Production	0.638*	0.552*
Political[†]	0.371*	—
Social[†]	0.397*	0.325*

*Indicates statistical significance at 5% level.
[†]For political dimension, last observation is 5 waves previously; for social dimension, 2 waves previously.
Sample present at two or more consecutive observations.
Source: Authors' calculations using BHPS Waves 1–8.

Table 3.7. *Exclusion over time, by dimension, Wave 8* (% of working-age population)

Number of waves at which excluded	Consumption	Production	Political engagement	Social interaction
0	63	70	76	77
1	12	12	17	13
2	8	5	7	6
3	5	3	n/a	3
4	4	2	n/a	1
5	3	2	n/a	n/a
6	2	2	n/a	n/a
7	3	1	n/a	n/a
8	n/a	3	n/a	n/a
Unweighted base* =100%	3562	4342	4563	4205

*Longitudinal sample (respondent at every wave) at Wave 8.
n/a: not applicable because data not collected for a sufficient number of waves.
Source: Authors' calculations using BHPS Waves 1–8.

Table 3.8 examines how the experience of exclusion on each dimension develops over time. Taking the consumption dimension as an example, at Wave 1, 16 per cent are excluded and 84 per cent are not (as also shown in Table 3.2). As time progresses, an increasing proportion of the sample have some experience of exclusion, and, correspondingly, a decreasing proportion have never

Table 3.8. *Cumulative exclusion, by dimension, Waves 1–8 (% of working-age population excluded at all, some, or none of waves since Wave 1)*

Wave	Consumption			Production			Political engagement			Social interaction		
	All	Some	None	All	Some	None	All	Some	None	All	Some	None
1	16	0	84	13	0	87	n/a	n/a	n/a	12	0	88
2	9	14	77	8	10	82	17	0	83	n/a	n/a	n/a
3	6	21	73	7	14	79	n/a	n/a	n/a	5	12	83
4	5	25	70	5	18	76	n/a	n/a	n/a	n/a	n/a	n/a
5	4	29	67	5	21	74	n/a	n/a	n/a	2	18	79
6	3	32	65	4	24	72	n/a	n/a	n/a	n/a	n/a	n/a
7	3	34	63	3	26	71	7	17	76	1	22	77
8	n/a	n/a	n/a	3	27	70	n/a	n/a	n/a	n/a	n/a	n/a

Note: Base is longitudinal sample at each wave.

Source: Authors' calculations using BHPS Waves 1–8.

experienced consumption exclusion during the panel. Interestingly, the proportion who are excluded throughout falls steeply over time, and continues to fall through to Wave 6—further evidence that the 'permanently excluded' are a small minority, even if we restrict our attention to a single dimension. Similar patterns are apparent for the other dimensions.

The proportion of the sample who experience some exclusion, but are not excluded throughout, is an indication of the degree of mobility in that dimension. In these terms, the consumption dimension shows the greatest mobility, followed by production, social, and political dimensions in that order. For social and political dimensions, this could be an artefact of the relative infrequency with which the questions are asked.

Finally, the multidimensional measure is combined with the longitudinal measure in a single index. For each individual, the score on the index is the number of dimensions on which he or she is excluded, multiplied by the total duration of that exclusion (in waves). Since not all four dimensions of exclusion are measured at every wave, the maximum score is 21, rather than 32 (4 dimensions multiplied by 8 waves).

Figure 3.1 plots the frequency distribution for the index, and shows a smooth curve. No member of the sample scores more than 17 (e.g. 2 dimensions at 7 waves and 1 dimension at 3 waves), while over 1 in 3 never experience exclusion on any dimension during the course of eight waves.

Table 3.9 shows how the experience of exclusion on multiple dimensions develops over time. Initially, a small minority of the sample have the maximum score (all possible dimensions at all waves which have elapsed). By Wave 4, this group has ceased to exist. Meanwhile, the proportion who have no experience of exclusion on any dimension during the period of observation falls from over two-thirds at Wave 1, to just over one-third by Wave 7. This kind of analysis

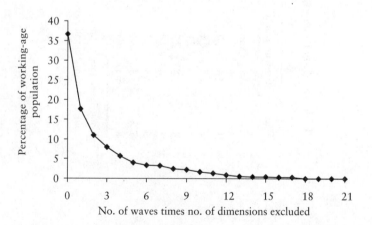

Figure 3.1. *Exclusion over time on multiple dimensions, by Wave 8*

Table 3.9. *Cumulative exclusion over time on multiple dimensions*
(% of working-age population excluded at all, some, or none of
total possible dimensions x waves, since Wave 1)

Wave	All	Some	None	Unweighted base[*]=100%	Maximum possible score
1	1.5	30	68	6854	3
2	0.2	45	55	5653	6
3	0.1	50	50	4836	9
4	0.0	53	47	4366	11
5	0.0	56	44	3898	14
6	0.0	58	42	3664	16
7	0.0	63	37	3418	20
8	0.0	63	37	3279	21

[*]Longitudinal sample at each wave.

Source: Authors' calculations using BHPS Waves 1–8.

highlights the sensitivity of results to the window of observation available—a shorter panel is more likely to indicate polarization in the population than a longer one—but also indicates that over a period as short as four years, the experience of some exclusion becomes a majority experience.

CONCEPTS AND MEASUREMENT, MEASUREMENT AND POLICY

The discipline of developing an empirical measure of social exclusion forces a degree of clarity over which outcomes are of interest—which social phenomena matter for their own sake, rather than simply as an indicator of another problem. Clarity over outcomes of interest has the potential to lead to better-focused research on the complex causes of social exclusion.

The attempt to define and measure social exclusion also brings to light areas where methodological development is needed. Perhaps the most significant gap between the concept and measurement tools available is the question of agency. Social exclusion is almost invariably framed in terms of the *opportunity* to participate, yet existing indicators measure actual participation or non-participation. We neither know whether the (non-)participation is regarded as problematic by the individual, nor whether he or she has other options.

Even a relatively crude measure can indicate the applicability of some concepts of social exclusion to contemporary Britain. For example, the evidence presented in this chapter does not fit easily with the idea of an underclass, cut off from mainstream society. Rather, inclusion and exclusion are found to be on a continuum, both across dimensions of exclusion and by duration. If anything, the results draw attention to the possibility of an 'overclass'—those who never dip below an exclusion threshold on any dimension during the eight waves for which we observe them—and their role in protecting a privileged position.

Measurement, and the kinds of measures used, can have an important impact on policy. The government's pledge to reduce child poverty was made distinctly more plausible by its simultaneous commitment to produce an annual poverty report. Similarly, if the government continues to make claims about social exclusion, it will be important that we have baseline data and subsequent measures. Such was the purpose of the New Policy Institute indicators (Rahman *et al.* 2000). But failing to distinguish between risk factors and outcomes, and the sheer number of indicators, creates the danger that the government will be able to highlight those areas where there has been progress (whether or not the result of government policy), while ignoring more politically sensitive issues, or areas where change is harder to implement, such as reducing material inequality.

The multidimensional, dynamic measure explored in this chapter could—if taken forward into the new century—act as a barometer of the effectiveness of government policy on reducing social exclusion. Some might argue that the social dimension is not one on which government policy could or should be focused, but policies on the family, cultural diversity, and regional labour markets could all have an indirect impact. The other dimensions are subject to more direct intervention from government. The longitudinal aspect of the measure could be important in assessing whether policies are succeeding in including the majority, at the expense of creating a more permanently excluded minority.

Appendix. BHPS Variables Used for Dimensions of Social Exclusion

Consumption
wHHNETDE (from Bardasi, Jenkins, and Rigg derived dataset see note 3): net current household income before housing costs, equivalized by McClement's scale and deflated to January 1998 prices. Includes income from earnings, benefits, pensions, investments, transfers, and 'other sources', for all household members. Includes some imputed data.

Exclusion defined as under half mean equivalized income for the year in question.

Production
wJBSTAT: self-defined economic activity (self-employed/employed/unemployed/retired/maternity leave/family care/full-time student or at school/long-term sick or disabled/government training scheme/other)

Exclusion defined as unemployed, not working and long-term sick or disabled, retired below state pension age, or 'other'.

Political Engagement
wORGMA-wORGAE (excluding *wORGMC* and *wORGAC*): whether a member of/active in any of the following organizations: political party, trade union, parents' association, tenants', or residents' association.

wVOTE7: whether voted in this/last year's general election (exact question phrasing depends on timing of interview within the fieldwork period)

Exclusion defined as did not vote in general election and not a member of, or active in, any campaigning organization.

Social Interaction
wSSUPA-wSSUPE: Is there anyone who ... 'you can really count on to listen to you when you need to talk?', 'you can really count on to help you out in a crisis?', 'you can totally be yourself with?', 'you feel really appreciates you as a person?', 'you can really count on to comfort you when you are very upset?'

Exclusion defined as lacking someone in any of these five respects.

Availability of variables, by wave

Wave	Net income	Economic activity	Organization membership + voting	Social interaction
1	✓	✓	✓+✗	✓
2	✓	✓	✓+✓	✗
3	✓	✓	✓+✗	✓
4	✓	✓	✓+✗	✗
5	✓	✓	✓+✗	✓
6	✓	✓	✗+✗	✗
7	✓	✓	✓+✓	✓
8	✗	✓	✗+✗	✗

4

The Dynamics of Poverty in Britain

SIMON BURGESS AND CAROL PROPPER

One central aspect of social exclusion under any definition is lack of income. The focus of this chapter is on movements in and out of income below the poverty line: what has come to be called poverty dynamics. Poverty was a major economic and political issue in Britain in the late 1990s. Recent figures show that in 1998/9 about one in five Britons had incomes that put them in poverty by one widely used measure (living in a household in which total income is less than half the national mean). The comparable figure in 1979 was less than one in ten. Poverty has risen among households with children: in 1979, one in twelve children were poor; in 1995/6 one in four were poor. Underlying these snapshots of poverty levels lie movements of people in and out of poverty over their lives. Many people will experience some poverty at some time, though only a minority of people are permanently poor. But the existence of income mobility does not mean that poverty should not be a major social concern. While poverty is a transient phenomenon for some, for most of the poor poverty is a persistent feature of their lives.

Poverty dynamics are complex and involve an analysis of the interconnections between the labour market, household formation and dissolution, and the welfare state. Britain has seen huge changes in all of these spheres since the mid-1970s. The nation as a whole has become much richer: national income has risen by 50 per cent in the 25 years since 1975. The unemployment rate more than trebled between 1975 and 1985, before falling back sharply in the later 1980s, then rising steeply again and then falling again. The dispersion of earnings has increased rapidly in Britain as in the USA, with those on the lowest earnings faring the worst. Marriage rates have fallen and divorce rates have escalated; the proportion of households containing one adult and children has risen substantially. The ethos of the welfare state has been challenged and the relative value of benefits eroded.

In this chapter we review the evidence on what has happened to the dynamics of poverty. We look at evidence produced from longitudinal surveys that document people's experiences of poverty over time. We argue that poverty is a complex issue to analyse and that to make progress we need a framework for analysing poverty, and we set out a number of ways this may be done.

POVERTY DYNAMICS IN THE UK

Poverty Levels: the Last 30 Years[1]

We begin by providing a brief overview of the patterns in poverty over the last 30 years. The UK has no official poverty line. There is considerable debate about the appropriate definition of poverty. Some researchers define poverty in terms of income (or rather, lack thereof). Others argue that poverty should be measured in terms of lack of access to social necessities. For a recent example of this latter approach in the UK, see Gordon *et al.* (2000). An example of this approach embodied in policy is the National Anti-Poverty Strategy (NAPS) in Eire, where the specific measure of poverty embodied in NAPS is related to both a relative income line and the experience of 'basic deprivation', as measured by individual's access to various non-monetary indicators (Layte *et al.* 2000). When an income-based measure is used, there is debate over whether this measure should be absolute (used in the USA) or relative (commonly used in the UK and Europe).

In this chapter we use an income-based measure. One of the most commonly used measures is the number of people whose income is less than half the average income. This is a *relative* measure of poverty, rather than an *absolute* measure: it depends on the prosperity of society as a whole, not the income needed to buy a fixed bundle of goods.[2] In UK official statistics, this measure is defined in two ways: before housing costs and after housing costs. The main advantages of deducting housing costs are twofold. First, this allows correction for one of the most important regional differences in living costs in the UK. Second, it provides consistency over time where rising rents have increased before housing cost incomes through increases in housing benefit, even though individuals are no better off. However, excluding housing costs omits any benefits individuals derive from higher (and more costly) housing quality.[3] In fact, whether incomes are measured before or after housing costs have been paid makes a considerable difference to the measured level of the number who are poor at any time, but has less impact on the trends over time. Income measured after housing costs (AHC) is more unequally distributed than incomes measured before housing costs (BHC), and the number who are recorded as poor is correspondingly higher. In this review we use both the BHC and AHC definitions. We also report results for people who have incomes in the bottom fifth of the income distribution.[4]

Figure 4.1(a) shows the proportion of the population with equivalized household income below half-average equivalized household income before housing costs (BHC) from 1961 to 1997/8. The figure shows the number of poor persons

---

[1] Much of the evidence reviewed in this section comes from Goodman, Johnson, and Webb (1997), and Hills (1998*b*).

[2] See for example Goodman, Johnson, and Webb (1997), chapter 1.

[3] For further discussion of these issues see Hills (1998*b*).

[4] All the measures of household income that we report are adjusted for differences in household composition: that is to say, they use *equivalized* income. All of these measures assume equal sharing of resources within households.

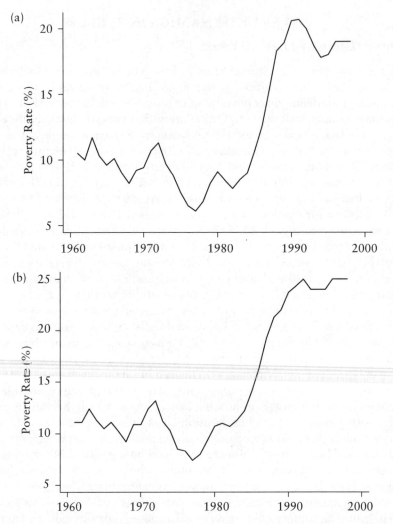

Figure 4.1. *(a) Percentage of individuals poor in the UK, 1961–1998 (before housing costs) (b) Percentage of individuals poor in the UK, 1961–1998 (after housing costs)*

Sources: Goodman, Johnson, and Webb (1997); DSS (2000*b*) and earlier editions.

was about 10 per cent of the population between the 1960s, fell during the early 1970s to a low of 6 per cent in 1977, then rose sharply during the last half of the 1980s to over 20 per cent in the early 1990s, since when it has fallen back to 19 per cent in 1997/8. The after housing cost measure in Figure 4.1(b) shows a more dramatic pattern, with a rise from 7 to 24 per cent of the population who had below half average income between 1977 and 1997/8.

The change from the gradual decline in poverty up to the early 1980s to the rapid rise since is very dramatic. While the USA also experienced an end to the long decline in poverty at the end of the 1970s, the subsequent rise was nothing like as dramatic: poverty rose from around 11 per cent through the 1970s to 15 per cent in the early 1980s and again in the early 1990s (see Danziger and Gottschalk 1995, fig. 3.8). However, poverty in the USA is measured against a fixed real value: the real income required to buy the basket of goods deemed to be necessary for subsistence living. The UK numbers quoted above measure the number who are poor against a standard which varies as the prosperity of the population changes. If we take a fixed standard in the UK (half the average equivalized income in 1979, adjusted for inflation) then we can define the numbers in absolute poverty as the number of individuals whose (equivalized) income fell below this level. Using this measure absolute poverty fell during the 1960s and 1970s: in 1961 just under 24 per cent of the population were poor in this sense, falling to 8 per cent in 1979. However, between 1979 and 1991 the numbers below this *fixed* standard fell only slightly on a BHC basis (to 7 per cent), despite national income rising by 23 per cent over those 12 years and average household income by more than a third. During the first half of the 1990s the number in absolute poverty fell to 5 per cent on a BHC basis.[5]

Individuals in all income groups shared the economic growth of the 1960s and 1970s, but that of the 1980s was concentrated in the top half of the distribution. During the first part of the 1990s economic growth once again improved the fortunes of the poorest, but between 1995/6 and 1998/9 inequality rose again and the relative position of the poorest worsened once again. Using an absolute poverty standard, the trend over the last 20 years has been similar in the USA and the UK, the latter faring better in that poverty continued to fall very slowly, rather than rising as in the USA in the early 1980s.

Poverty Dynamics in the UK: the Facts

Much of the popular and policy debate on poverty understandably focuses on those people who are poor at the time. This would be appropriate if poverty (and non-poverty) was essentially a permanent state of affairs. But this is unlikely to be the case.

The statistics above show that around a fifth of individuals in Britain are currently in poverty using the definitions adopted here. At one extreme an average poverty rate of 20 per cent may mean that those same 20 per cent of individuals are always poor. At the other extreme every individual may have a one in five chance of being poor at any time. The nature of the poverty problem is clearly dependent on which of these is closer to the truth. The stock of people in poverty at any point in time is driven by two flows: the numbers falling into poverty and the numbers escaping. To determine the chances that an individual will

---

[5] The AHC figures tell a similar story, though the levels are slightly higher.

experience these movements requires not a single 'snapshot' of income at one time, but information about people's income over time. Thus we need longitudinal data of the kind that can be obtained from a survey that follows individuals over time and from which we can determine their poverty status.

Until recently, lack of data meant that relatively little has been known about poverty dynamics in the UK, but the advent of the British Household Panel Survey (BHPS) has meant that we are beginning to establish facts about poverty dynamics in the UK. These BHPS data reinforce the point that any snapshot picture masks the extent of mobility. Many people will experience low income at some point in their life. Over half the household population spent at least one year in the bottom 30 per cent of the income distribution between 1991 and 1996. For most people this was transitory and lasted no longer than a year. But for some it was a longer term experience (HM Treasury 1999).

Jarvis and Jenkins (1998) have analysed movements in and out of poverty between 1990 and 1994/5 using the BHPS. Their analysis indicates the following. First, if poverty is defined as having an income (BHC) of less than half the average income in the BHPS at the first interview (1990/1), then almost a third of individuals in the survey were poor at least once during the four-year period. For those starting a low-income spell, the exit rate within one year is around 54 per cent (Jarvis and Jenkins 1996). Those who leave poverty have a 30 per cent chance of returning within another year. Defining persistent poverty as being poor in all 4 of the years 1991–5, then just under 5 per cent of persons in the sample were in persistent poverty. These analyses have been repeated for these years and the following 4 (DSS 2000*b*) using a definition of poverty as having an income in the lowest fifth of the income distribution. These analyses show that about 37 per cent of individuals were poor in at least one year out of each four-year window, but a smaller proportion were poor in most of the years. Only 7 to 8 per cent were poor in all 4 years, 14 per cent poor in at least three, and 23 per cent poor in at least two. The figures also show little change in these patterns between the two four-year periods. As the time period is increased, the numbers who are poor all the time falls: only 3 per cent of the population have incomes in the bottom fifth for all 8 years between 1991 to 1998 (see Tables 3.7 and 3.8 in Chapter 3 of this volume for similar results).

Although people do move out of the lowest income groups, they often do not move far. Table 4.1 shows Jarvis and Jenkins' comparison of the income (quintile) groups of individuals for average 1991 and 1992 income and for average 1993 and 1994 income.[6] If there were complete immobility, individuals would never change income group. If movements were random, 20 per cent of each starting group would fall into each ending group. If we define being poor as

---

[6] This table refers to individuals in the BHPS sample with income reported in each year. Income is net of tax, summed over all household members and over all sources of income. It relates to the month prior to the interview. The averaging is intended to reduce measurement error.

Table 4.1. *Income mobility in the BHPS*

Quintile income group 'W12'	Quintile income group 'W34'					
	Bottom	2	3	4	Top	All
Bottom	64	24	9	2	0	100
2	22	48	22	5	3	100
3	10	20	46	20	4	100
4	3	5	19	53	19	100
Top	1	2	5	20	74	100

Notes: The table gives the percentage of individuals in each quintile group in averaged waves 1 and 2 moving to the column quintile in averaged waves 3 and 4. Quintile Income Group 'W34' means quintile income group of the averaged wave 3 and wave 4 income.

Source: Jarvis and Jenkins (1998), table 2.

being in the lowest quintile group of the income distribution, the table shows 64 per cent of those who were poor in 1991/2 were also poor in 1993/4, and 88 per cent were either poor or in the next quintile of the income distribution. Analyses based over the eight-year period 1991 to 1998 show a very similar pattern of limited mobility out of the lowest income quintile group (DSS, 2000*b*).

Another way of looking at this is to compute what proportion of income differences across individuals is long term i.e. persists across years. We do not have access to people's lifetime incomes, but estimates can be made from the BHPS. Jenkins (1999) estimates that long term inequality accounts for around 88 per cent of the income inequality observed in an average year.

Movements in and out of poverty are not random. That is to say, people who have low income at one time are likely to have low incomes at another. From the first four waves of the BHPS, Hills (1998*a*) has compared Jarvis and Jenkins' findings on how often individuals are found in poverty (defined as half average BHPS incomes) with what would be expected if income movements were uncorrelated over time. He shows that in the BHPS 64 per cent of individuals were never in poverty, compared to 41 per cent if poverty inflows and outflows were uncorrelated. Similarly, 14 per cent of individuals are poor three or four times out of 4 years, compared to 2.7 per cent if movements in and out were uncorrelated. These results show how poverty and non-poverty are concentrated in the population.

Another way of seeing this is to compare entry and exit rates for all individuals compared with those for individuals that have been poor (or not poor) for a certain time. Jarvis and Jenkins found that the exit rate from low income after a year on low income is 54 per cent (the figure given above), but for those who are poor for 2 years this falls slightly to 51 per cent. Amongst those leaving poverty, the poverty re-entry rate after one year out of poverty is just under 30 per cent, but the re-entry rate after 2 years out of poverty is considerably lower at 11 per cent.

These pictures of movements in and out of poverty come from observing income at two points in time. Transition matrices of the sort provided in Table 4.1 provide a compact way of summarizing such information about income dynamics. However, they do not provide a very intuitive view of the process, nor do they allow for differences across people, as the transitions are averages over everyone. An alternative presentation of the data has been developed by Gardiner and Hills (1999). This involves classifying individuals into a set of income trajectory types depending on the evolution of household income over 4 years. Using the BHPS dataset and income percentile boundaries, the following types were defined on the basis of the number of boundaries crossed and the general direction of income change: flat, rising, falling, blips, and others. The results are shown in Table 4.2. They reinforce the idea of substantial income mobility in general: only 40 per cent of the population have an income profile over 4 years that is 'flat'. Indeed, only 60 per cent have what could be described as 'straightforward' income profiles (flat, rising, or falling)—the remaining 40 per cent experiencing substantial and erratic changes in their income. However, the authors show that this mobility does not mean that all poverty is transient and therefore of little concern to policy-makers. They show that 41 per cent of poverty-years are spent

Table 4.2. *Types of income trajectory*

Trajectory type	Per cent of cases	Per cent of low income observations
Flat:		
Poor	8.7	40.5
Non-poor	32.5	1.6
Rising:		
Out of poverty	2.6	5.4
Non-poor	3.5	—
Falling:		
Into poverty	1.5	3.6
Non-poor	2.5	—
Blips:		
Out of poverty	5.6	20.6
Into poverty	5.1	7.1
Non-poor	19.2	—
Other:		
Repeated poverty	5.2	13.7
One-off poverty	5.8	7.5
Non-poor	8.0	—

Notes: Income paths or trajectories are categorized on the basis of the number of crossings allowed of income percentiles. Details are provided in the source paper.

Source: Gardiner and Hills (1999).

in the context of 'poor flat' income trajectories. A further 34 per cent are spent in trajectories characterized as 'blipping out of poverty' or 'repeated poverty'. All of these income histories indicate that poverty is a persistent fact of life for most of the poor.

In summary, the emerging British evidence suggests that, compared to a picture of a mass of people permanently poor, there is both considerable movement in and out of the population in poverty. There is also evidence that poverty persists for a small but not insignificant group: most of the people poor at any point in time will experience a lot of poverty. How does this compare to other countries?

Poverty Dynamics in Other OECD Countries

A study comparing poverty dynamics across six countries for the first half of the 1990s (Germany, the Netherlands, Sweden, the UK, the USA, and Canada) found that poverty dynamics shared several common features. While care must be taken in drawing strong conclusions from data across countries, Oxley *et al.* (2000) found:

• In all six countries, the poverty situation is both better and worse than the picture suggested by looking just at numbers in poverty at any one time. The share of individuals who are poor (below half median equivalized income) throughout a six-year window is small and typically makes up between 2 to 6 per cent of the population. On the other hand, the share of the population that was poor at least once in the six-year window was large, ranging from 20 to nearly 40 per cent. This number was considerably larger than the poverty rate 'snapshot' in all six countries.

• People experiencing longer spells of poverty have a lower probability of exit and the chances of exiting fall with previous experiences of poverty. For those who exit, there is a high probability of falling back into poverty.

Table 4.3 breaks down the share of individuals experiencing any poverty over the six-year period on the basis of the number of years spent in poverty.[7] For example, 26 per cent of those experiencing poverty in the UK spent one year in poverty, and 28 per cent of those experiencing poverty were poor for 5 or more years of the six-year window. The average number of years spent in poverty is similar across all the four countries, but this average masks significant differences between the countries. The table shows that the UK and the USA are rather different from the other four countries. For example, in Germany, just over 46 per cent of those who experienced poverty did so for only one year. The comparable figure for Britain was 26 per cent and for the USA 33 per cent. On the other hand, nearly 28 per cent of the poor were poor for 5 or more years in the

---

[7] This includes repeat spells.

Table 4.3. *Time spent in poverty over a 6-year window*

		\multicolumn{6}{l}{Share of individuals in poverty for 1 to 5+ years (%)}					
		1 year	2 years	3 years	4 years	5 or 6 years	Average years in poverty
Canada	1990–95	36	27	14	9	14	2
Germany	1991–96	46	19	12	8	16	2
Netherlands	1991–96	48	21	12	8	12	2
Sweden	1991–96	41	22	13	9	16	2
UK	1991–96	26	19	14	13	28	3
USA	1988–93	33	19	11	10	28	3

Notes: Numbers rounded to nearest decimal place. Income is post-tax and transfers. Poverty line is taken as 50% of median equivalized disposable income.

Source: Oxley *et al.* (2000).

UK and the USA, whilst the comparable figures for the Netherlands, Sweden, Germany, and Canada were all under 16 per cent.

The share of all poverty spells experienced by those in poverty for at least 5 years is 30 per cent in Canada, 36 per cent in Germany, 29 per cent in the Netherlands, and 35 per cent in Sweden, but in the UK and the USA it is around 50 per cent. Given these figures, it is not surprising that the chances of escaping poverty are in general lower in the UK and the USA than in the other four countries. And having exited, the probability of re-entering within 2 years is higher in the UK and USA, where around 50 per cent re-enter within 2 years, than in all the other four countries.[8]

In summary, the position of the UK appears to be closer to that of the USA than other European countries. Fewer poor individuals have short spells and more have longer spells in poverty. In other words, poverty in the UK appears more persistent than in other OECD countries.

Of all these countries, the USA has the longest runs of longitudinal data. However, whether we take this longer run perspective, or examine different groups, or look at slightly different periods, doesn't change the basic picture much. The data indicate again considerable differences between the stock of individuals who are poor at any one time and the number who are frequently in poverty over a 'lifetime'. In an early study of US data, Duncan (1984) used 9 years of data from the Panel Study of Income Dynamics (PSID) and found that 33 per cent of the sample experienced poverty in at least one year, but only about 5 per cent were persistently poor (which he defined as being poor for 8 out of 10 years).

---

[8] This picture of greater numbers of long-term poor to some extent conflicts with the view of the USA, and to a lesser extent, the UK, as more mobile societies than Germany. For examination of this, see Schluter (1998).

Bane and Ellwood (1986) found most poverty spells in the 1970s (1971–81) in the USA were short: 45 per cent of spells were terminated within a year and 70 per cent of the spells were over within 3 years. Huff Stevens (1994) reported almost identical figures for the period 1970–87. Note that the finding that most poverty spells are of a short duration does not mean most observed poverty is short term, as individuals who spend longer time in poverty are more frequently observed when we take a 'snapshot' picture (i.e. look at the stock of the poor). Using data on young people—individuals aged between 14 and 30 years of age in the 1980s (from NLSY data for 1979–91)—Burgess and Propper (1997) found that an average poverty rate of 13 per cent masked considerable differences between individuals: 40 per cent of individuals were poor at least once during 13 years, but 4 per cent were poor for at least 10 years out of 13.

WHO EXPERIENCES POVERTY TRANSITIONS?

Being poor is having income below a certain level, where generally the calculation of income is adjusted for household needs. Being poor will depend on the household's participation in the labour market and other sources of income, and also on the number of household members. So underlying changes in poverty are due to changes in these factors, and so poverty dynamics are related to the dynamics of these processes.

For this reason, one way of beginning to answer the question of who experiences poverty transitions is to look at the events associated with becoming poor and moving out of poverty. These events can be grouped into three sets. The first is employment-related events—changes in labour market participation or in earnings—of any of the household members. The second is family structure related events, for example marriage, divorce, the birth of a child. The third are events associated with changes in income which fall into neither category, for example changes in the amounts received from unearned income, or from the tax and benefit system.

The Impact of Labour Market Events

An analysis of the BHPS for 1991–6 by Oxley (1999) showed that around 28 per cent of entries into poverty and 41 per cent of exits from poverty were associated with employment-related events. The figures for households for which there was a working-age head were, not surprisingly, higher: 35 per cent of entries into poverty and 51 per cent of exits were associated with employment-related events for these households. Further analysis of the relationship between these employment-related events and the chances of moving into poverty showed that it was households where all members lost their jobs, or had a fall in hours, who were most likely to become poor. For exits, the presence of a second worker who increases hours is most likely to lead to an exit from poverty.

Given this association between entry and exit into poverty and employment, the distribution of work across households will affect the distribution of poverty

movements. Lack of work is an important risk factor for short-term and persistent low income. Two-thirds of working-age households on low income are
workless and 8 out of 10 are not fully employed. Among those on persistently
low incomes of working age, 60 per cent are in workless households compared
to just 13 per cent who are fully employed (HM Treasury 1999*b*). The last three
decades have seen a substantial change in the distribution of employment across
households. Table 4.4 shows that the number of households in which there are
no earners and the number in which there are two earners have both risen, while
the number in which there is only one earner has fallen. In other words, work has
become more concentrated within certain households.

In addition to a concentration in employment, there has been a widening of
earnings differentials. This widening gap has been characterized by increased
occupational and educational differentials. This increase in earnings differentials
is not peculiar to the UK, but has occurred also in the USA, Canada, Australia,
and New Zealand. If there were a lot of movement up and down the earnings distribution this widening gap would be of less concern. However, the data from
panel surveys shows that there is relatively little earnings mobility over short time
periods, that low pay persists, and that much mobility is short range. The result is
that there is considerable immobility in earnings. Data from the Lifetimes Labour
Market Data base (Table 4.5) shows that 27 per cent of individuals who were in
the lowest earnings group for their age group in 1978 at age 25 were in the

Table 4.4. *Households by number of earners (%)*

	1971	1981	1991
No earner	3	7	9
One earner	51	42	31
Two earners	46	51	60

Source: HM Treasury (1999*b*), table 2.11.

Table 4.5. *Earnings mobility of men*

Earnings group in 1978 at age 25	Earnings group in 1992–3 at age 40					
	Bottom fifth	Next fifth	Middle fifth	Next fifth	Top fifth	No longer in class 1 employment
Bottom fifth	27	18	9	7	7	33
Next fifth	15	17	22	15	6	26
Middle fifth	11	17	19	16	11	26
Next fifth	9	14	15	20	19	22
Top fifth	4	7	12	20	37	19

Figures are percentages of earners from that age group.
Source: HM Treasury (1999*b*), table 2.19.

lowest earnings group 15 years later at age 40. Most of those who moved up the earnings ladder moved up only to the next fifth. A large proportion of those in the lowest earnings group when young actually moved out of employment, either to self-employment or, more commonly, into unemployment or out of the labour force. Such persistence of low pay, or cycles of low pay and unemployment, contribute to the numbers in poverty. (For further discussion of these cycles, see Abigail McKnight, Chapter 7 in this volume).

The Impact of Family-Related Events

Employment and/or earnings changes are the most important events associated with entry and escape from low income. But changes in family composition such as divorce, marriage, and childbirth are also associated with changes in income. For a significant minority of people—one in three—the birth of a child results in a fall in their living standards. For some—between 10 and 15 per cent—it leads the family into poverty (HM Treasury 1999*b*). A tenth of all entries into low income are associated with separation or divorce. Oxley (1999) has calculated that 26 per cent of all entries into poverty and 9 per cent of exits are associated with a family event. Jenkins (1999) and Jarvis and Jenkins (1999) find similar qualitative results: 38 per cent of transitions into low income and 18 per cent of transitions out are associated with demographic events.

Just as there are links between the chances of unemployment in one period and the chances of unemployment in the next, so there are links between household events. These may be links across generations as well as over time for the same individual, as discussed by John Hobcraft in Chapter 5 in this volume. Kathleen Kiernan (Chapter 6 in this volume) examines the impact of parental divorce on the chances of their children forming partnerships in adulthood. Young women who experience parental divorce are more likely than their peers to commence sexual relations earlier, to cohabit or marry at young ages, to have children in their teens, and have children outside marriage. Men and women whose parents have divorced are in turn more likely to experience the break-up of their own marriage. Men and women from divorced families are also more likely to become parents at a young age.

In addition, family and work-related events are not mutually exclusive. For example, a divorce may lead to a loss of a job if the single mother cannot make adequate childcare arrangements. It is well established that lone parents face more problems with combining work and parenthood, which in turn puts them and their children at greater risk of becoming and remaining poor (HM Treasury 1999*b*). Alternatively, a marriage may be associated with greater labour market participation by both partners in the marriage. This indicates that to understand poverty dynamics we need to understand the transitions in and out of single motherhood as well as in and out of employment.

Kiernan and Mueller (1999) found that divorced men are less likely to be in employment than their married counterparts. Unemployment is higher amongst the unmarried, both single and divorced. For example, younger childless male divorcees were over twice as likely to be unemployed than the analogous group of women. Reliance on state benefits and disability were also features of the currently divorced. These factors also appear to be precursors of divorce. While it is difficult to distinguish causality, Kiernan and Mueller's analysis of longitudinal data suggests that poor economic and social well-being may be important stressors in a relationship and that the selection of vulnerable groups into divorce may be an important aspect of the poverty amongst divorced groups. This suggests that the deprived are more at risk of divorce, and that divorce may well compound their deprivation.

Oxley (1999) has shown for the UK that the probability of entry into low income from divorce and separation rises sharply when they occur at the same time as employment-related changes. On the other hand, the impact of additional work on exit from poverty appears to be the same whether it occurs alongside a marriage or partnership or whether it is not accompanied by a change in partnership status. This last result seems quite specific to the UK. For the other countries he examined—Germany, the USA, and Canada—the chances of escaping poverty were higher when both a marriage or partnership occurred at the same time as an increase in labour market participation of the household.

Given these patterns in employment and family formation, movements into and out of poverty are associated with employment and family status. Jarvis and Jenkins (1998) used the BHPS to examine the characteristics of those who are poor (defined as in the bottom fifth of the income distribution) in all 4 years for which they were interviewed. They compared these to the characteristics of those who are only poor in the first year of the survey. They found that although many of the people who are persistently poor are the same people as the Wave 1 poor population, there are some differences.[9] The 'poor at Wave 1 only' population mostly comprises elderly persons and non-working families with children. In the 'persistently poor' population there are more people belonging to lone parent families (26 per cent compared to 17 per cent) and to non-working families with children (25 per cent compared to 13 per cent). As a result persistent poverty is more associated with being unemployed or lone parenthood than once-off poverty, and there are more dependent children amongst the low-income stayers than those observed as poor only once.

METHODS OF ANALYSING POVERTY DYNAMICS

We should not be content simply to measure poverty and characterize the events associated with poverty dynamics. In addition, we would like to understand the dynamics of the underlying processes which lead in and out of poverty. This is

---

[9] Given that some individuals who were poor only at Wave 1 may have been poor before Wave 1, and that the analysis uses only 4 years of data, we might not expect large differences in the two groups.

necessary to understand the causes of poverty, and to formulate anti-poverty policies. In this last section we review attempts to model poverty dynamics.

The general message that comes from the literature surveyed above is that an understanding of poverty dynamics requires considerably more than an analysis of earnings. While at its simplest, poverty (defined, as here, in terms of a money amount) depends on the income individuals have, the probability of being poor is about more than lack of earnings. Individuals live in households and poverty is calculated as a function of household income, since it is assumed that individuals who live in households have access (implicitly equal) to the total income of that household. So the probability that an individual will be poor will depend not only on her own earnings or benefits, but also on those of others in the household. Household income will depend on the size of the household, and earnings from work of each member in the household and other sources of income, such as benefits or pensions. To quote a leading analyst of poverty in the UK,

even where income dynamics are more closely associated with labour earnings dynamics, we need to recognise that earnings dynamics are often a mixture of the earnings dynamics of several persons, not just the household head . . . Moreover, there are some households, especially the elderly, for whom the main events are changes in non-labour income. And the incidence of demographic change as the main event is not insignificant for large numbers of persons in the population. (Jenkins 2000)

Approaches to the Analysis of Poverty Dynamics

Approaches to the analysis of poverty dynamics therefore need to take into account the impact of work and household composition on household income, and also to understand the links between work and household formation and dissolution decisions. This is clearly a complex task. Most of the analyses to date have focused on part of the picture, often in an attempt to answer a specific question.

Jenkins (2000) identifies four main types of dynamic models that have been applied in the income and poverty dynamics literature to date. These are:

- The analysis of longitudinal poverty patterns
- Transition poverty models
- Variance components models
- Structural models.

These methods are reviewed in some detail in Jenkins (2000), so here we concentrate on the last method which we have adopted (Burgess and Propper 1998), sketching only the outlines of the other three. The interested reader is referred to Jenkins for further details of all four approaches.

The first method essentially describes different patterns of poverty dynamics in terms of the fixed characteristics of the individual. The dependent variable is the longitudinal sequence of income for an individual, for example a year spent in poverty followed by a year out of poverty, or 8 years of poverty out of a ten-year window. The 'explanatory' variables are the fixed characteristics of the individual, for example, their education or race. There is no focus on dynamics per se, so rather than providing an analysis of the dynamics of the poverty process, this method answers the question of who experiences certain types of poverty transition. The Gardiner and Hills (1999) analysis of who experiences different trajectories is an example of this type of analysis.

The second approach examines the chances of exit from, or entry into, poverty, as a function of observed characteristics of the individual. This approach answers the question of who experiences these events. So, for example, it provides an answer to who has the highest chances of becoming poor, or who has the highest chances of leaving poverty in the event they become poor. The most econometrically complex example of such a model is Huff Stevens (1999) who analyses exit and re-entry rates using the longest available run of individual income data (the PSID data from the USA).

A key issue with this approach is whether the current state the individual is in (for example, their marital state, or employment state), should be used to 'explain' their current income. It is clear that this will explain a lot of the variation in poverty flows—for example, an individual who is unemployed at a particular time is much more likely to have low income than one who is not unemployed. On the other hand, when two or more events occur at the same time, such as a marriage or unemployment, the choice of which to condition on is arbitrary. And there is a deeper issue as well. Analysing a movement in or out of poverty as a result of an event such as marriage or unemployment is essentially explaining poverty by the same processes that drive poverty transitions. For example, movements in and out of marriage are associated with education, income, and employment. These same factors are associated with poverty transitions. Controlling for events such as marriage, and arguing that they account for poverty transitions, ignores the fact that such events are, in part, caused by exactly the same factors that cause poverty. So explaining poverty transitions in terms of such events does not give information about the importance of the processes underlying the event and nor does it allow us to identify the relative importance of the factors that cause these processes.

The third approach focuses on income and seeks to explain the path of income of an individual or a household in terms of observed characteristics of the individual (for example, her age and education), and other non-observed processes. The dependent variable is not the binary variable, being poor or not poor, but income at any point in time, observed at several time points for all individuals in the sample. The model was originally developed for the analysis of the dynamics of earnings of individuals. (The unobserved processes in this context may be a 'shock' which hits the macro economy, causing unemployment to rise for all, but to rise disproportionately for some.) The question that this approach seeks to answer is whether we can discover regularities in the process driving household income, and so poverty dynamics. However, while the statistical approach can be extended to examine household income, the processes that are used to model earnings dynamics are not likely to provide a good fit to the large and discontinuous jumps that occur in household income as a result of, say, divorce, child birth, or unemployment (Burgess and Propper 1998).

The final approach is to model the economic processes that underlie poverty transitions as a function of observed and unobserved characteristics of the individual. The question this approach seeks an answer to is what are the fundamental characteristics of an individual or events that cause both poverty transitions and associated events. If households were fixed through time, then analysis of the probability of being poor would be relatively easy. The key issue would be the determination of the household labour supply and the level of human capital available to the household. To understand how poverty evolved, we would need to model dynamic processes, such as the labour supply responses of one partner to the other losing a job. Even in this simple case, individual decisions and events have an impact on the poverty status of all household members. So for example, if an individual loses her job, the nature of the benefit system may mean that if her partner earns a low amount, it is not worth her partner continuing to work. Modelling the income dynamics of the household (and so poverty dynamics) requires, among other things, modelling labour supply in the presence of job loss risk, and the interaction of the benefit system and earned income at a household level.

But households are not fixed through time. Individuals form, dissolve, and then re-form households. For example, young adults leave the parental home, form partnerships, have children, split up and see their own children leave home. These events may occur more than once in an individual's life and in different sequences. The individuals who make the economic decisions on employment and earnings are being continually re-sorted into different household groups. These household transitions are not exogenous: they are influenced by the behaviour of individuals. Thus an economic model of household income (and so of poverty) is a mix of individual decisions taken in a household context and decisions on household formation. The probability of a single identified individual being poor depends on the income flows into the household in which the individual lives and the household's needs. The aggregate poverty rate for a group of individuals depends on the earnings available to the group, and how the group organizes into households. These are the economic processes that constitute the poverty transition process. The central components are labour market factors such as labour supply and earnings generation, and household formation and dissolution processes such as marriage, divorce, and fertility.

So any model of poverty dynamics requires modelling of the underlying economic processes: labour supply and earnings in a household context, plus the decisions on household formation and dissolution (marriage, divorce, and fertility). To fully explore such a model is beyond the scope of this chapter. However, an approach along these lines is proposed and implemented for poverty in the USA in Burgess and Propper (1998) and we outline the approach and report some of their analysis here.

To model poverty dynamics, we model changes in employment, changes in marital status and having children as three interrelated processes. We use this framework to derive the probability of any individual being poor at any date. From this we can plot changes in poverty over time for an individual or group of individuals. The usefulness of this approach is that it allows examination of how poverty dynamics are affected by changes in the factors that affect the three underlying processes. Using simulation methods, the effect of these factors can be examined whilst holding others constant.

An example of how this framework can be used to examine poverty dynamics is given by an analysis of poverty dynamics of young women in the USA. In Burgess and Propper (1997) we first examine the impact of family background factors, such as parental income, marital status of parents, education of the individual. We compare and contrast the experience of black and white women between the ages of 19 and 29. We find that the impact of a range of background variables on poverty rates varies across the races. Changes in the income level of the family of the individual at 14 has a negligible impact on the poverty rates (in US terms) at 29 of white women, but more effect for black women at the same age. Unemployment at age 18 has a large effect on poverty rates of white women at age 29 but a smaller effect for black women. But the background variable with the largest effect on poverty rates is education. Having a college education basically eliminates the chances of poverty for both black and white women, partly by affecting women's chances of employment and partly by affecting the level of income earned in employment.

The second set of factors are the individual's current marital, employment, and family status at age 19. The results indicate that starting in unfavourable states has a downward impact on income over the next ten years. Starting at age 19 with a child as a single parent who is not in work means that the individual will still be poorer at age 29 than individuals who did not have a child at 19, even though the individuals will experience some amelioration in their relative position in the income distribution over that time.

The framework can also be used to pose the question, 'What would poverty rates be like for one group if they had the labour market or marital behaviour of another group?' These results indicate the importance of marital behaviour in accounting for the differences in poverty rates and poverty transitions for young black and white women. They also indicate that where the individual is by age 19 is more important for black than white women: in other words escaping from an initial poor position may be harder for black than white women.

These results are illustrative, but they indicate the way in which poverty dynamics can be modelled, and the benefits of focusing not on income transitions but on the behaviours underlying these transitions. But to carry out such analyses requires longitudinal data over a number of years. Until recently such data were not available in the UK: however, the advent of the British Household Panel, which now has over eight waves, means that such analysis can now be made.

CONCLUSIONS

Knowledge about the changes in individuals' poverty over time—poverty dynamics—has increased dramatically for the UK as longitudinal data have become available. What is emerging from these data is a picture of a society in which a large minority of individuals experience poverty at least once in a number of years. While for many this is a once-off event, many who escape do not move far from poverty, and among those who are poor, there is a group who experience repeated and persistent poverty. In other words, poverty experiences are widespread and are not random: individuals who experience poverty once are more likely than the rest of the population to experience it again. These patterns appear to be closer to those of the USA than those of Canada or Germany. As in the USA, relative poverty is concentrated amongst a group who suffer poverty often.

While our knowledge of the facts has increased considerably in the last decade, understanding of the factors that cause these patterns is considerably less developed. Much research to date has examined the correlates of poverty dynamics. This has identified certain groups as vulnerable to falling into poverty, and others as less vulnerable. What this research has not been able to do is to distinguish between causal factors—factors which prevent individuals from becoming poor, or get them out of poverty quickly should they fall into that state—and events which happen around the time of becoming poor or escaping poverty. The challenge is to take forward modelling approaches that allow this distinction to be made, so that policy can be focused to bring about long- rather than short-term changes in individuals' poverty status.

5

Social Exclusion and the Generations

JOHN HOBCRAFT

This chapter focuses on the pathways into social exclusion, especially during young adulthood. More specifically, I set out to discuss some of the issues involved in assessing the influences on adult social exclusion of parental endowments, of childhood circumstances, attributes, and behaviour, and of prior experiences during adulthood. Thus, both inter-generational and intra-generational aspects of the transmission of social exclusion are considered. The conceptual and practical issues involved are illustrated with examples drawn from my ongoing research programme within CASE, using results from analysis of the experiences of the cohort of children born in the first week of March 1958, who comprise the target population for the National Child Development Study (hereafter NCDS).

WHAT IS SOCIAL EXCLUSION?

One of the greatest difficulties faced in trying to analyse social exclusion is that of finding a working definition of what comprises social exclusion (a recurring theme in other Chapters, especially 1 and 3). Social exclusion is unequivocally more than poverty, but undoubtedly poverty is a key precursor, marker, or component of social exclusion. Equally, social exclusion goes beyond other economic variables, such as employment status or occupational class. An as yet unresolved question is what else is included among social, welfare, demographic, housing, psychological, and health circumstances. Clearly lack of interaction, benefit dependency, lone parenthood, living in a 'sink' estate, and having mental or physical health problems (to give but a few examples) are also precursors, markers, or components of social exclusion. Moreover, in so far as social exclusion is relative rather than absolute, the bundle of circumstances deemed to exclude an individual from (full and 'normal') inclusion in society must inevitably change with age. In the face of such uncertainty, the pragmatic solution is to explore a wide range of attributes that might be deemed indicative of social exclusion and the interplays among these attributes and then gradually to refine the definition.

These conceptual issues are further exacerbated in practical analysis by the availability in existing surveys of measures of the different aspects of social exclusion (at least until we are much surer of a definition of social exclusion in clearly measurable terms and one is regularly implemented in national surveys).

In looking at these issues longitudinally, especially across the life-course, we shall inevitably be constrained by the limits of secondary data sources for a long time to come.

A further serious problem is the difficulty of capturing a multifaceted concept such as social exclusion in a single indicator. The theory required to measure a complex construct with a single indicator inevitably takes much time and thought to develop and cannot usually be uncontroversial. How do we combine the differing elements or dimensions of social exclusion in a meaningful way? To answer this we need to develop an understanding of the relative importance of these elements and also examine very carefully the ways in which they are inter-related. In the meantime, pragmatic solutions involve examining individual attributes one at a time, or in closely related bundles, or rather simple aggregations across the differing domains of social exclusion. Whilst not being perfect, such approaches are likely to help us to progress in our understanding and a genuine theory may well prove beyond our grasp for a long time yet. 'Theory' that does not have empirical underpinnings and that cannot be subjected to reasonably rigorous testing (including exposure to alternatives) is speculation and does not deserve the label of theory.

Both because of these difficulties and for narrow disciplinary reasons, most work hitherto on inter-generational and intra-generational mobility has focused on single outcome variables (e.g. income or employment status for economists; occupational class for sociologists) and has also tended very much to limit the precursors studied to the outcome variable or to the disciplinary domain (good exceptions are Gregg and Machin 1998; and Feinstein 2000). Whilst acknowledging that such analysis is itself often difficult and challenging, the failure to grapple with the greater complexity of the undoubtedly interconnected nature of life circumstances has to be deeply regretted. There have been many occasions in my own attempts so far to face up to the complex issues involved when I have seen the benefits of running away from this daunting challenge. However, I believe that these issues are of fundamental importance and that the future programme for social scientific research has to involve breaking away from current disciplinary hegemonies, has to be multidisciplinary, and needs to engage with the biological and behavioural sciences, particularly genetics and brain science.

Illustrations of Issues in Adult Social Exclusion: Interplays

In order to illustrate some of these issues further, let us consider the potentially excluding adult outcomes by age 33 which were included in separate analyses in an earlier report (Hobcraft 1998). In that work a wide range of parental and childhood precursors were considered and their associations with each of the adult outcomes in turn were considered separately for men and for women. The relevant adult outcomes were young parenthood, extramarital births, three or more co-residential partnerships, a high malaise score, living in social housing, receipt of non-universal benefits, adult homelessness, lack of qualifications, and low income, plus adult unemployment for men only. The study explored the extent to which these were linked to common or specific antecedents among the parental and childhood variables, but did not properly take account of the obvious fact that these adult outcomes are themselves interrelated. This inter-relationship is central to the importance of social exclusion.

One simple multivariate approach to exploring these interplays is to examine for each outcome in turn its dependency on the other outcomes considered. Since the outcomes were all treated as binary responses (yes/no), a logistic model is appropriate and we chose to use a stepwise selection procedure in order to remove 'noise', with the significance level for inclusion being one in ten thousand. The results are shown in Table 5.1. Reassuringly, with very few exceptions, there was considerable symmetry in the relationships observed, in the sense that both the magnitude and statistical significance of the relationship between pairs of variables were very similar whichever of the pair was taken as the dependent variable, net of the other factors included in the selected models. For example, the net odds ratio for a young father being in social housing is 2.69 and for someone who is in social housing being a young father is 2.70 (this latter ratio indicates that someone who lives in social housing has odds of 2.7 to one of having been a young father, compared with an individual who was not in social housing). Thus, for women, being a teenage mother (looking at the first column in Table 5.1) is strongly associated with having had an extramarital birth (odds ratio 3.22), with living in social housing (odds ratio 3.38), with having no quali-fications (odds ratio 3.11), with there being no other significant relationship with any other outcome (multiple partners, malaise, benefit receipt, homelessness, or low income).

The results of this exploration are summarized in Figures 5.1 and 5.2, which show the odds ratios for the significant relationships (averaged when both are significant, because the magnitude was always close). The extent of multiple interconnections is evident from these diagrams. A notable feature is that being in social housing at age 33 is connected with more of the other adverse outcomes than any other, for both men and women. There is a direct and reciprocal net relationship of social housing with early parenthood, extramarital births, lack of qualifications, low income, and benefit receipt for both men and women, and with malaise for women, and with experience of unemployment for men. In addition, social housing predicts adult homelessness for both men and women, but homelessness does not feature in the models for social housing. The only adult outcome without a direct link to social housing for either sex is having been in three or more cohabitational partnerships by age 33, which is the least clear measure of disadvantage examined here; on closer examination, multiple partnerships are associated both with considerable advantage and disadvan-tage, which perhaps explains this less clear association.

Thus, we see that living in social housing at age 33 is associated with a wide range of other adverse outcomes in adulthood and might in some senses be regarded as the best single summary measure of social exclusion among those

Table 5.1. *Relationships between adult outcomes by age 33: odds ratios from stepwise logistic models of each outcome on other outcomes*
(p > 0.0001)

Women

Odds ratio for:	Teenage mother	Extra-marital birth	Many partners	Malaise	Social housing	Any benefits	Homeless	No qualifications	Low income	Ever unemployed
Teenage mother	xxxx	3.21	—	1.74	2.71	1.74	—	3.11	—	—
Extramarital birth	3.22	xxxx	3.50	—	2.43	1.80	—	—	—	—
Many partners	—	3.56	xxxx	—	1.93	—	7.04	2.00	—	—
Malaise	3.38	—	—	xxxx	—	1.74	—	—	—	—
Social housing	—	2.93	—	2.07	xxxx	3.49	2.60	3.16	3.72	—
Any benefits	—	1.96	—	1.74	3.26	xxxx	—	—	8.72	—
Homeless	—	—	5.93	—	2.60	—	xxxx	—	—	—
No qualifications	3.11	—	—	2.01	2.89	—	—	xxxx	1.71	—
Low income	—	—	—	—	3.57	8.76	2.30	1.85	xxxx	—

Men

Odds ratio for:	Young father	Extra-marital birth	Many partners	Malaise	Social housing	Any benefits	Homeless	No qualifications	Low income	Ever unemployed
Young father	xxxx	3.24	—	—	2.70	—	—	2.53	—	—
Extramarital birth	3.17	xxxx	—	—	—	2.00	—	—	—	1.78
Many partners	—	—	xxxx	—	—	—	4.27	—	—	—
Malaise	—	—	—	xxxx	—	—	—	—	—	—
Social housing	2.69	2.12	—	—	xxxx	2.95	2.85	3.66	2.80	2.80
Any benefits	—	—	—	—	2.78	xxxx	—	—	2.60	—
Homeless	—	—	4.35	—	—	—	xxxx	—	—	—
No qualifications	2.31	—	—	2.27	3.75	—	—	xxxx	2.96	—
Low income	—	—	—	—	2.87	2.63	—	3.02	xxxx	1.83
Ever unemployed	—	1.79	—	1.83	2.80	—	—	—	1.83	xxxx

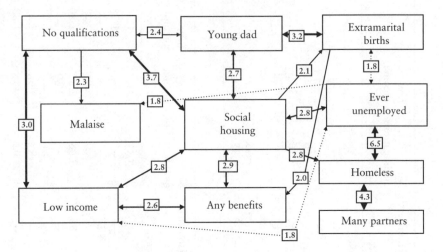

Figure 5.1. *Outcomes by age 33: Men*

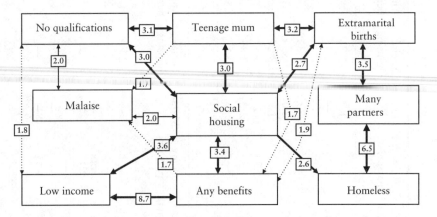

Figure 5.2. *Outcomes by age 33: Women*

considered here. However, this begs the question of the pathways and causal directions involved: clearly, for example, early parenthood and lack of qualifications occur well before age 33 and cannot be caused by being in social housing at age 33. To a considerable extent, being in social housing at age 33 reflects the cumulative impact of one or more of the other aspects of social exclusion considered here. But we cannot rule out the possibility of some causal links in the reverse direction, for example that people trapped in the worst estates are less likely to find employment or to obtain higher income as a result of 'labelling' by location, or that such residence contributes significantly to their malaise. These issues are discussed more fully in Chapter 8.

For both men and women, early parenthood is strongly associated with lack of qualifications, extramarital births, and social housing; for women there appears to be a further consequential link to malaise and to benefit receipt at age 33. Although these outcomes are all nominally measured at age 33, it is clear that lack of qualifications will often have been prior to early parenthood (though in principle repairable by age 33), though early parenthood could also contribute to early termination of education. Extramarital births and early births are highly likely to have been contemporaneous, though not completely overlapping. Early parenthood will often have preceded and sometimes caused entry into social housing, often well before age 33. These interplays thus serve to point up that social exclusion is not an event, but rather a process and that disentangling the relative timing of pathways is of critical importance in understanding its genesis.

Other associations are:

- *Extramarital births* are related to early parenthood and social housing for both men and women, but not significantly to lack of qualifications. But for men those with extramarital births are more likely to have experienced unemployment (a less obviously comprehensible link) and for women extramarital births are also strongly related to repeated cohabitational partnerships and to receipt of non-universal benefits at age 33.

- One of the most powerful linkages observed for both men and women is between having had *three or more cohabitational partnerships* and experience of homelessness between ages 23 and 33. The only other significant direct association of repeated partnership is that already mentioned for women with extramarital births.

- *Adult homelessness* is in turn powerfully linked to multiple cohabitational partnerships and to social housing at age 33 for both men and women; low income women are also more likely to have been homeless.

- A *high malaise score* is more common for women and linked to lack of qualifications, teenage motherhood, social housing, and benefit receipt. For men, the association is again with lack of qualifications, but the only additional link is to any experience of unemployment.

- *Receipt of non-universal benefits* is, as might be expected, particularly strongly related with low household income for women, but also with low earnings for men. Both men and women are more likely to receive benefits at age 33 if they had an extramarital birth and if they are in social housing; in addition, teenage mothers are still more likely to get non-universal benefits at age 33.

- *Lack of qualifications* is linked to early parenthood, social housing, and low income for both men and women, and to malaise for women.

- *Low income* is unsurprisingly associated with benefit receipt, social housing, and lack of qualifications for both men and women, and to any experience of unemployment for men.

- Finally, *experience of any unemployment for men* is linked to low earnings at age 33, living in social housing, and to having had an extramarital birth.

The brief account of this exploratory analysis and the observed interlinkages raises at least as many questions as it answers, especially about the timing and pathways of the transitions involved. Nevertheless it suffices to remind us of the very strong interplays that are crucial to the notion of social exclusion itself and should be salutary for those who focus on any one single outcome. Multiple disadvantages are interconnected, but there are also associations which do not show up clearly once some of the other outcomes have been controlled.

So how do we cope with these issues? We have already indicated the need to explore the relative timing of events involved in the genesis of social exclusion and are pursuing that further. But we also need to tease out the implications of this longitudinal approach for any attempts to measure social exclusion from cross-sectional surveys and to devise ways of judging how excluded individuals are at any point in time. Attention to the pathways into social exclusion also helps to indicate which policy levers *might* help to reduce the incidence and impact of exclusion.

The list of adverse outcomes considered above is in part an arbitrary one and alternative outcome measures, especially ones which are more focused in time, need considering. We have proposed a further and slightly more coherent set of indicators for women along these lines in more recent work (Hobcraft and Kiernan 1999).

Illustrations of Issues in Adult Social Exclusion: Summary Measures

A further issue already touched upon is the advantage of having one (or possibly very few) summary indicators of the extent of social exclusion. Among the problems are: which outcomes should comprise indicators of social exclusion; should these outcomes be treated as 'switches' (dummy variables such as lack of qualifications or low income) or should we introduce gradations (quartiles or deciles of income, age at first birth etc.); and how to combine 'apples' and 'pears'.[1] At the moment, it seems simplest and most comprehensible to combine indicator measures through very transparent (perhaps weighted) summation procedures.

As an illustrative example, I have taken a simple count of the number of negative adult outcomes by or at age 33 in the NCDS on: young parenthood, extramarital birth, multiple partnerships, malaise, social housing, non-universal benefit receipt, homelessness, and lack of qualifications. (Note that a measure of low income is not included here, in part because non-response problems mean that this indicator is not available for many sample members still observed.) This 'adult social exclusion score' is almost certainly too heavily weighted by demographic outcomes and the multiple partnership component should probably be

---

[1] Although statistical theory and software are becoming available for latent trait and latent class models with mixed continuous and categorical variables (Moustaki 1996) and for ordinal variables, the assumptions involved may be too strong (and perhaps too impenetrable) for practical analysis at this stage of knowledge concerning the latent construct of social exclusion.

removed. However, a simple construct of this kind can be used to illustrate some of the advantages of a single measure. Firstly, it is possible to explore the associations of bundles of adult outcomes with their childhood and family background precursors, which can provide insights into common antecedents (using a Poisson or negative binomial regression model, despite concerns about the combination of disparate elements). Secondly, it can provide a simple way of exploring links to a wider range of adult outcomes. In due course, if and when we are clear which elements comprise social exclusion and how they should be combined, this could permit assessment of other correlates that are important and may be antecedents or outcomes of social exclusion. At the exploratory stage this screening process is part of the exploration of possible precursors, markers, or components of social exclusion.

Table 5.2 shows the outcome of such a simple exploratory analysis. For the whole sample the average adult social exclusion score thus defined is 0.94 for the women and 0.67 for the men; outcomes with an average score greater than twice these sample means are shown in italic type. The first cluster of outcomes by age 33 shown in Table 5.2 are those that comprise the inputs to the adult social exclusion score; by definition these are self-referent and every young parent will score one (shown in parentheses) plus whatever is the score on the other seven indicators. The average scores for these eight outcomes are fairly bunched, which is indicative of the interlinkages explored above and it will come as no surprise that the score is highest for those living in social housing (but only just for women).

Of more interest are the scores based on these eight outcomes for other outcomes by age 33. There is a very high score indeed for those currently on income support (who are in receipt of benefit and therefore have the score for this shown in parentheses), which exceeds the score for every one of the components of the social exclusion score. In addition, those who were currently unemployed or sick, especially among men, show very high exclusion scores. Clearly there is a very strong case for including these indicators of poverty and employment status among the indicators of social exclusion. Relatedly, low income is a further candidate, though not as strongly related to the preliminary bundle and having additional problems of restricting sample size; a further time-diffuse indicator of poverty, having ever experienced rent or mortgage arrears is also clearly differentiated.

Another very strong candidate variable for an indicator of social exclusion for both sexes is lack of access to a telephone in the household, which shows very high scores on this indicator and indicates both poverty and social isolation, a further dimension of social exclusion. Experience of lone parenthood (though extremely rare for men) also shows very high scores on adult social exclusion for both sexes and is evidently linked with the demographic and housing elements of the score.

Only one further adult outcome measure shows above twice the average adult social exclusion score for both sexes, namely the subjective report that life is

Table 5.2. *Average 'adult social exclusion' scores for different outcomes by age 33*

	Women	Men
Total sample	0.94	0.67
Young parent	1.98 (+1)	1.35 (+1)
Extramarital birth	1.95 (+1)	1.26 (+1)
Multiple partners	1.80 (+1)	1.17 (+1)
Malaise	1.69 (+1)	1.33 (+1)
Social housing	2.01 (+1)	1.47 (+1)
Any benefits	1.64 (+1)	1.33 (+1)
Homeless	1.99 (+1)	1.38 (+1)
No qualifications	1.85 (+1)	1.36 (+1)
Low income	1.98	1.40
Ever unemployed	1.06	1.20
Current unemployed or sick	2.24	2.58
Income support (current)	2.15 (+1)	1.78 (+1)
Ever SB or IS	1.65	1.14
Ever rent arrears	2.06	1.48
No telephone	2.70	1.99
Ever lone parent	2.42	2.10
Current smoker	1.57	1.09
Morning cough	1.83	1.16
Fried food or chips weekly	1.67	1.01
Emotional—specialist	1.66	1.45
Ill health	1.85	1.28
Ill last year	1.84	1.71
Lousy life	1.98	1.37
Life unsatisfactory	1.43	0.98
Did not vote in 1987	1.36	0.91
Anti-establishment	1.92	1.24
Assault/Rape	2.48	0.95

'lousy' (derived from a summary of several scales), which could join the more specific malaise indicator as a measure of mental health. Women who have experienced assault or rape (a very small group) are evidently very socially excluded, and those who hold anti-establishment views somewhat so. Men who were ill in the year before age 33 and who had ever seen a specialist about emotional problems (another very rare group) were also relatively excluded.

This kind of exploratory work can thus help to speed up the process of refining the bundle of indicators of adult social exclusion, although there are counterarguments in favour of trying to find independent (i.e. indicators that are not highly interlinked) dimensions too. By the processes outlined here we can aid the empirical clarification of what elements comprise social exclusion and how they are interrelated, while also paying close attention to theoretical considerations. The full process involves several iterations and much further unpacking.

PARENTAL ENDOWMENTS AND LIFE-COURSE EXPERIENCES

There is overwhelming evidence from many domains that children 'inherit' from their parents; such inheritance includes their genes, the family environment, and childhood experiences during the life-course. This association is unequivocally established for genetic inheritance and the linkage is indisputably causal. It is fundamentally implausible and empirically untrue to maintain that our genetic endowments play no part in shaping outcomes through the life-course. Yet, many social scientists persist in either denying or ignoring this and seem never to engage with the possibility that human behaviour is shaped in any way by genetic endowments, instead regarding humans as being a Hobbesian *tabula rasa* at birth, who are then entirely shaped by individual experiences or structural constraints.

To accept otherwise is neither to fall into the trap of genetic determinism nor to deny the importance of non-biological factors in shaping outcomes. This fact is increasingly understood and being explored empirically and theoretically by behavioural geneticists and developmental psychologists (see, for example, Dunn and Plomin 1990; Plomin 1994) and much more speculatively and sometimes deterministically by sociobiologists or evolutionary psychologists (e.g. Buss 1994; Diamond 1997; Ridley 1996; and Etcoff 1999). Many of the arguments advanced involve subtle interplays between genetics and environment or between nature and nurture. (For very differing treatments of these interplays see Plomin 1994; Rutter *et al.* 2000; Frank 1998; and E. O. Wilson 1998).

Most empirical work that sets out to assess the relative importance of genes for behavioural outcomes is done by behavioural geneticists and developmental psychologists (for a perceptive and well-written review of these issues see Plomin 1994). Much of this work has involved trying to tease out separate components of variance, which can be ascribed to genetic inheritance, to 'shared environment', and to non-shared environment (usually including residual variance too). For these purposes a shared environment explicitly means being in the same family or household, rather than experiencing directly measured similar influences (such as parenting styles or childhood poverty). Moreover, the procedures for estimation often sweep any gene-environment interactions into the 'genetic' component of variance and thus can overstate the direct genetic component of inheritance. For a very good review of these issues see Rutter *et al.* (2000).

In order to tease out these components of variance, particularly the separation of genetic and non-shared environment, increasingly complex quasi-experimental designs have been used and include comparisons of monozygotic (identical) and dizygotic (fraternal) twins, siblings, and a frequent emphasis on those reared together and apart (usually adopted). A crucial assumption in order to proceed is usually that children reared apart are in completely uncorrelated environments (in the sense of the shared environment component), which seems at least implausible in the context of shared characteristics, especially given the constraints of adoption and the likelihood that separately adopted twins will be placed by the same agency or individual. Equally, co-resident twins (and sometimes siblings) are usually assumed to experience an identical shared environment (for a very perceptive and full review of these issues see Rutter *et al.* 2000). However, for a few behavioural markers estimation has taken place using different study designs that involve differing identifying assumptions and this work may indicate that these seemingly dangerous assumptions may not be of critical importance.

More complex still are the attempts to identify different types of genotype–environment correlations (often conceptualized as 'passive, reactive, and active', see Plomin 1994); as always, it proves much easier to conceptualize differing types of interplay of genotype with environment than to distinguish between these in statistical models. Some progress has been made through clever use of differing quasi-experimental designs, but identifying assumptions become ever more complex too (Plomin 1994). In many cases, a strong theoretical structure is required for identification purposes, but sometimes this becomes an act of faith rather than of theoretical or empirical evidence. This kind of fallacy can happen among proponents and opponents of such research.

One of the unsatisfying aspects of this otherwise exciting work is that the components of variance are just 'black boxes': the complexities of sample design and the rarity of key groups (e.g. twins reared apart or adopted children) mean that sample sizes are often too small to permit more elaborate analysis, though recent progress is being made in this respect.

'Black-box' Fixed-effects Approaches by Economists

The recent fashion among economists for 'fixed-effects' models which look at siblings with differing outcomes is another black-box component of variance approach, though in some ways even less satisfactory. Fixed-effects models are usually described as controlling for the shared environment in the family and often make no mention of possible genetic similarities, although both must be swept into the same black box.

An example of this approach is provided by Geronimus and Korenman (1992) in the context of assessing the socio-economic consequences of teenage childbearing, a topic we shall examine further in due course. Their approach is not dissimilar to earlier (and now primitive) approaches to twin studies that did not use a modern model-based approach in order to utilize all of the available information. In essence, they argue that we can only recover information about consequences of teenage childbearing by looking at sisters where one did have a teenage birth contrasted with one who did not, so as to net out the shared environmental effects (and of course the unacknowledged genetic similarities); the presumption that sisters born perhaps several years apart share an identical home environment, are treated the same way by their parents etc. is almost certainly too strong.

Thus, sisters who both had a teenage birth are removed from the analysis and comparisons, as are those where neither had a teenage birth. Only about half of the teenage births are thus included in the 'fixed-effects' analysis and there is no way of knowing whether the changes in the estimated 'consequences' are largely due to sample selection differences. Our own work on this issue (Hobcraft and Kiernan 1999, for Britain rather than the USA), although unable to control for shared individual family environment, shows clear evidence that women who have children in their early twenties also experience subsequent disadvantage compared with those who have not had a birth by age 23. Since many of the sister pairs with one teenage and one non-teenage birth were probably not too far apart in their ages at first birth in the US sample, that would be almost certain to attenuate apparent 'effects' in the Geronimus and Korenman analysis. The latent variable structural approaches used by psychologists or a multilevel modelling approach seem more appropriate and would make fuller use of available information.

More on Nature–Nurture

Let us return briefly to 'black boxes' and issues to do with peering into them. On the environmental side, most social scientific studies collect information on a wide range of characteristics of the experience of individuals and thus try to peer into the shared and non-shared environmental boxes, but risk serious bias of misattribution of possible genetic endowments to environment. Shared environment is not usually treated as identical family background, but rather attempts are made through multivariate models to assess the association of outcomes to marker variables. The interpretation of any observed association is complex and great care has to be taken against assuming too much, since many studies fail to control for a wide range of contemporaneous factors, for earlier events in the life-course, and for parental genetic and environmental endowments.

The possibilities of peering into the genetic black box are only recently beginning to open up, but over the next ten or twenty years we might expect very considerable progress in exploring the links of quantitative trait loci (QTLs, which are markers on the human genome) to behaviour and experience. Serious progress in this arena would be likely to reduce the emphasis on siblings and twins within families, since the QTLs might be directly identifiable and could then be used as markers in multivariate analysis. A trivial example of the difference would be for a characteristic that is completely related to a single marker on the genome. At the moment, for siblings or dizygotic twins we can uncover a 50 per cent commonality; but with the identification of the marker there would either be complete concordance or none. If the outcome associated with the marker is only expressed with certain environmental stimuli, we shall be able to examine such interplays with much greater precision than hitherto.

The estimates of heritability from existing studies for many behavioural characteristics make it almost certain that genetic linkages will not be to a single marker, but at best to multiple markers. The time, sample sizes and investment required to identify the relevant QTLs and whether the combinations are interactive or additive and how their expression interplays with environmental factors is going to mean that progress in this arena will be slow. Moreover, these difficulties make it essential to identify (through simpler variance-component decompositions) whether there is heritability or genotype–environment correlation to be explained before undertaking expensive explorations among QTLs.

One observation that has long puzzled developmental psychologists in family studies is the often quite small proportion of variance attributed to the shared (or family) environment (Maccoby and Martin 1983). One response to this has been a greater realization of the need to explore the extent to which children within the same family do indeed share the same environment, since perhaps quite subtle differences in parenting or childhood circumstances, or in genotype-family environment interplays, might be associated with quite different outcomes.

Others have taken these findings to show that parental inputs have virtually no impact on outcomes for children and that it must (by a rather naïve *reductio ad absurdum* argument) therefore be the case that all the non-shared environment component of variance is attributable to interaction with peers (Harris 1998 takes this argument to its extreme). Among other factors, these approaches ignore the facts that the 'non-shared environment' variance component includes the residual error variance in its black box and is thus mislabelled and that all gene–environment correlations are swept into the 'genetic' black box.

ILLUSTRATIONS USING THE NCDS

We shall illustrate some of the issues in intergenerational and life-course transmission of social exclusion using examples drawn from analysis of the results of the NCDS. We are unable to introduce controls for genetic endowments because the very design of the study, with its focus on a cohort of births, means that the only siblings that can possibly be included are the very few multiple births. There are far too few of these to get much leverage on genetic components of variance for the range of outcomes that I have tried to examine. Moreover, there are indications that twins are more likely to have been lost to consecutive waves than singleton births, making selective attrition a further complication. For these reasons it has only been possible to consider environmental precursors of adult outcomes for the survey members and we have no way of knowing what fraction, if any, of observed association with either parental characteristics or earlier experience of the individual originates from or is mediated by their genes.

Nevertheless, the complexities of analysis are considerable. Information was first collected about the parents and birth characteristics when the survey members were born in March 1958. Subsequently, a rich array of information was gathered at ages 7, 11, and 16 from the parents, from schools and teachers, from medical sources, and from tests of the individuals who were also interviewed in their own right at age 16. The individual survey members, and their partners if relevant, were again interviewed at ages 23 and 33 and a wide range of information collected, including fairly detailed event histories on childbearing, partnership, labour force participation and employment, training, and housing.

Of course, a major difficulty with any secondary analysis is that the information collected is given and determined with other purposes in mind than understanding the generation of social exclusion. Moreover, the questionnaire content reflects the interests of sponsors and is inevitably limited by the state of knowledge at the time—with hindsight there might be much we would wish to modify. But the art of secondary analysis is to try to tease out whatever can be achieved from the existing information, without dwelling more than is necessary upon these practical limitations.

A further important difficulty arises from missing information: in a longitudinal study some individuals are not included in each wave and these can differ between waves; moreover, at each wave there can be differential non-response to the various questionnaires and also to different items for each instrument. An advantage of the repeated measurement over time is that it becomes possible (unlike cross-sectional surveys) to get some purchase on selectivity in non-response, but it also becomes ever more dangerous to ignore this (e.g. by omitting all but complete responses) and ever more difficult to handle due to the complexity of the patterns involved.

From the beginning of this chapter it has been made clear that a major consideration has been to examine the wide range of factors that are available and to avoid disciplinary hegemony. This requires us to find ways of rising above the full detail of the available information. For example, tracing detailed pathways through childhood for each variable considered, especially in the face of missing information, is perhaps too ambitious, at least until we have discovered what is really important in broader terms. Thus, for example, we have reading and mathematics test scores (among other tests) measured at each of ages 7, 11, and 16. The approach adopted has been to summarize this information into a single overall measure based on relative performance at each age (see Hobcraft 1998 for details). There are a number of arguments for such summarization: we can use incomplete information (missing at one or two of the rounds); test scores include some unreliability of measurement and multiple observations can help reduce this; it may also be that it is experience over the whole of childhood that is most important (more true for repeated exposure to childhood poverty). But there are also some inevitable losses with summarization, especially the inability to disentangle detailed pathways and to ask whether experiences at a particular age have greater impact in adulthood.

The incomplete but fairly rich evidence on parental endowments or childhood family environment that is available in NCDS is shown in schematic form in

Figure 5.3 and includes summaries of repeated information (Hobcraft 1998): on family structure at ages 0, 7, 11, and 16; on occupational class and employment status of the father (or father figure) at ages 0, 7, 11, and 16 (further information is available on social class of origin concerning both grandfathers); on mother's and father's interest in their schooling at ages 7, 11, and 16 (albeit through the observational lens of a teacher); some indicators of poverty at 7, 11, and 16 ('financial hardship' and free school meals); and housing tenure at 7, 11, and 16. In addition, some behavioural measures (aggression, anxiety, and restlessness) and test scores were available for ages 7, 11, and 16. Hobcraft (1998) also makes use of a summary of three separate reports on whether the child had been in contact with the police by age 16. Other information is available in the childhood waves of NCDS, but is not used here. For this range of a dozen summary indicators of childhood experience we have explored linkages to the range of adult outcomes (measured by age 33) shown in Figure 5.3 (see Hobcraft 1998 and Hobcraft and Kiernan 1999 for details).

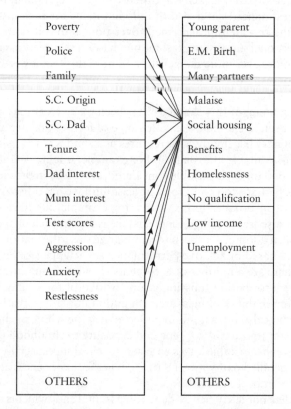

Figure 5.3. *Pathways from childhood to adulthood*

Pervasive associations

Among the more important results to emerge from this work is an assessment of which childhood factors emerge as pervasive predictors of a wide range of adult outcomes. The negative outcomes are shown in Figure 5.3, with nine being considered separately for men and women plus experience of unemployment for men. For these 19 combinations of adverse adult outcomes by sex, we can see in Table 5.3 that 4 of the childhood precursors stand out as having particularly prevalent associations. Educational test scores are the most powerful of any childhood precursor (taking account of the magnitude of associations in addition to the pervasiveness), followed by childhood poverty, contact with the police, and experience of family disruption (including being born out-of-wedlock and having been in care, as well as widowhood, divorce, and remarriage). These 4 childhood precursors show strongly significant relationships with 14 or 15 of the 19 possible sex-outcome combinations.

The remaining 8 childhood precursors are only strongly associated with fewer than half of the 19 sex-outcome combinations. The two which indicate levels of parental interest in schooling (as judged by teachers) are the next most pervasive and to some extent are close competitors for entry into the models—taken together they have a strong association for 11 of the sex-outcome combinations. The structural (tenure and social class) and behavioural measures show less pervasive influence for adult outcomes.

Table 5.3. *Pervasive continuities: numbers of strongly significant associations of childhood variables with negative adult outcomes*

Adult outcome	Number of strong associations (of 10 male and 9 female negative outcomes)
Test scores	15
Poverty	15
Contact with police	15
Family type	14
Father's interest in school	8
Mother's interest in school	6
Aggression score	5
Social class of origin	5
Social class of father	4
Housing tenure	4
Anxiety score	4
Restlessness score	1

Specific Associations

However, some childhood factors can nevertheless have strong and interesting specific associations with particular adult outcomes, even though not affecting a wide range. Table 5.4 shifts attention to these specific continuities. For each childhood precursor we show the adult outcome for which the odds ratio in the stepwise logistic models is largest; for educational test scores we also provide the next few largest odds ratios. Entries in Table 5.4 where the adult outcome is specifically similar to the childhood precursor are shown in *italic* type: test scores and educational qualifications; parental interest in schooling and educational qualifications; out-of-wedlock childbearing in parental and childhood

Table 5.4. *Specific continuities: adult negative outcomes showing largest odds ratio for each childhood variable (including non-largest for poverty and for test scores)*

Child factor	Men		Women	
	Outcome	Odds ratio	Outcome	Odds ratio
Clear poverty	No qualifications	2.8	No qualifications	2.6
Clear contact with police	No qualifications	3.7	No qualifications	2.4
Low test scores	No qualifications	45.9	No qualifications	26.8
	Social housing	4.3	Teenage mother	3.7
	Low income	3.9	Social housing	2.7
	Young father	3.4		
Low father's interest in school	No qualifications	4.3	No qualifications	3.7
Low mother's interest in school	Extramarital birth	2.1	No qualifications	2.5
Born out-of-wedlock	Extramarital birth	2.0	Extramarital birth	2.5
Ever in care	Malaise	2.1	Extramarital birth	3.7
Divorce	3+ partners	3.2	3+ Partners	2.3
Remarriage	Homeless	2.8	Extramarital birth	1.7
Low housing tenure	Social housing	2.5	Social housing	1.8
Low social class of origin	Malaise	1.5	Social housing	2.4
Low social class of father	Young father	2.5	Social housing	1.4
High aggression	3+ partners	1.8	Teenage mother	1.9
High anxiety	Malaise	1.6	Malaise	1.7
High restlessness	No qualifications	1.9	Homeless	1.7

generations; parental divorce and multiple cohabitational partnerships; inter-generational 'inheritance' of social housing; and childhood anxiety linked to adult malaise; moreover, the links of homelessness for men and extramarital births for women to remarriage are possibly indicative of specific 'escape' pathways. This is a formidable list of specific continuities, especially since some of the childhood measures do not have direct adult analogues included in the analysis (e.g. social class, aggression, restlessness, and contact with the police).

Educational failure (lack of qualifications by age 33) is the most strongly linked outcome for several childhood precursors, which is remarkable given that the huge association with test scores might have suppressed all other associations but clearly did not. Test scores (massively), contact with the police, childhood poverty, lack of parental (especially father's) interest in schooling, and male restlessness at school are all most strongly linked to educational failure. One possible reason for this multiplicity of most powerful associations of childhood precursors with educational failure is simply that most of the failure to get qualifications had already occurred by about age 16, so that this outcome is more proximate to childhood than the others (however, further work has shown the power of qualification levels as a predictor of social exclusion at ages 23 and 33 (see Hobcraft 2000); for further discussion of education and social exclusion, see Chapter 11).

We illustrate the strong association of childhood educational test scores with several adult outcomes by showing a few additional large odds ratios. Not only is there the very powerful and hardly unexpected association with lack of qualifications, but both women and men with low test scores are very much more likely to have become young parents and to live in social housing at age 33 and the men also have much higher incidence of low income.

In addition to the very specific continuities already referred to (both test scores and parental interest in schooling with educational qualifications; out-of-wedlock childbearing; parental divorce and multiple cohabitational partnerships; inter-generational 'inheritance' of social housing; and childhood anxiety linked to adult malaise) there can also be observed a more general coherence to the links between childhood and adult circumstances: demographic behaviour is so linked, especially for women; structural variables (housing tenure and social class) are also especially linked for women; men seem perhaps more emotionally vulnerable to childhood circumstances (links of malaise, early fatherhood, and multiple partnerships in adulthood to childhood family circumstances, social class, and aggression).

Pathways through Intermediate Outcomes

A number of additional issues arise when we consider intermediate adult outcomes (by age 23) in the context of the relative importance of childhood precursors and very early adult experience for outcomes by age 33. Figure 5.4 shows in schematic form some of the pathways involved, while a detailed exploration of

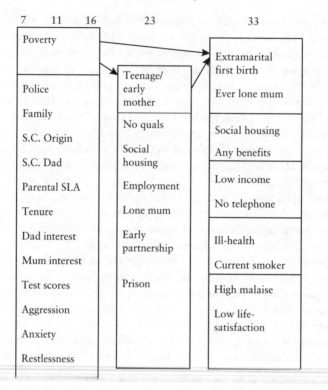

Figure 5.4. *Pathways from childhood through early to later adulthood*

the relative importance of childhood poverty and of early motherhood net of the wide range of other childhood factors shown is provided by Hobcraft and Kiernan (1999). The additional complexity is partly illustrated by the arrows shown in Figure 5.4. Childhood poverty is not just a precursor of outcomes by age 33, but also by age 23. Thus we have to consider pathways whereby childhood poverty can exert an indirect effect on an outcome at age 33 (through early motherhood for example) and an additional direct effect. Evidently, the addition of other childhood precursors complicates this picture further, since they also interplay with (and are in part contemporaneous with) childhood poverty and can also exert both direct and indirect influences through early motherhood. Examining multiple intermediate factors and the related proliferation of potential pathways clearly can add even further complexity.

Some very simplified illustrations are provided in Table 5.5, which summarizes the percentages of women experiencing four of the adult outcomes considered by Hobcraft and Kiernan (1999): ever a lone parent, living in social housing, no telephone in the household, and a high malaise score. These percentages are shown for three different levels of childhood poverty and for three ages at first birth. Note first that teenage motherhood is much more common among those

Table 5.5. *Percentages of women experiencing selected outcomes at age 33 by simplified childhood poverty status and age at first birth*

Outcome and age at first birth	Childhood poverty level		
	No evidence	Some poverty	Fairly poor
Number of cases			
Teenage	362	116	167
20–21	614	138	152
22–32	2,107	251	225
Per cent by age			
Teenage	12	23	31
20–21	20	27	28
22–32	69	50	41
All	100	100	100
Ever lone parent			
Teenage	54	52	51
20–21	33	33	42
22–32	12	16	24
Social housing			
Teenage	38	43	62
20–21	27	34	44
22–32	7	15	27
No telephone			
Teenage	13	20	28
20–21	8	13	27
22–32	3	9	11
Malaise			
Teenage	19	30	31
20–21	15	22	29
22–32	7	11	13

women who experienced significant amounts of childhood poverty (31 per cent) compared with only 12 per cent for those with no evidence of childhood poverty. Conversely, over two-thirds of women without indications of childhood poverty who have had a first birth by age 32 delay their first birth to age 22 or later, compared with only 41 per cent for those who were fairly poor as children.

It is clear that having been a lone parent by age 33 is strongly related to the age at first birth and barely related to experience of childhood poverty—just over half of all teenage mothers have been lone parents by age 33 regardless of their childhood poverty circumstances. Nevertheless, there appears to be a small additional risk of lone parenthood for those who first become mothers after their teens if they were fairly poor as girls (42 per cent compared with 33 per cent).

In contrast, living in social housing, lacking a telephone, and showing high malaise at age 33 are clearly related both to age at first birth and to childhood poverty levels, though with some minor variations in the patterns—for example higher poverty in childhood seems to extend the range of ages at first birth which are associated with particularly high levels of disadvantage for both lack of a telephone and high malaise.

Hobcraft and Kiernan (1999) examine these issues more thoroughly with controls for a very wide range of other childhood circumstances and some key results of that analysis are summarized for the full range of outcomes in Figure 5.5. We see that both childhood poverty and early motherhood are generally associated with higher odds of experiencing adverse outcomes at age 23, though the 'effects' of early motherhood are often somewhat stronger. The first part of the next chapter also takes up these issues at greater length, looking at teenage mothers in particular.

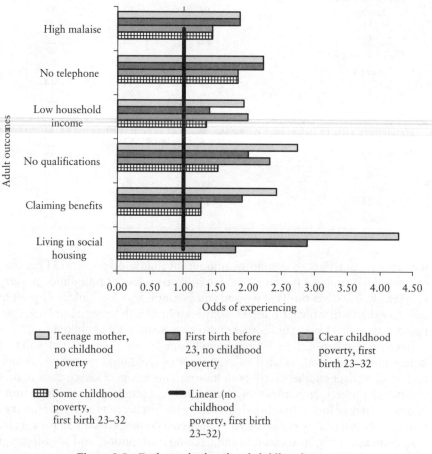

Figure 5.5. *Early motherhood and childhood poverty*

CONCLUSION

We have discussed many of the issues involved in trying to tease out the linkages between and within generations that are associated with adult social exclusion and in deciding what constitutes adult social exclusion. We emphasized that social exclusion is more than poverty or other economic outcomes. We discussed the problems posed by genetic inheritance for most survey analysis and looked at some of the difficulties involved in tracing pathways through various ages to adulthood. We recommend a judicious use of careful but brutal summary, of pragmatic and theoretical approaches, and sufficient care for analytic niceties and missing information. We have provided a number of illustrative examples drawn from our work to date. However, the complexity of the research agenda being tackled means that not all problems can be solved and many of the approaches and partial solutions outlined here are interim or partial steps along the way.

6

Disadvantage and Demography—Chicken and Egg?

KATHLEEN KIERNAN[1]

INTRODUCTION

Children in Britain are amongst the most likely of European Union children to grow up in poverty (Bradbury and Jantti 1999; Piachaud and Sutherland 2000; and Table 9.4 in this volume). An important engine behind this vulnerability is significant differences in the demography of family life in Britain compared with other European countries. British children, compared with their European contemporaries, are more likely to be born to young mothers and to solo mothers, are more likely to see their parents separate and to live in lone-mother families, all of which enhance the chances of growing up disadvantaged (Kiernan 1997b, 1999; Bradshaw et al. 1996). Overall, in Britain 40 per cent of children live in low-income households (if measured as being in the bottom 30 per cent of the income distribution) whereas 68 per cent of children with young mothers (aged 16–24 years), 79 per cent of children in never-married lone-parent families, and 66 per cent of children in separated or divorced lone-parent families do so (DSS 1999a). Youthful parenthood, solo motherhood, and fragile unions are hallmarks of British family life that have far-reaching consequences for the adults and children involved.

In this chapter we examine the links between demographic and socio-economic vulnerability. In particular, we focus on youthful parenthood, unmarried families, and parental divorce to investigate the extent to which family demographics are selective of the more vulnerable, and the implications of demographic behaviour for subsequent vulnerability.

YOUTHFUL PARENTHOOD

Across Europe in recent decades couples have been becoming parents at increasingly older ages. Men and women may be having children later in their lives

[1] The research support of the ESRC, UK is gratefully acknowledged. The Office for National Statistics provided the General Household Survey data used with the permission of the Controller of TSO and these data along with the NCDS were provided by the ESRC Data Archive.

because they have more life-style choices combined with highly effective means of controlling their fertility. Spending longer as a dual-earner couple before becoming parents generally improves a couple's position in terms of housing and consumer goods as well as allowing time for career development and leisure activities. Moreover, the increased participation in tertiary education and train-ing as well as accrual of qualifications to meet the demands of modern economies has led to an extension of the period of dependency into the third decade of life. Consequently, the time span of the transition to adulthood, from leaving education, entering the labour market and marrying and becoming parents has become more protracted. For the majority of young men and women there has been an upward shift in their social, economic, and demographic timetable, but for particular social groups this is not happening, or the pace of change may be slower.

In Britain, there is a noteworthy deviation from the trend to later childbearing. Not only do we have the highest teenage fertility rate in Western Europe but unlike other European countries there has been no decline in the rate over the last two decades. There is a growing concern on the part of government and policy-makers with the high and stable rates of teenage fertility to be found in Britain compared with other European countries (Social Exclusion Unit 1999a). Evidence from British longitudinal studies shows that, even after allowing for a wide range of background factors, teenage mothers compared with older mothers (particularly those who become mothers after their early twenties) are more likely in later life to be living in low-income households and to be relying on state benefits to support themselves and their children. Young mothers are also the most likely to be living in social housing and to have experienced homelessness, and their general physical health and mental well-being tends to be poorer than that reported by older mothers (Kiernan 1980, 1995; Maughan and Lindelow 1997; Hobcraft and Kiernan 1999).

Who become teenage mothers? There is now a considerable body of evidence from longitudinal studies which shows that teenage mothers are disproportion-ately drawn from the more disadvantaged groups and have the least propitious childhood and adolescent experiences (Kiernan 1980, 1995, and 1997b; Maughan and Lindelow 1997; Hobcraft 1998; Meadows and Dawson 1999). In sum, young mothers are the most likely to come from economically disadvan-taged families, to have lower educational attainment and to have exhibited higher levels of emotional problems, particularly during adolescence, and to have come from disrupted families. Moreover, with respect to more proximal factors, it is known that teenage mothers tend to become sexually active at younger ages, have lower rates of contraceptive use and the majority of the preg-nancies are unplanned (Wellings *et al.* 1996; Kiernan 1997b; and Meadows and Dawson 1999).

Our research and that of others has shown that two of the most powerful background factors implicated in the timing of motherhood are educational attainment and experience of poverty during childhood. The research outlined by John Hobcraft at the end of the previous chapter already examined the links between early motherhood, childhood poverty, and later outcomes. Here we focus specifically on teenage mothers and examine in more detail the combined impacts of experience of poverty during childhood together with lower educational attainment. Both of these feature strongly in the backgrounds of teenage mothers, and may account for the fact that women who become mothers in their teens tend to experience more disadvantaged outcomes in adulthood. We use data from the National Child Development Study (NCDS) which has followed up a birth cohort of children born in 1958 at ages 7, 11, 16, 23, and 33 (for details on the study see Shepherd 1985, and Ferri 1993).

Childhood Poverty and Educational Performance

Initially, we focus in on two sub-samples of women from the NCDS, those who had had no experience of poverty at the time of interviews at ages 7, 11, and 16 and those where there was evidence of having experienced poverty on one of these three occasions. To investigate in more depth some of the associations already seen in Table 5.5 in the previous chapter, these two groups of women were further subdivided according to whether, when they were tested at ages 7, 11, and 16 on a range of educational tests, their scores were in the lowest quartile or in the uppermost quartile of the distribution on 2 out of 3 occasions (see Hobcraft 1998 for detailed construction of the poverty and educational test variables).

These four groups of women were further subdivided according to whether they had a baby in their teens or not. The proportions of women in these categories who experienced a given outcome are shown in Table 6.1. We see that amongst the children who experienced childhood poverty and who had test scores in the lowest quartile of the educational test distribution those who became a mother in their teens were much more likely by age 33 than the analogous group of women who had a baby later to be living in social housing, to be in receipt of benefits (universal benefits are excluded), to be in the lowest quartile of the household income distribution, and to have experienced lone parenthood. The differences between the two groups of women with respect to having no qualifications or scoring highly on the malaise index (a measure of incipient depression) were not statistically significant. The number of women who experienced childhood poverty and whose test scores were in the upper quartile of the test distribution was too small for reliable analysis and are not included in the table. That there should be such a small number of cases in this group alerts us to the potency of poverty in the realm of educational attainment.

Turning to the young women who had not experienced poverty during childhood, we see that on all the outcomes women who became mothers in their teens, whether or not they had high or low scores on the educational tests, were more likely to have experienced less advantaged outcomes in their thirties, although the proportions with such outcomes tend to be lower amongst teenage mothers with higher test scores. The inference from this simple analysis is that teenage mothers are not only disproportionately drawn from disadvantaged groups but disadvantaged girls who do not become teenage mothers fare better in later life than their sisters who become teenage mothers, and even women with relatively advantaged backgrounds who become mothers in their teens fare relatively badly.

A series of multivariate analyses were also performed that addressed a number of questions. We enquired: to what extent childhood poverty and educational performance separately and in combination, attenuated the association between teenage motherhood and disadvantage in later life; and whether the inclusion of a range of other background factors together with the measures of poverty and educational performance affected the association between teenage motherhood and experiences in later adulthood. These additional factors included social class of origin, parent's school-leaving ages, housing tenure in family of origin, level of parental interest in education, and level of child's emotional well-being and family type (for a detailed description of these variables see Hobcraft 1998). For the multivariate analyses we used the full distribution of poverty and educational test scores rather than just the extremes of the distribution shown in Table 6.1.

The results are shown in Table 6.2 and are expressed in terms of odds ratios. From Table 6.2 we see that teenage mothers have 5.6 times the odds of being in social housing at age 33 compared with their contemporaries who did not become teenage mothers. The introduction of experience of childhood poverty

Table 6.1. *Proportion (%) of teenage mothers with specified outcomes by age 33 according to experience of poverty and educational test scores in childhood (numbers in parentheses)*

	Social housing	In receipt of benefits	Lowest quartile household income	No qualifi- cations	High malaise score	Ever lone parent
Childhood poverty-LQ Tests						
Not teenage mother	41 (154)	40 (165)	47 (106)	52 (161)	25 (163)	29 (163)
Teenage mother	65 (80)	51 (82)	64 (55)	61 (79)	34 (82)	54 (81)
Childhood poverty-UQ Tests						
Not teenage mother	— (15)	— (15)	— (13)	— (15)	— (15)	— (15)
Teenage mother	— (2)	— (2)	— (2)	— (2)	— (2)	— (2)
No Childhood poverty-LQ Tests						
Not teenage mother	22 (200)	24 (214)	34 (146)	27 (208)	16 (216)	13 (213)
Teenage mother	50 (46)	52 (46)	53 (34)	64 (47)	32 (47)	48 (46)
No Childhood poverty-UQ Tests						
Not teenage mother	4 (538)	10 (535)	14 (401)	1 (559)	4 (565)	6 (555)
Teenage mother	21 (14)	36 (14)	20 (10)	0 (13)	21 (14)	43 (14)

— Cell sizes too small for reliable analyses.

Source: Analysis of NCDS data.

Table 6.2. *Odds ratios of outcomes at age 33 for teenage mothers compared with other women according to background factors*

	Social housing	In receipt of benefits	Lowest quartile household income	No qualifi- cations	High malaise score	Ever lone parent
Baseline odds	5.55	3.51	2.48	4.83	2.67	6.94
Childhood poverty	4.58	3.05	2.11	3.74	2.23	6.26
Educational test scores	4.16	2.76	1.96	3.13	2.08	5.80
Childhood poverty and educational test scores	3.74	2.57	1.78	2.74	1.88	5.51
Childhood poverty and educational test scores and other* background factors	3.07	2.29	1.55	2.25	1.72	5.02

*See text for list of variables.
All odds ratios statistically significant at <.001.

Source: Analysis of NCDS data.

lowers the odds to 4.6, the inclusion of educational scores lowers them to 4.2, and experience of childhood poverty and educational performance in combination lowers the odds to 3.7, and the odds are further lowered to 3 with the introduction of the rest of the background factors. However, the odds of a teenage mother being in social housing in her thirties are still 3 times those of a woman who did not become a teenage mother. A similar story pertains for the other outcomes. The introduction of controls for childhood poverty and measures of educational performance are important factors in effecting a reduction in the odds, and all the other factors have a somewhat lower impact once childhood poverty and educational performance are taken into account. But the association between becoming a teenage mother and adversity in later life remains substantial and significant. Teenage motherhood matters, in that it substantially increases the chances of such families living in poorer social and economic circumstances, even 15 or so years after the birth of the child.

Context of First Birth

Young mothers, compared with older mothers, are more likely to commence family life as a lone parent, to have their first child in a cohabiting union rather than within a marital one, and amongst those who partner or marry are also the most likely to become lone parents. As an indication of solo motherhood birth registration data for 1998 showed that 29 per cent of all teenage mothers solely registered the birth of their baby compared with 13 per cent of mothers aged 20–24 and 6 per cent of those aged 25–29 years (ONS 1999). Analysis of the 1996/7 General Household Survey showed that amongst couples with a dependent child, 31 per cent of the cohabiting mothers had had their first child in their teens as compared with 12 per cent of married mothers. Additionally, a substantial proportion of lone mothers in the population had their first child in their teens. Amongst mothers under age 40 years in 1996/7, 49 per cent of the never-married mothers had had a child in their teens and 24 per cent of the separated and divorced mothers had had a child in their teens as compared with 15 per cent of married mothers. Yet, these young mothers have accumulated the least human capital on their way to adulthood and thus are the least likely to be self-sufficient if they become lone mothers. The higher incidence of teenage mother-hood may well form part of the explanation as to why British lone mothers are more likely to be living in poverty compared with lone mothers in other Western European countries (Kiernan 1996).

UNMARRIED FAMILIES

Children living with never-married lone mothers are amongst the poorest children in Britain (DSS 1999*a*). It is to the issue of unmarried families that we now turn. These children have either had cohabiting parents who separated or were born to a mother on her own, i.e. the father was not living with the mother when the child was born. Amongst this latter group, which we refer to as solo-mother families, the father may have been living elsewhere or the relationship may have terminated prior to the birth of the child.

Here, again NCDS data were used to examine the extent to which poverty and educational background were associated with partnership context of first birth. We examined three groups of women: those who had their first child on their own, solo mothers; those who had their first child within a cohabiting union, cohabiting mothers; and those who had a child within marriage, married mothers.

Using the same definitions of poverty and educational attainment used for the analysis on teenage motherhood in Table 6.1, we see from Table 6.3 that around 40 per cent of the solo mothers and cohabiting mothers, compared with 23 per cent of the married mothers, were drawn from poorer families of origin. Similarly, both solo mothers and cohabiting mothers were more likely than married mothers to have been on 2 out of 3 occasions in the lowest quartile of the educational tests. Thus, with respect to these background indicators solo mothers and cohabiting mothers are more likely to be drawn from less advantaged groups.

We also examined family circumstances in later life according to the partnership context of first birth and again express the findings in terms of odds ratios. It is apparent from Table 6.4 that women who have their first child within marriage are more likely to be living in more advantaged situations at age 33 than women who had their child on their own or in a cohabiting union. For example, the odds ratio of a solo mother living in social housing at age 33 were nearly 7 times those

Table 6.3. *Partnership status of women at first birth according to childhood poverty and educational test scores (women with a first birth by age 33)*

Partnership status at first birth	Per cent who experienced poverty on at least one occasion in childhood (ages 7, 11, or 16)		Per cent in lowest quartile of educational tests on at least two occasions (ages 7, 11, or 16)	
	%	N	%	N
Solo mother	43	(300)	30	(300)
Cohabiting mother	42	(219)	27	(219)
Married mother	23	(3351)	17	(3351)

Source: Analysis of NCDS data.

of a married mother. For a cohabiting mother the odds were almost 4 times higher, and the odds ratio of a solo mother and a cohabiting mother being in receipt of benefits at age 33 were over 4 times and nearly 3 times respectively that of a married mother.

However, it is the case that younger mothers are more likely to have their first child on their own or in a cohabiting union than older mothers. Thus, it is possible that the differences observed according to partnership context of first birth merely reflect earlier entry into motherhood. The second row of figures in Table 6.4 presents the odds ratios for the specified outcomes controlling for age at first birth in single years. We see that controlling for age at first birth substantially reduces the odds of experiencing a given outcome and this is particularly noticeable for solo mothers. However, the odds of experiencing disadvantaged outcomes compared with married mothers persist. This is also the case (with one exception malaise score at age 33 which is no longer significantly different across the groups) when we introduce the measure of childhood poverty (row 3) and then the educational test scores and in the final model where we enter these latter two variables and the other background factors (social class of origin, parent's school-leaving ages, housing tenure in family of origin, level of parental interest in education, and level of child's emotional well-being and family type). In all but the case of malaise scores the odds ratios for solo mothers and cohabiting mothers are significantly different (at 5 per cent or less and in most instances at 1 per cent or less) from the women who had their first child within marriage.

This analysis has shown that young women from more disadvantaged backgrounds are more likely to become solo mothers or cohabiting mothers than their more advantaged peers, and that these behaviours are associated with poorer outcomes in later life. It might be expected, other things being equal, that a mother having a child on her own is commencing motherhood at a marked disadvantage, but why should this be the case amongst cohabiting couples? Ermisch (2001), in his analysis of BHPS has shown that women who became

Table 6.4. *Odds ratios of experiencing a specified outcome according to context of first birth*

	Social housing	In receipt of benefits	Lowest quartile household income	No qualifications	High malaise score	More than one episode of lone parenthood
Baseline odds						
Solo	6.72***	4.75***	3.82***	3.51***	2.26***	6.69***
Cohabiting	3.87***	2.84***	2.76***	2.78***	1.83**	3.60***
Married	1.00	1.00	1.00	1.00	1.00	1.00
Controls: age at first birth						
Solo	3.13***	3.05***	2.54***	1.80***	1.36+	2.60***
Cohabiting	3.34***	2.54***	2.50***	2.32***	1.55**	2.50***
Controls: age at first birth; childhood poverty						
Solo	2.93***	2.90***	2.32***	1.57***	1.27	2.50***
Cohabiting	2.99***	2.37***	2.33***	1.93***	1.38+	2.34**
Controls: age at first birth; test scores						
Solo	3.08***	2.91***	2.38***	1.69***	1.29	2.57***
Cohabiting	3.04***	2.31***	2.30***	1.91***	1.39+	2.42**
Controls: age at first birth; childhood poverty; test scores						
Solo	2.91***	2.82***	2.24***	1.49*	1.23	2.49***
Cohabiting	2.79***	2.24***	2.21***	1.73**	1.30	2.30**
Controls: age at first birth; childhood poverty; test scores; plus other† background factors						
Solo	3.04***	2.83***	2.37***	1.48*	1.21	2.62***
Cohabiting	2.69***	2.18***	2.11***	1.65**	1.18	2.34**

†See text for list of variables.
+ =significant at the <.10 level; * significant at the <.05 level; ** significant at the <.01 level; *** significant at <.001 level.

Source: Analysis of NCDS data.

mothers in a cohabiting union were more likely to have partners who were unemployed or who were in partly skilled or unskilled occupations. We have shown (Kiernan and Estaugh 1993) that cohabiting couples with children are amongst the poorest two-parent families. Why do the poor choose to cohabit rather than marry, if it is a choice? One might point to a range of reasons. Pregnancy is an important precipitating factor in cohabitation, just as bridal pregnancy was an important precipitator of marriage before the advent of wide-scale cohabitation (Kiernan, Land, and Lewis 1998). With the decline in the stigma attached to having a child outside marriage, cohabitation for some may be preferable to solo motherhood or marriage. As Smart and Stevens (2000) show in their small-scale in-depth study of cohabiting families some mothers preferred cohabitation to lone motherhood or to marrying a man whom they were uncertain they could rely on for support. These finding resonate with W. J. Wilson's (1987) thesis developed in his book on the USA *The Truly Disadvantaged* of the shrinking pool of 'marriageable' (that is economically stable) men and the influence that joblessness has had on family structure. He argues that the decline in marriage amongst US blacks is associated with the declining economic status of black men. This may have a corollary in Britain in the declining status of men who have uncertain job prospects. Cohabitation, for some, may be a rational choice in the face of uncertainty, insecurity, unemployment, and socio-economic disadvantage. Public policy that promotes marriage per se (HM Government 1999) is unlikely to be the solution to these issues. Tackling the underlying disadvantage is likely to have more impact and extend the range of choices in the lives of these men, women, and children.

PARENTAL SEPARATION AND DIVORCE

Parental separation continues to be the major route into becoming a lone parent with its all too frequent attending deprivations. Divorce (here we use divorce as an inclusive term to cover all parental separations emanating from marriages and cohabitations) often brings with it a loss of economic resources and severe economic deprivation for some (Jarvis and Jenkins 1997). Even children from relatively advantaged backgrounds experience reduced economic circumstances when their parents live apart. In Britain in the 1990s around 80 per cent of lone mothers relied on state benefits to support themselves and their children (Ford and Millar 1998). Limited finances may affect a child's school attainment since many lone mothers may not be able to afford the toys, books, sports equipment, home computers, and other goods that can aid school success (see Middleton and Ashworth (1997) for a detailed study on spending on children). Low incomes may also mean that lone-mother families are more likely to be living in areas with poorer quality schools. Moreover, children living with lone mothers may leave school early, so as to seek employment in order to assist with family finances, or even work long hours whilst still at school to compensate for the lack of family finances for their own needs and social activities. Low educational attainment and early entry into the labour market in turn increase the likelihood of low occupational attainment, low incomes, and unemployment and state dependency.

There is now evidence for a range of countries that children who experience the break-up of their parent's marriage, have lower educational attainment, lower incomes, are more likely to be unemployed, and to be in less prestigious occupations in adult life than their contemporaries brought up with both parents (McLanahan and Sandefur 1994; Dronkers 1995; Jonsson and Gahler 1997; Elliott and Richards 1991; and Kiernan 1997*a*). Young women who experience parental divorce are also more likely than their peers without this experience to commence sexual relations earlier, to cohabit or marry at young ages, to have children in their teens and have children outside of marriage (Kiernan and Hobcraft 1997; Kiernan 1992; Cherlin, Kiernan, and Chase-Lansdale 1995; and Kiernan 1997*a*) and men and women from such families are in turn more likely to experience the break-up of their own marriage (Mueller and Pope 1977; Kiernan 1986; Glenn and Kramer 1987; Kiernan and Cherlin 1999).

However, as our research and that of others have shown, divorce is more likely to occur amongst couples with personal, social, and economic problems. For example, our analysis of cross-sectional data from the Family Resources Survey (FRS) and longitudinal data from the British Household Panel Survey (BHPS) showed that unemployment, reliance on state benefits, and disability featured as characteristics of the currently divorced in the FRS and these factors (unemployment, being in receipt of benefits, and having a disabled spouse) along with financial difficulties, were also found to be important precursors of divorce from our analysis of the BHPS (Kiernan and Mueller 1999). This suggests that poor economic and physical well-being may be important stressors in a relationship and that the selection of vulnerable groups into divorce may be an important aspect of the poverty observed amongst the previously partnered, in addition to the deprivation that may be a by-product of the divorce itself. Thus one of the challenges in assessing the legacy of divorce for children is being able to sort out the conditions that lead couples to separate and their potential effects on children, from the consequences of the dissolution itself. Additionally the selective nature of the population of children who experience parental divorce may lead to an overstated impression of the effects of divorce by conflating pre-existing differences amongst children from disrupted families with the fallout from marital dissolution.

Again, we made use of NCDS data to address some of these issues. Specifically, we enquired whether the link between experience of parental divorce and adult experiences weakens after taking into account financial circumstances of the family prior to divorce. To address this question the sample who had experienced parental divorce during childhood were divided into two groups: those whose parents divorced when they were under age 7 years and those who experienced parental divorce when they were between 9 and 16 years of age. Age 9 unambiguously post-dated the age-7 interview, which allowed us to assess whether attributes that chronologically preceded parental separation were implicated in later life experiences. We also examined the 7-year-old attributes of those children who experienced parental divorce before age 7 to assess whether they moderated or amplified subsequent behaviour, but for this group we do not know whether differences were due to the aftermath of the separation or pre-disruption factors.

A number of socio-economic and demographic outcomes in adulthood were examined. The socio-economic ones include having no qualifications at age 33 and living in social housing at age 33. By the time the cohort members were aged 33 years, those who had experienced parental divorce as children (16 and under) were almost twice as likely to lack formal qualifications as others: 20 per cent compared with 11 per cent. Children who experienced parental divorce were also under-represented amongst graduates. Insights into whether the lower educational attainment of children arose from pre-divorce or post-divorce factors can be gleaned from Table 6.5 which shows the odds ratios of having no qualifications relative to children brought up with both parents for those who experienced parental divorce in later childhood between ages 9–16 years inclusive, those who experienced it under age 7, and then for the entire period from birth to age 16. The analysis was carried out in a series of steps. Firstly financial hardship was included in the model on its own and then a range of age 7 characteristics (educational test scores, social class of the family, and behavioural problem scores) were added. Focusing in on the 9–16 years column we see clear evidence that financial hardship in the family at age 7 substantially attenuates the difference between children from divorced families and those from intact families with respect to having no qualifications in adulthood. For example, the baseline odds ratio of 2.04 is reduced to 1.3 in the case of the women, and in the case of the men, where the relationship is somewhat weaker, from 1.44 to 0.91. Controlling for the other age 7 factors leads to some further attenuation, but of a lesser order that that seen for financial problems. Turning to consider the children who experienced parental divorce prior to age 7 we see amongst the women that the chance of having no qualifications as compared with those who had not

Table 6.5. *Odds ratios for effects of parental separation by age of child on having no qualifications in adulthood*

	Men			Women		
	9–16 years	0–6 years	0–16 years	9–16 years	0–6 years	0–16 years
Baseline	1.44*	2.11***	1.62***	2.04***	2.37***	2.16***
Financial hardship age 7	0.91	1.80*	1.19	1.30	1.53 +	1.44**
All age 7 factors	0.88	1.63	1.10	1.27	1.16	1.24

+ =significant at the <.10 level; *significant at the <.05 level; **significant at the <.01 level; ***significant at <.001 level.

experienced a parental divorce by age 7 is also much less when we control for financial well-being. This is less the case amongst the men. Where parental divorce occurred prior to age 7, we cannot disentangle whether differences in educational outcomes are due to parental separation, or to selection, or a combination of selection and an amplification of financial problems. However, the findings with respect to the post age-9 group suggest that selection may be an important element, but not an exclusive one, in the interplay between the divorce process and the educational attainment of children. Poverty appears to reduce educational success and parental divorce can amplify it.

Adults who experienced parental divorce in childhood were more likely than others to be living in property rented from a local authority or housing association and less likely to be home owners. Overall, 15 per cent of the sample were in social housing at age 33 whereas 24 per cent of those who experienced parental divorce were in social housing.

Multivariate analysis shown in Table 6.6 suggests that the relationship between coming from a divorced family and being in social housing in adulthood was largely an indirect one, in that controls for financial adversity at age 7 reduced the odds of being in social housing at age 33. For example, amongst the men who experienced parental divorce at age 9 or later the odds ratio was reduced from 1.4 to 1.1 and amongst the women from 2.1 to 1.5. The importance of financial hardship in accounting for why children who experience parental divorce are more likely to end up in social housing resonate with the findings in relation to being unqualified. Controlling for the other age-7 factors reduces the differences between the two groups still further, but the difference for all women who experienced parental divorce in childhood compared with those who did not persists. Further examination showed that some of the residual difference between the two groups of women could be accounted for by early motherhood, which is more prevalent amongst women who experienced parental divorce, as well as being an important factor in precipitating entry into social housing (Murphy 1984).

Table 6.6. *Odds ratios for effects of parental separation by age of child on being in social housing at age 33*

	Men			Women		
	9–16 years	0–6 years	0–16 years	9–16 years	0–6 years	0–16 years
Baseline	1.35+	2.00***	1.66***	2.10***	2.10***	2.00***
Financial hardship age 7	1.13	1.71*	1.38*	1.50**	1.80**	1.60***
All age 7 factors	1.14	1.56+	1.43+	1.56*	1.53*	1.48**

+ =significant at the <.10 level; *significant at the <.05 level; **significant at the <.01 level; ***significant at <.001 level.

FIRST PARTNERSHIPS AND PARENTHOOD

Turning to consider demographic outcomes in adulthood, we found that men and women who experienced parental separation during childhood were more likely to form cohabiting rather than marital unions, and to cohabit or marry at a younger age than those whose parents stayed together. Men and women from divorced families were also more likely to become parents at a young age. Partnership break-up was also greater amongst children who had experienced parental divorce. But across all these demographic outcomes, controlling for the influence of childhood (and adolescent) background factors produced at most only a modest reduction in the odds ratios (Kiernan 1997a).

Evidence from our research suggests that pre-divorce factors, especially financial hardship, play a part in explaining some of the increased odds that children whose parents divorced lack qualifications and are to be found living in social housing as adults. However, pre-divorce circumstances were far less influential in accounting for why children who experienced parental divorce differed in their personal relationships and parenthood behaviour in adulthood.

CONCLUSION

There is evidence (Haveman and Wolfe 1994) that resources provided by parents have a more direct influence on children than those provided by the community or government. Family resources are important for children's development particularly their social, intellectual and emotional development which tends to be more pliant than at later stages in life. Undoubtedly, childhood poverty and educational experiences are two of the most powerful influences on how an individual's life course unfolds, and they also affect and interact with one another. We have seen that socio-economic vulnerability in childhood is powerfully associated with early parenthood and with the partnership context within which a child is born and that these demographic behaviours are also associated with disadvantage further along the life course. Additionally, socio-economic vulnerability is implicated in parental separation and parental separation can confound the disadvantage. Parental separation in turn has important implications for the demographic life course of the children involved, being as it is associated with experiences such as youthful parenthood, solo motherhood, and partnership dissolution. Reducing childhood poverty alongside major pedagogic investments, other things being equal, should reduce the chances of subsequent generations engaging in 'risky' demographic behaviours such as early parenthood, which in turn should reduce the risk of lone parenthood or at least temper the disadvantage associated with lone mother-hood—thereby breaking the nexus of childhood poverty and adult poverty for parents and their children. Until then, disadvantage and demography will continue to matter, both as direct and indirect mutual influences on adult experiences in the realm of social exclusion.

7

Low-paid Work: Drip-feeding the Poor

ABIGAIL MCKNIGHT

This chapter turns the focus of attention on to the low-wage labour market, specifically looking at how low-wage employment is linked with social exclusion and poverty over different time horizons. It shows how the overlap between low pay and poverty at one point in time understates the extent to which they are related over longer time horizons. Poverty and low pay are entwined over the life course and across generations. The interrelationship between low pay and poverty is demonstrated by examining the extent to which childhood poverty is associated with adult low pay, persistence in low pay can lead to poverty, and how low pay during the working life can lead to poverty in old age. The chapter concludes with a discussion on a selection of policies targeted at reducing the overlap between low pay and poverty by tackling either the causes or the consequence.

Unemployment and economic inactivity among individuals of working age play an important role in determining an individual's chance of being or becoming socially excluded. One of the dimensions of social exclusion used in Chapter 3 (Burchardt, Le Grand, and Piachaud) was whether or not an individual is productively active. Individuals who are unemployed, long-term sick or disabled who are not working, or who have retired earlier than the State retirement age are considered to be excluded on this dimension. For the majority of individuals, unemployment or economic inactivity results in reliance on low levels of welfare income and as a consequence can lead to social exclusion through low income and/or wealth. Current government thinking about the best way to tackle rising levels of inequality, high levels of unemployment, and increases in child poverty is through welfare reform based on the philosophy of 'work for those who can, security for those who cannot' (DSS 2000a). But due to the prevalence of low-paid work, a job does not guarantee that work alone will raise income enough to escape poverty. Recent government initiatives have attempted to tackle this through a raft of policies designed to 'make work pay'.

As unemployment and low-wage employment are linked with poverty, unemployment and low pay are also interconnected. The unemployed are more likely to find work in low-paid jobs than well-paid jobs and low-paid workers are more likely to experience unemployment than are higher-paid workers. This relationship has been referred to as the 'low-pay no-pay' cycle characterizing the precarious nature of many low-paid jobs and highlighting the fact that a job may only represent a turn in the cycle of poverty.

WHO IS LOW PAID AND WHY?

There is no precise definition of low pay. It is a relative concept and different from the notion of being underpaid, although many low-paid workers may be underpaid. Low-paid workers are simply defined as the *lowest*-paid workers. In empirical work a range of definitions are used. Some definitions use fixed proportions such as the lowest 10, 20, or 30 per cent of earners, others define low-paid workers relative to average earnings or the earnings of the median worker. In minimum-wage research a fixed wage rate is commonly used, and multiples of this wage, to define workers earning at or around a low-pay threshold. Low pay is commonly defined in terms of the hourly wage but in some instances weekly, monthly, or even annual earnings are used to define low-paid workers. In this chapter various definitions of low pay are used and there will not be a discussion on the merits of using one particular definition over another.[1] None of the findings presented below are greatly affected by the definition of low pay used, although the actual numbers involved will vary slightly.

Interest in the low-wage labour market in the UK grew in the 1980s and 1990s in an environment of increasing earnings inequality, deteriorating labour market position of low-skilled workers, high youth unemployment, and increases in economic inactivity rates among men over 55 years of age. Employment protection of low-wage workers gradually diminished over the 1970s and 1980s with a decline in trade union representation and power and the gradual removal of the Wages Councils.[2] Other institutions championing the rights of low-wage workers grew and the Low Pay Unit, which campaigns for social and economic justice for low-paid workers, has been a strong and growing force since 1974. Low pay is, unsurprisingly, a political issue and concern about low-wage employment led the Labour Party to pledge to introduce a National Minimum Wage upon winning the 1997 General Election. The establishment of the Low Pay Commission (LPC) in 1997 and the lead up to the introduction of a National Minimum Wage (NMW) in April 1999 resulted in a substantial amount of research on low-wage employment.[3] This means that our knowledge of the causes and consequences of low pay has improved markedly in recent years.

---

[1] For discussion of the relative merits of the different definitions, see for example Stewart and Swaffield (1998) or the OECD *Employment Outlook 1996*.

[2] The Wages Councils set minimum wage rates in 26 industries in the early 1990s, down from a peak of 60 in the early 1960s. In 1993 the remaining Wages Councils were abolished. Dickens *et al.* (1999) show that the Wages Councils were effective in protecting the wages of the lowest-paid employees but their effectiveness diminished from the 1980s up to their dissolution in 1993.

[3] The LPC has been responsible for commissioning research on the low-wage labour market and has collated a substantial amount of existing research in this area through seminars and the publication of collections of papers.

From these previous studies we know that some individuals are more likely to be low paid than are others. They include:

- Women;
- Young people;
- People with low levels of qualifications;
- Older (male) workers;
- Long-term sick and disabled;
- Ethnic minorities;
- People with little or no work experience.

Low-paid work is concentrated in certain industries:

- Textiles;
- Agriculture;
- Hotels and catering;
- Retail;
- Residential care.

Workers within certain occupations are consistently low paid:

- Hairdressers;
- Cleaners;
- Catering assistants;
- Care assistants;
- Sales assistants;
- Security guards.

In addition, low pay has a regional dimension and is more prevalent in the North-East of England and Northern Ireland than elsewhere. Although low-paid workers are found in all firm types, they are more likely to be employed in small and medium-sized enterprises than large enterprises.

Why are some workers low paid? Low-paid workers are those workers who for one reason or another do not obtain a high reward in the labour market. We might think of them as individuals who have low-earnings power as a result of low levels of 'intrinsic' productivity (due to low levels of human or social capital, innate ability, etc.), and for many this is likely to be true. Other workers can be low paid because their job does not take advantage of their full potential due to skill mismatch. Skill mismatch can arise when there are not enough jobs around which require the skills available in the workforce, individuals' skills may have become redundant due to technological and industrial change, or discrimination may prevent some individuals from finding work commensurate with their level of skill. Trainees may also be on low rates of pay during their training when a lower wage represents an employee's contribution to the cost of training in return for a higher wage in the future.

While low pay has an important economic dimension it also has an important social dimension. The recent debate on the NMW has considered the (normative) question: how low is too low? With the introduction of the NMW in April

1999 this was the key question uppermost in the deliberations of the Low Pay Commission. At that time it was decided that anything below £3.60 per hour for adult workers was unacceptably low. In assessing the appropriate rate the LPC considered evidence on the proportion of the workforce likely to benefit from a NMW, potential for negative side effects (such as loss of employment and knock-on effects higher up the earnings distribution), its likely impact on poverty, and its potential impact on productivity (LPC 1998). Early evaluations suggest that the NMW has been a success in raising workers wages without having detrimental effects on employment (LPC 2000).

TRENDS IN LOW-WAGE EMPLOYMENT

Two important questions concerning trends in low-wage employment are considered in this section. Firstly, an assessment is made about whether or not there has been an increase in low-wage employment in Britain since the mid-1970s. Secondly, we examine changes in real and relative earnings of low-paid employees over time.

In this section data from the New Earnings Survey (NES) are used. The NES is the largest regular survey of pay conducted in Britain (earnings data for approximately 160,000 employees is collected on an annual basis). The sample is effectively a random sample of approximately 1 per cent of all employees identified through the National Insurance system. Employers are required under a statutory obligation to provide pay information on the selected sample of employees. One of the disadvantages of the NES is that its coverage of low-paid workers is incomplete as the sample is largely selected on earnings being above the income tax threshold (see Wilkinson 1998; and Orchard and Sefton 1996). Due to changes in collection procedures its coverage has also changed through time (McKnight *et al.* 1998). However, the advantages with the NES in terms of the quality of information collected and the time span which it covers make it the most important source of information on trends in pay in Britain.

Two low-pay thresholds are used here to examine trends in low pay over time. Low-wage employees are defined here as employees whose hourly wage is either less than two-thirds of the wage of the median employee or less than half the wage of the median employee. Figure 7.1 plots the proportion of employees who are low paid according to these two definitions over the period 1975 and 1999. It is clear that the proportion of employees in low-wage employment has increased markedly since 1977. The percentage of employees earning less than two-thirds of the median employee has increased from 12 per cent in 1977 to 21 per cent in 1998, increasing by three-quarters over this period. There has also been a substantial increase in the proportion of employees on even lower wages. The percentage of employees earning less than half the earnings of the median employee fell slightly between 1975 and 1978, and then increased from 3 per cent in 1978 to 6 per cent in 1998, doubling in twenty years. However, since 1998

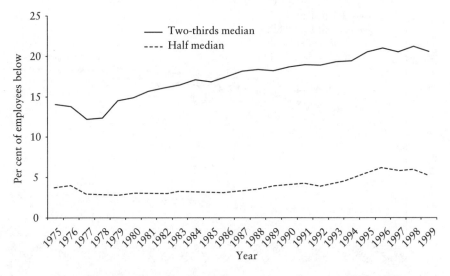

Figure 7.1. *Change in the share of low-wage employment, 1975–1999*
Source: New Earnings Survey Panel Dataset.

there has been a fall in the share of low-paid workers. This fall is likely to be the result of the introduction of a National Minimum Wage in April 1999.

It was noted earlier that coverage of very low paid workers in the NES is incomplete because the sample is largely drawn from employees earning above the tax threshold. If the coverage of the NES has improved over time then such an increase in low-wage employment as that shown in Figure 7.1 could result. To test for the effect of change in coverage, trends in low pay are assessed for a group of employees whose coverage is unlikely to have changed over this period—employees earning above the Lower Earnings Limit (LEL) for National Insurance contributions. The median earnings are redefined for this group of employees as are the proportions of employees earning below the two low-pay thresholds. Figure 7.2 compares the trends in low pay for all employees in the NES between 1980 and 1999 with employees earning above the LEL.[4] The dispersion in wages is lower among employees earning above the LEL than among all employees, which is not surprising given that this restriction truncates the weekly earnings distribution and therefore the hourly earnings distribution due to the high overlap between low weekly pay and low hourly pay. The result is that a smaller proportion of employees with earnings at or above the LEL than employees below the LEL have earnings below the low-pay thresholds. There is a similar rise in low pay among both groups of employees over this period although the increase in employees earning below the lower-pay threshold (half

---

[4] The LEL is set at roughly the same level as the basic State Retirement Pension. For example, in 1998/9 it was set at £64.70 per week.

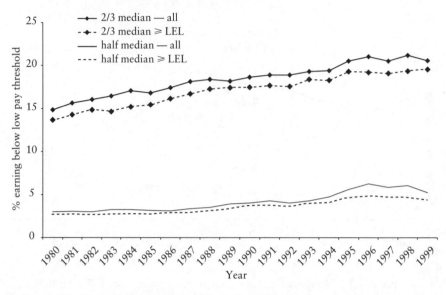

Figure 7.2. *Trends in low-wage employment with and without employees earning below the LEL, 1980–1999*

Source: New Earnings Survey Panel Dataset.

median earnings) in the second half of the 1990s is less marked when only employees earning above the LEL are considered. This may be due to changes in coverage, although an increase in the proportion of employees earning below the LEL on low hourly rates of pay cannot be ruled out.

Turning to the relative position of low-wage employees, Figure 7.3 shows the wage of employees at the tenth percentile (demarcating the lowest-paid 10 per cent) relative to employees at the fiftieth percentile (the median employee) and the ninetieth percentile (demarcating the highest-paid 10 per cent). The figure shows a compression in the distribution of earnings in the mid-1970s, but since 1977 the wage of the lowest-paid employees relative to the median and the highest-paid employees has deteriorated. In 1977 employees at the tenth percentile were earning around one-third of the wage of employees at the ninetieth percentile, falling to around one-quarter in 1999.

It is sometimes argued that concentration on relative earnings is inappropriate and that we should be more concerned about changes in real earnings. Figure 7.4 plots the evolution of real wages (expressed in 1996 prices) for three points in the earnings distribution—the tenth percentile (demarcating the lowest-paid 10 per cent), fiftieth percentile (the median employee) and the ninetieth percentile (demarcating the highest-paid 10 per cent).

The results are fairly dramatic. The real wage of employees at the lowest decile of the earnings distribution increased from £3.03 per hour in 1975 to £3.75 per hour in 1999. Whether this is considered to be a small increase or a large increase

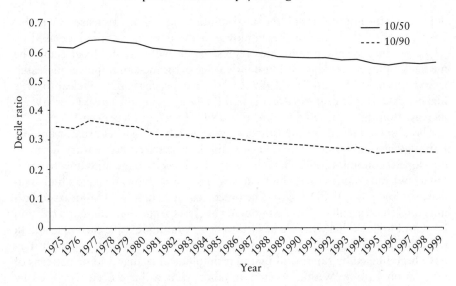

Figure 7.3. *Relative earnings of low-paid employees, 1975–1999*
Source: New Earnings Survey Panel Dataset.

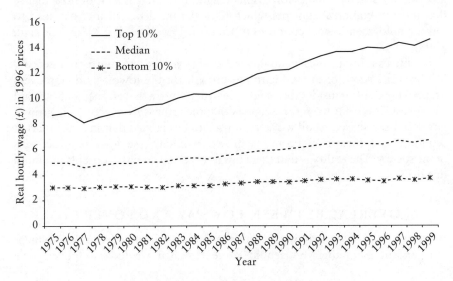

Figure 7.4. *Real earnings, 1975–1999*
Source: New Earnings Survey Panel Dataset.

depends on the importance placed on absolute or percentage increases. Over this 25-year period the wage of the employee at the tenth percentile increased by 72 pence. In percentage terms this represents an increase of 24 per cent. The median employee fared better. The hourly wage of the median employee increased from £4.95 in 1975 to £6.71 in 1999 (£1.76, or 36 per cent). But it is clear that the highest-paid 10 per cent of earners fared the best, seeing their real hourly wage increase from £8.77 in 1975 to £14.72 in 1999 (£5.95, or 68 per cent).

The observed trends in the British low-wage labour market are not unique. Earnings inequality has increased over the last quarter of a century in many developed economies (USA, Canada, Australia, New Zealand, and Italy to name but a few) and countries with high earnings inequality typically have a high incidence of low pay (OECD 1996). The precise cause behind what appears to be a universal trend is still in dispute but many analysts argue that a demand shift[5] in favour of high-skilled workers has led to deteriorating relative earnings, and in the USA falling real earnings, of low-skilled workers. This demand shift may have been fuelled by rapid skill-biased technological change and/or patterns of international trade. Within country trends appear to have been tempered by changes in labour supply, the effectiveness of the welfare state, the power of collective wage setting agreements, and minimum wages.

The USA and Britain experienced some of the greatest increases in earnings inequality (and incidence of low pay) over the last twenty-five years; both countries also undertook fairly radical reforms of labour market institutions designed to protect the wages of low-skilled workers. Some would argue that as a consequence both the USA and Britain have enjoyed higher employment growth, but international comparisons suggest that there is little or no evidence that institutional arrangements which limit the incidence of low pay lead to lower employment across countries (Card *et al.* 1996; OECD 1996; Keese *et al.* 1998).

The increase in earnings inequality in Britain over the last quarter of a century has been the result of limited earnings growth for the lowest-paid employees accompanied by considerably higher earnings growth for the highest-paid employees. It is clear from these figures that the returns from economic growth have not been shared by all workers. It used to be claimed that in a free market economy the returns from economic growth would trickle down to all sections of the society. The reality is that there has not been so much of a trickle but more of a drip.

OVERLAP BETWEEN LOW PAY AND POVERTY

When we look at low pay we consider individuals' income from employment independent from their household context. When we look at poverty we

---

[5] A demand shift in favour of high-skilled workers can only be a partial explanation because earnings inequality increased both between and *within* skill groups.

consider individuals' earnings only in the context of their contribution to overall household income. This means that an individual can be high paid and poor, low paid and rich or anywhere in between. In this section we consider the extent to which individuals at the bottom of the earnings distribution (low paid) are also at the bottom of the income distribution (poor).

We know that the unemployed are not necessarily living in poverty, as the unemployed can be protected from poverty through income of other household members. Likewise, finding a job does not automatically mean that an individual is protected from poverty. This again depends on income of other household members and the availability and generosity of in-work benefits. Some individuals are able to offset low hourly wages by working very long hours, working overtime, or holding down more than one job.

When we move from individual earnings to household income to identify those at the bottom of the distribution we are considering other forms of income—welfare transfers—benefits, tax credits, etc., and income from investments—'unearned income'. We also have to consider assumptions about the extent to which income is pooled across household members, economies of scale, and differences in needs.

The overlap between low pay and poverty has been found to vary across countries. A strong positive association exists between the incidence of low-paid work and the non-elderly adult poverty rate across OECD countries. At the start of the 1990s the greatest overlap was found in the USA where 25 per cent of all low-paid prime age workers were living in poverty,[6] followed by the Netherlands (18 per cent), the UK (13 per cent), and Canada (12.5 per cent). The lowest rates were found in the Nordic countries: Sweden (3.7 per cent), Finland (4.9 per cent) (Marx and Verbist 1997). Millar *et al.* (1997) shows that for the UK the overlap between low pay and poverty in the 1970s and early 1980s was only around 3–4 per cent but by the early 1990s had increased to 13 per cent. This means that a higher proportion of the poor is now made up of working poor than in the past. A number of factors are likely to have contributed to this rise.

Any change in the number of households in poverty over time depends on changes in the demographic structure of households and the share of poor individuals within a household type. The first two columns of Table 7.1 show changes in the distribution of individuals across household types, where households are defined in terms of employment status, between 1968 and 1996. The final two columns show the proportion of individuals within a household type who are living in poverty.

As discussed in Chapter 4, there has been an overall rise in the proportion of the population living in relative poverty (below half median equivalized household income after housing costs), from 10 per cent in 1968 to 23 per cent in

---

[6] Poverty is defined as below half average equivalent household income, low-paid workers are defined as full-year, full-time workers earnings less than 66 per cent of the median.

Table 7.1. *Employment status of households and the extent of poverty, 1968 and 1996*

	Distribution of population (%)		% of group living in poverty	
	1968	1996	1968	1996
Workless	3	13	70	73
Employed	70	55	4	10
1 low-paid	1	3	24	53
1 high-paid	28	17	6	16
2 both high-paid	16	19	1	2
2 at least 1 low-paid	10	8	3	10
Self-employed	10	13	10	20
Pensioner	19	19	26	27
All			10	23

Notes: Further configurations of employed households are not shown. A workless household has no household member of working age in work. 'Low pay' is defined as the lowest quintile group of the hourly earnings distribution and 'high pay' is anything above this level. Poverty is defined as below half median income (adjusted for household composition) after housing costs.

Sources: Family Expenditure Survey. Author's calculations from tables in Dickens (1999, 2000).

1996. Some of this rise has been due to an increase in the proportion of the population living in household types which are most vulnerable to poverty. Households most at risk of poverty are workless households, and the proportion of the population living in workless households increased from 3 per cent in 1968 to 13 per cent in 1996. On average, employment protects a household from poverty, but the proportion of individuals living in employed households decreased from 70 per cent in 1968 to 55 per cent in 1996. Households containing only a low-paid worker are at higher risk of poverty, and the share of households with only a low-paid worker increased from 1 per cent to 3 per cent. Having a single 'high-paid' (i.e. not low-paid) worker protects a household from poverty but the proportion of the population living in a household with a single 'high-paid' worker decreased from 28 per cent to 17 per cent.

A second factor that affects any overall change in poverty is the extent of poverty within a household type. The figures in the final two columns of Table 7.1 show that there has been an increase in the proportion of individuals living in poverty within each household type. Importantly, employment is now less likely to protect a household from poverty than in the past. These two changes together show that the share of households with a single low-paid employee has increased and the proportion of those households in poverty has doubled. The proportion of households with one high-paid employee has decreased and the extent to which this type of household is protected from poverty has decreased; in 1996 16 per cent of individuals in this household type were living in poverty compared with 6 per cent in 1968. A single 'breadwinner' (male or female) is now less likely to be able to protect a household from poverty than in the past.

At any point in time low-paid workers are more likely to be living in poor households than higher-paid workers. Stewart (1998) shows that low-paid workers (earning below £3.50 per hour in April 1997 terms) are more than seven times more likely than higher-paid workers to live in poor households (below half average income)—15 per cent compared with 2 per cent. In addition, because the workless are even more likely to be living in poverty and the high propensity for low-paid workers to experience unemployment/non-employment, the relationship between low pay and poverty is even higher when considered over the longer term.

At the household level Dickens (1999) looks in detail at the overlap between employment (particularly low pay) and poverty to assess the potential effect of a National Minimum Wage on household poverty. He shows that a minimum wage will help more individuals in poverty over the longer term due to the movements between non-work and low pay. Stewart (1999) examines a four-year period (1991–4) and shows that nearly half of all individuals who are 'permanently' low paid (low paid (£3.50 per hour) at least once and never higher paid) are in poor households, compared with 29 per cent of individuals who are 'temporarily' low paid (low paid at least once and higher paid at least once), and 10 per cent of individuals who are never low paid.

Low-paid jobs tend to be more precarious than higher-paid jobs. This is not because low-paid workers move quickly into high-paid jobs. Tracking individuals over time shows that low-paid workers are more likely to go on to experience unemployment, or periods out of the labour market, than higher-paid workers (Stewart 1999; McKnight 2000). Little is known about the reason why these low-paid jobs are more likely to terminate than higher-paid jobs. We know that in economic downturns it is the low-skilled/low-paid workers who tend to lose their jobs first but the cycling between low-pay and no-pay appears to be present regardless of the state of the economy. It may be that employers prefer to maintain a high turnover of staff to maintain productivity in low-paid monotonous jobs or they may be attempting to avoid firing costs.[7] Some low-paid work is seasonal and naturally comes to an end at the end of a season. In some cases low-paid jobs do act as recruitment channels into higher-paid jobs. If employers operate an 'up or out' policy then a proportion of these employees will be without work after a trial period.

---

[7] Until recently (June 1999) employees were not entitled to bring a case of unfair dismissal against an employer before two years of continuous employment. In June 1999 this was reduced to one year. In the past, employees on fixed-term contracts were often asked to sign a waiver agreeing to forgo their right to unfair dismissal related to expiry of a contract without renewal. This practice has been outlawed since 25 October 1999. Employees only qualify for redundancy payments after two years of continuous employment.

There are a number of reasons why individuals may seek short-term work. Due to caring responsibilities (such as caring for elderly relatives or dependent children) an individual may only be able to work for short periods of time (such as school term time). Students may only be able to, or want to, work during vacations. An individual may terminate a job if they find that the work is not what they expected, or they are unhappy with their employer. Although we know that low pay is often associated with short-term employment we do not yet know enough about the reason why these jobs frequently end in periods of non-employment.

CHILDHOOD POVERTY AND ADULT LOW PAY

Over the last 30 years the UK has experienced a large increase in the proportion of children living in poverty. In 1968 one in ten children were living in relative poverty increasing to one in three by 1996 (Gregg, Harkness, and Machin 1999; Piachaud and Sutherland, Chapter 9 in this volume). This is partly due to the increase in the number of children in workless households (where the extent of poverty is high) and an increase in the proportion of children living in working poor households.

Focusing on the distribution of the population of children across household types and how it changed between 1968 and 1996, the figures in Table 7.2 show that children in 1996 were more likely to be living in households at greater risk of poverty than were children in 1968 (where poverty is defined as below half

Table 7.2. *Childhood poverty in 1968 and 1996*

	Distribution of child population (%)		% of child population living in poverty	
	1968	1996	1968	1996
Workless	4	20	81	89
Employed	80	63	7	17
1 low-paid	2	5	33	69
1 high-paid	43	21	9	24
2 both high-paid	15	22	3	2
2 at least 1 low-paid	11	10	5	15
Self-employed	12	16	13	27
All			10	33

Notes: Pensioner households and further configurations of employed households are not shown. A workless household has no household member of working age in work. Low pay is defined as the lowest quintile group of the hourly earnings distribution and 'high paid' is anything above this level. Poverty is defined as below half average income (adjusted for household composition) after housing costs.

Sources: Family Expenditure Survey (Dickens, 1999, 2000).

average income (adjusted for household composition) after housing costs). The proportion of children living in workless households increased from 4 per cent to 20 per cent (higher than 16 other OECD countries examined by Gregg, Harkness, and Machin 1999). There also appears to be a polarization within employed household types. The share of children living in households with one low-paid employee increased, with one high-paid employee decreased but the share of children in households with two high-paid employees increased.

Employment protects children from the risk of poverty, but a higher proportion of children in employed households were living in poverty in 1996 than in 1968, increasing from 7 to 17 per cent. Having only one employee in a household is even less likely to protect children from poverty in 1996 than in 1968. In 1968 one-third of children in households with one low-paid employee were living in poverty compared with over two-thirds living in this household type in 1996. If the employee is 'high paid' (i.e. not low paid), 9 per cent of children living in these households were poor in 1968 compared with 24 per cent in 1996. Overall this suggests that worklessness is a problem that has increased over time, both in terms of the proportion of children living in workless households and the proportion of children in workless households living in poverty. In addition, while employment to some extent protects children from poverty, children in households where there is only one earner, even if the earner is high paid, are now more likely to be living in poverty than in the past.

Poverty has detrimental consequences on individuals at the time but it can also have long-lasting effects. John Hobcraft's chapter in this volume highlighted the long-term detrimental effects suffered by children from households with reported financial hardship or children who had received free school meals. In addition, individuals from low income and poor households are more likely to experience unemployment and non-employment than individuals from higher income backgrounds (McKnight 2001a). Childhood poverty is also linked with lower earnings in adulthood. In Table 7.3 the position of young adults (age 23/26) in the earnings distribution is shown by household income at age 16. The results in this table show that individuals from low-income and poor households are much more likely be among the lowest paid employees in adult life. Comparison of two birth cohorts, one born in 1958 and one born in 1970, shows that this relationship has strengthened through time. This means that these young people are less likely to be able to improve their position through earnings from employment. The consequence of this is that inequality and poverty are likely to perpetuate across generations.

Some of the difference in earnings by household income background is due to education. Children from low-income and poor backgrounds perform less well in standard literacy and numeracy tests at a young age and go on to attain fewer educational qualifications than their counterparts from higher-income households (McKnight 2001b). A formal analysis of earnings and unemployment shows that these differences do explain some, but not all, of the inequalities in labour market outcomes (McKnight 2001b). Even after controlling for differences

Table 7.3. *From childhood poverty to low-wage employment (%)*

Wage (quintile group)	Cohort born in 1958, household income age 16			Cohort born in 1970, household income age 16		
	High income	Low income	Poor	High income	Low income	Poor
Bottom	17	22	28	13	26	30
2nd	19	21	22	16	23	25
3rd	20	19	18	20	20	17
4th	21	19	17	24	16	16
5th	22	18	15	26	14	12
All	100	100	100	100	100	100

Notes: High-income households have at least average income, low-income households have below average income and poor households have below half average income. Hourly wages in the 1958 cohort are measured at age 23 and in the 1970 cohort at age 26.

Source: National Child Development Study, British Cohort Study 1970.

in educational attainment, children from low-income and poor households are more likely to be unemployed, and if they are in work their earnings are, on average, lower than children from higher-income households.

LOW PAY, POVERTY, AND POLICY

Low pay and the overlap between low pay and poverty (in-work poverty) can be tackled in a number of ways. These policies can be usefully grouped into those that tackle the root causes and those that tackle the consequence (although some policies attempt to address both). In the long term it is clearly the causes which need to be tackled, but in the short term it is often necessary to relieve in-work poverty by tackling the consequence and supply-side issues. It was noted above that there are significant educational inequalities among young people related to parental resources. As long as education provides the key route to good jobs, through productivity enhancements or access to well-paid occupations, it will be important to break the cycle of poverty by assuring access to high-quality education for all (for further discussion see Chapter 11).

Two policies designed to tackle the consequence of in-work poverty covered here are the Working Families Tax Credit, Housing, and Council Tax Benefits. In terms of policies that can address the cause of the overlap between low pay and poverty, two policies are described—improvements to the National Insurance system and the National Minimum Wage. This is by no means an exhaustive list of policies which impact on the low-wage labour market and relieve in-work poverty but is included to illustrate some of the benefits and potential pitfalls of such policies.

(i) The Working Families Tax Credit

To ensure that individuals with dependent children can support their families through work, where low-paid jobs are the only option, working families with dependent children on low incomes have received various forms of 'top up' through the benefit and tax system over time. The Family Income Supplement was introduced in 1971, replaced by Family Credit in 1988 and succeeded by the Working Families Tax Credit (WFTC) in October 1999. Although WFTC and its predecessors vary in terms of generosity and eligibility criteria they have all been broadly designed to meet the same policy objective. These in-work benefits have been designed to overcome what has become known as the 'benefit trap'. The benefit trap arises when the difference between in-work income (earnings) is not sufficiently greater than out-of-work income (benefits) to provide the necessary incentive for individuals to find work. This usually occurs when an individual can only find a low-paid job or where other caring responsibilities limit the number of hours that they can work (also one of the causes of in-work poverty). In effect, these in-work benefits are designed to reward the efforts of individuals who are prepared to take a low-paid job rather than rely solely on benefits.

The WFTC reduces the overlap between low pay and poverty by topping up the incomes of working families in low-paid jobs. In the longer term, an additional benefit may be realized through increased work experience as individuals are able to maintain contact with the labour market even when their out-of-work benefit income is higher than their earnings. The increased work experience can lead to higher earnings and/or rates of employment in the future. There may also be an additional benefit of having a working parent(s) to act as a role model for the children.

There are two main side effects that can arise from such a system of in-work wage supplementation. Firstly, employers may pay lower wages than they would in the absence of the benefit. This may be because they know that the benefit system will increase the disposable income of low-paid workers. However, employers do not have to be aware of the benefit system, for the fact that individuals are prepared to take very low-paid jobs or accept low or no pay rises due to the income 'top up' means that employers can pay lower wages. The result is that individuals who do not qualify for the benefit can lose out in favour of those who do, not only because they do not receive the additional income but also because the wage offered by the employer is now lower. Employers pay lower wages and the difference is met via general taxation and as a consequence some of the benefit then goes directly to the employers.

The second side effect is that in a two-parent household there is very little incentive for a second person to find work and this may have long-term damaging effects on the non-employed individual's longer-term employment prospects. It may also have beneficial effects if it means that one parent can now afford to stay at home and care for their children.

The current provision of wage supplementation to low-income working families with children is likely to be extended to single people and couples without dependent children. Results from a three-year pilot programme of an in-work benefit made available to low-paid workers without dependent children (Earnings Top-up), suggest that such a wage supplementation programme can successfully raise the incomes of this group without having negative secondary effects for other groups and with small positive effects on unemployment (falls in inflows into unemployment and increases in outflows) (Marsh 2001). The Treasury (2000a) has set out the future for wage supplementation in the modernization of Britain's tax and benefit system. The current plan is that by 2003 the WFTC will be divided into child and adult components with the adult Working Tax Credit (WTC) being made available to most low-paid workers in low-income households. The detail on rates and thresholds is yet to be agreed but the objectives of the WTC are to increase work incentives for low-paid workers *and* to relieve in-work poverty.

(ii) Housing Benefit and Council Tax Benefit

These two benefits are not strictly speaking in-work benefits but the fact that they are available to working as well as non-working individuals on low incomes means that they play an important role in the low-wage labour market. Council Tax Benefit is the most widespread of all means-tested benefits, yet has been largely overlooked in discussions of welfare reform. One of the key issues is how these benefits interact with other benefits available to low-paid workers. Raising the generosity of one in-work benefit such as WFTC may have very little effect if the increase gives rise to a pound-for-pound reduction in, for example, Housing Benefit. A recent assessment of the likely impact of WFTC showed that the overall affect on employment participation is expected to be fairly small (Blundell *et al.* 2000). This is due, in part, to the fact that for many the increase in the generosity of WFTC is offset by reductions in Housing Benefit entitlement. A major reform of Housing Benefit and its interaction with other benefits is now seen as long overdue. The very high withdrawal rates of Housing and Council Tax Benefits as incomes rise contribute to the poverty trap—i.e. reduce the incentive to gain higher earnings as only a small fraction of any increase is retained due to the removal of benefits (Hills 2001).

The impacts of Housing Benefit and Council Tax Benefit are hard to assess because the variability in living costs around the country is directly related to the amount that can be claimed. The amount of Housing Benefit payable depends on other income, value of savings, personal circumstances (household composition, disability) and the eligible rent.[8] The same conditions apply to Council Tax Benefit awards although, of course, the amount of Council Tax due rather than the eligible rent is assessed. A recent assessment of the effectiveness

---

[8] The eligible rent may be lower than the rent charged if the rent is higher than the local reference rent, the accommodation is deemed too large, or the claimant is single and under 25 years.

of Council Tax Benefit (Clark *et al.* 2000) offers some suggestions for future reform but concludes that the current system provides an effective safety net, although low levels of take-up (probably due to its complexity) threaten its ability to achieve its objective.

Due to the way in which Housing Benefit and Council Tax Benefit effectively increase the incomes of low-paid workers (by reducing living costs), the secondary effects of Housing Benefit are very similar to those from Family Credit/WFTC. While in-work benefits play an important role in raising the incomes of low-paid workers they can result in an in-work benefit (poverty) trap and reduce the prospects of escaping poverty. The fact that their existence effectively subsidizes low-paid work means that they may well 'crowd out' better-paid work.

(iii) National Insurance and Low Pay

The National Insurance system in the UK is based on a contributory principle. Individuals in work pay National Insurance Contributions (NICs) and then in certain times of need claim benefits based on their, or in some cases their spouse's, contribution record, subject to meeting various qualifying conditions. The main benefits involved are Jobseeker's Allowance, Incapacity Benefit, Maternity Allowance, Widowed Parent's Allowance, Bereavement Payment, Bereavement Allowance, and Retirement Pension. In addition, although Statutory Sick Pay and Statutory Maternity Pay are non-contributory benefits, entitlement does depend on average earnings at least equal to the Lower Earnings Limit (set at £67[9] per week in 2000/1) over a qualifying period. If an employee earns below the Lower Earnings Limit (LEL) they are not liable to make NICs. As soon as earnings reach this threshold employees pay a proportion of their earnings. In the past NICs were payable on all earnings once earnings reached the LEL. This meant that some individuals, earning just above the LEL, paid very high marginal tax rates. This created an incentive for low-paid employees (and their employers) to keep earnings below the LEL. In the short term this meant that they maximized their take-home pay but in the medium to long term it increased the likelihood that they would have to depend on means-tested benefits. The operation of the National Insurance system therefore created a low-wage trap— there was a strong incentive to keep wages below the LEL—and led to a greater dependency on the means-tested benefit system in the longer term.

A recent study (McKnight *et al.* 1998) has shown that far from being a marginal issue a large number of employees at any one time have earnings below the LEL. In 1998, approximately 3 million employees were earning below the LEL, accounting for one in five female employees and one in twenty male employees. Moreover, many of these employees remained in jobs paying below the LEL for prolonged periods of time and were more likely to cycle between low pay

---

[9] The LEL is set at approximately the same level as the basic State Retirement Pension.

and non-employment than improve their earnings and move up the earnings distribution.

A number of changes have been made to the NI system and contributions schedule in recent years. Changes affecting employees are outlined here, although changes to thresholds and rates have also been made to the employers' NI contribution schedule. In April 1999 the so-called 'entry fee', which created high marginal tax rates just above the LEL, was abolished. This meant that employees are now only required to make NICs on earnings above the LEL, at a rate of 10 per cent on earnings up to the Upper Earnings Limit (UEL). From April 2000 a new primary threshold of £76 per week (increased to £87 in April 2001) was introduced. Employees earning between the LEL (£67 per week in April 2000, raised to £72 in April 2001) and the primary threshold are not required to make NICs but will build up entitlement to contribution based benefits, creating in effect a zero-rated band. The primary threshold, since April 2001, is set at the weekly equivalent of the income tax personal allowance, forming part of the alignment of National Insurance and Income Tax systems. The NIC threshold to the Income Tax threshold whilst protecting entitlement to contribution-based benefits for low-paid workers through the zero-rated band. The introduction of a zero-rated band is a fairly radical move because it signifies a departure from the contributory principle underlying the National Insurance system (although individuals have been able, in particular circumstances, to build up entitlement to contribution-based benefits through a system of credits). For example, primary carers of dependent children at home full-time or earning below the LEL, qualify for Home Responsibilities Protection (HRP) which protects entitlement to a basic State Retirement Pension by reducing the necessary number of qualifying years against which a pension may be drawn.

The current situation is an improvement on the old situation but there are still a number of key issues that remain to be addressed. It is still the case that employees must have a complete contribution record for a whole year for that year to count as a qualifying year. This means that employees who are employed for only part of a year—who are most likely to be low-paid workers—have an incomplete contribution record for that year and will not be able to benefit from these contributions in the future (precise rules governing entitlement vary across benefits). Unlike Income Tax these workers cannot reclaim these 'lost' contributions. A fairer system would take into account actual contributions rather than calculations based on 'qualifying years'. Low weekly paid workers are now artificially divided into those below the LEL who do not make NICs and do not build up entitlement to contributory based benefits, and those above the LEL but below the primary threshold who do not make NICs but do build up entitlement to contribution-based benefits through what is effectively a zero-rated band. It seems extremely unlikely that such a system can survive in the long term.

It is still the case that many low-paid workers do not build up sufficient contribution records to qualify for a basic State Retirement Pension. DSS statistics for 1996 show that 60 per cent of women did not have a sufficient contribution record to qualify for a full basic State pension (DSS 1997). Low pay during the working life has implications for poverty and social exclusion in old age.

(iv) National Minimum Wage

The National Minimum Wage tackles in-work poverty by addressing one of the causes: very low (what some people call 'exploitative') wages.

In 1997 the Low Pay Commission (LPC) was established by the Labour Government to recommend the level at which the NMW should be introduced, its coverage, and how it should apply to young workers. In June 1998 the LPC recommended that an initial adult rate (21 years and over) of £3.60 per hour should be introduced in April 1999, rising to £3.70 in June 2000. Alongside the adult rate a Development Rate (18–20 years and adults for the first six months of an accredited training programme) of £3.20 per hour, rising to £3.30 in June 2000.

The Government partly implemented these recommendations, introducing a NMW in April 1999 for adults at £3.60 per hour (increased to £3.70 in October 2000), a Youth Rate of £3.00 per hour for workers aged from 18 to 21 (increased to £3.20 in June 2000) and a six months 'training rate' for adults at £3.20.[10] In October 2001 the Government has agreed to raise the adult rate to £4.10 per hour and recommendations for the Youth and Training Rate are currently being developed.

The arguments against a minimum wage are fairly well rehearsed and basically centre on the opinion that a minimum wage will hurt exactly the people it is aimed to help by destroying jobs of low-paid workers (the low-pay versus no-pay debate). For many years it was regarded as received wisdom in economics that minimum wages were harmful because they destroyed jobs (based on the standard neoclassical model of the labour market). In more recent times this view has been challenged through the work of, among others, Card and Krueger (1995) and Dickens, Machin, and Manning (1994) who offer alternative models of the labour market and demonstrate through empirical work that minimum wages do not necessarily lead to decreases in employment.

Although it is still too early to estimate the longer-term impact of the introduction of the NMW in the UK, early estimates (nine months after its introduction) suggest that if it has had a negative effect on employment, it is negligible (LPC 2000).

The objectives for introducing a NMW in the UK were to remove 'exploitative wages', make work pay and thereby improve the work incentives of individuals at the bottom end of the labour market, and help tackle in-work poverty. A NMW also plays an important role in the presence of employment tax credits by

---

[10] See DTI (1999) for more information.

creating a wage floor and thereby preventing employers from reducing wages to the extent that they reap all (or at least a large proportion of) the rewards. It is still too early to tell the extent to which the NMW has reduced in-work poverty. The LPC estimated that the NMW would improve the wages of approximately 1.5 million workers. Their early assessment suggests that around one million workers (in the formal sector of the labour market) have benefited (LPC 2000).

CONCLUSIONS

Simon Burgess and Carol Propper showed in Chapter 4 of this volume that relative poverty in Britain has increased dramatically since the late 1970s. The increase in poverty has been even greater among households with children (see Chapter 9). This increase is cause for concern not only because of the obvious disadvantages faced by people living in poverty at that point in time but because of longer-term impacts of poverty. It has been shown in this chapter (and Chapter 5) that poverty can have long-lasting effects through education and labour-market disadvantage faced by individuals who experience childhood poverty.

Work provides a means through which individuals can improve their income but due to the complex relationship between low pay and poverty a job may not be enough to raise a household out of poverty. Low-paid workers are more likely to live in poor households than rich households and the overlap between low pay and poverty has increased over the last thirty years. Viewed over a longer time horizon the interrelationship between low pay and poverty is even greater. This is largely because low-paid workers are more likely to experience periods of no-pay (unemployment or economic inactivity) than higher paid workers, and workless individuals are the most likely to be poor.

Low-paid work has increased over the last twenty-five years and the relative earnings of low-paid workers have fallen. The fall in the relative pay of these workers is due to lower growth in low paid-workers' earnings compared with much higher growth in the pay of the highest earners. Falling relative wages of low-paid workers are likely to explain much of the increase in the overlap between low pay and poverty over the last thirty years.

The final section of this chapter reviewed a number of government policies designed to tackle the causes and consequences of the overlap between low pay and poverty. Policies designed to tackle the consequence of in-work poverty, such as the Working Families Tax Credit, Housing Benefit, and Council Tax Benefit, have an important role to play in the short term by increasing the incomes of these households and relieving poverty. However, as a long-term strategy they can bring some undesirable effects. In-work benefits can reduce the incentives to move out of low pay into higher-paid jobs, reduce the incentive for a second earner to find work and allow employers to keep wages artificially low. The extent to which they can continue to relieve in-work poverty will also depend on their generosity. If the value of tax credits is uprated with prices rather than earnings then their effectiveness in relieving (relative) in-work poverty will be limited.

While worklessness virtually guarantees poverty, work is now less likely to lift a household out of poverty than in the past. This means that the current emphasis on encouraging parents to find work may not lift children out of poverty but will mean that parents will have less time to devote to the care of their children. In-work benefits in the form of the Working Families Tax Credit may go some way in reducing the overlap between work and poverty but in-work benefits are not new. In-work benefits for families with dependent children have been around since the early 1970s and, although they have become more generous over time, the overlap between employment and poverty has increased.

A constructive long-term strategy should tackle the root causes of low-pay by reducing the chances of individuals entering low-paid work in the first place and secondly, helping individuals in low-wage employment move out of low-paid jobs into better-paid jobs. It is low-pay 'careers' in the form of persistence in low pay, or cycling between low-pay and no-pay, that has the most damaging effects rather than a temporary experience of low pay. Longer-term policies include improving education, in particular ensuring that children from low-income backgrounds have access to good-quality education and the necessary support to fulfil their potential, a shift in the emphasis of welfare-to-work programmes away from a concentration on moving benefit claimants into any job (usually low-paid work supported by in-work benefits) to helping individuals move off benefits altogether and into financial independence.

While global trends may limit the extent to which a low-wage labour market can be reduced there are clearly lessons to be learned from countries which have managed to keep a check on their growth. An education and training system which compresses the skill distribution by ensuring high minimum standards of education and training seems to limit the size of the low-wage labour market (such as in Germany), effective minimum wage rates and collective wage-setting agreements have also had some success in a number of countries (e.g. France, Belgium, and the Netherlands) as do strong social welfare institutions which limit inequality (found in Scandinavian and other Nordic countries). One thing is clear, ignoring the growth in inequality and low-wage employment will result in increases in in-work poverty. The greatest danger in ignoring in-work poverty is that children are both very exposed to poverty and then tend to carry the scars into their adult lives.

8

Social Exclusion and Neighbourhoods

RUTH LUPTON AND ANNE POWER

Economic and demographic studies contribute to an understanding of the social exclusion of individuals and their families. In this chapter, we introduce a spatial dimension, exploring the relationship between neighbourhood and exclusion.

Poverty and social exclusion in Britain are spatially concentrated. This is not a new pattern. Industrial Britain has always had poor areas and indeed, has always had studies of poor areas (Glennerster *et al.* 1999). However, there is evidence that over the last century, the relative deprivation of the poorest areas has got worse as absolute poverty has diminished (Gregory *et al.* 1999). Even at local authority level, the gap between the poorest areas and the rest is widening. Moreover, the 1980s saw a particular increase in intra-urban polarization, with increasing contrasts between poorer and more affluent electoral wards *within* cities (Hills 1995). It appears that poverty is becoming more concentrated in certain neighbourhoods.

The Social Exclusion Unit has identified up to 4,000 neighbourhoods which are not only poor but which are, 'pockets of intense deprivation where the problems of unemployment and crime are acute and hopelessly tangled up with poor health, housing and education. They have become no-go areas for some and no-exit zones for others.' (Social Exclusion Unit 1998*b*: 9)

We shall argue that the concentration of problems in particular neighbourhoods is not coincidental; that the nature of neighbourhoods actually contributes to the social exclusion of their residents, in three ways.

Firstly, neighbourhoods have intrinsic characteristics, well established and difficult to change. These include their location, transport infrastructure, housing, and economic base. Such characteristics are not wholly determined at neighbourhood level; for example, an over-supply of housing might be the result of national trends or local depopulation; weak labour market prospects might reflect wider regional trends. However, some neighbourhoods are more affected than others and these characteristics differ sharply even between neighbourhoods in the same town or city. Intrinsic neighbourhood characteristics impact directly on individual residents, reducing opportunities and increasing challenges. Unemployment, isolation, and poor health are examples of these direct consequences. Intrinsic characteristics can also impact through 'concentration effects'—changes in attitudes, behaviour, and interactions with others that occur when many people clustered together are similarly disadvantaged.

Secondly, residential sorting takes place, concentrating the most disadvantaged people in the least advantaged neighbourhoods. Part of the sorting process is driven by market responses to intrinsic neighbourhood characteristics, such as the quality of the housing or the type of work available, which affect the desirability of neighbourhoods. However, public policy also plays a part in determining who lives where, for example through tenure.

Thirdly, once this concentration of disadvantage is established, neighbourhoods can acquire even more damaging characteristics. Acquired characteristics include the area's reputation, its environment, services and facilities, levels of crime and disorder, and aspects of social life such as the extent of social interaction and residents' levels of confidence in the neighbourhood. When these characteristics are negative, they limit opportunities for residents and reduce the quality of life, and they can contribute to a sense of powerlessness and alienation that is in itself excluding. Of course these neighbourhood characteristics also fuel the process of residential sorting, because they make some neighbourhoods more attractive than others.

This chapter explores these links between neighbourhood and social exclusion, drawing both on existing evidence and on CASE's ongoing areas study. This is tracking twelve of the poorest neighbourhoods in England and Wales to understand the dynamic processes of social exclusion at neighbourhood level, and to see how these neighbourhoods fare, over time, in comparison with the cities and regions around them. We show how economic trends and public housing policy are exacerbating intrinsic differences between neighbourhoods and illustrate the impact of these intrinsic characteristics. We then explore how residential sorting takes place at neighbourhood level, and how neighbourhoods acquire negative characteristics as a result. However, we also demonstrate that these processes of neighbourhood decline are neither standard nor inevitable, and suggest how policy interventions at national and local level could make a difference.

LOCAL ECONOMIES AND CHANGES IN SOCIAL HOUSING: INCREASING NEIGHBOURHOOD DIVERGENCE

Location, economic structure, and housing type account for much of the spatial distribution of poverty. Areas with low-skill, low-wage economies (which are concentrated in certain cities and regions), and those with state-subsidized housing inevitably have higher concentrations of people on low incomes.

Our analysis of 'poverty wards' at the 1991 Census (those which were among the poorest 5 per cent of wards on measures of both deprivation and worklessness)[1]

---

[1] We used the Breadline Britain Index (percentage of deprived households in each ward) and a measure we called 'work poverty' which was the proportion of people of working age not working, studying, or on a government training scheme. For more details of this analysis see Glennerster *et al.* (1999).

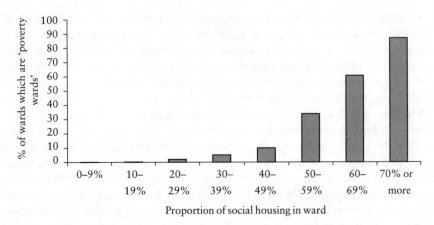

Figure 8.1. *Relationship between concentration of social housing and poverty*
Source: 1991 Census.

showed that the area concentration of poverty is overwhelmingly an urban, industrial problem. Overall, 57 per cent of the poverty wards and 71.3 per cent of the poverty ward population is in one of the six metropolitan counties,[2] or in a London borough, although these districts account for just 17 per cent of all electoral wards and 35 per cent of the total population between them. Of the twelve areas we chose to include in our study as representative of the poorest in England and Wales, seven are in major conurbations, and four others are in former mining or industrial areas. Only one, a declining seaside town, does not match the urban/industrial norm.

The majority of the poorest areas are dominated by social housing. The average electoral ward in England and Wales has 16 per cent social housing.[3] 63 per cent of the 'poverty wards' in our analysis have more than 50 per cent. When we look at all wards in England and Wales, we can see that the majority which have a high concentration of social housing are very poor. Overall, just 3 per cent of wards come into our classification of 'poverty wards' (in the top 5 per cent for both worklessness and deprivation), but 87 per cent of wards which have more than 70 per cent social housing are poverty wards (Figure 8.1).

The associations between economic structure, tenure, and poverty are long established. The Joseph Rowntree Inquiry into Income and Wealth noted

[2] Merseyside, Tyne and Wear, Greater Manchester, West Midlands, South Yorkshire, and West Yorkshire.
[3] Across the country as a whole, 23 per cent of households are in social housing, but these are not evenly distributed between wards. A relatively small number of wards have high concentrations of social housing while most wards have little. Thus the unweighted average for wards is lower than the overall proportion of households.

'depressing continuities' in the spatial distribution of poverty (Hills 1995). However, the evidence does suggest that the poor are becoming increasingly concentrated in certain areas, even *within* the worst affected cities and regions. During the 1980s the greatest increases in polarization nationally were at ward, rather than local authority level. Continuing economic restructuring and changes in the tenant profile of social housing are exacerbating long-established patterns of neighbourhood polarization.

The change in Britain's economy over the last three decades has three key features that affect low-income areas particularly harshly:

• The decline in manufacturing. Manufacturing accounted for one-third of all jobs in 1971, but for just 17 per cent by the mid-1990s—a loss of some 3 million jobs. Low-skilled jobs have declined in number. There were 0.8 m fewer people employed in unskilled occupations in the mid-1990s than in 1981. Jobs in skilled craft trades have also declined (Green and Owen 1998).

• The growth in service industries. This has brought an increase in managerial, administrative, and professional occupations, placing a greater premium on higher-level skills. These jobs have not offered replacement work for manual workers, because upward mobility from manual to managerial and professional positions is low (Elias and Bynner 1997). There has also been an increase in inter-mediate non-manual jobs, particularly part-time jobs, but these have tended to be filled by women. Men who were formerly employed in skilled manual work are more likely to have been downgraded into less skilled work or unemployment and casual work (Turok and Edge 1999). Thus there has been a general shift away from full-time manual jobs held by men, to part-time service sector jobs held by women. Women now account for almost half of the employed, compared with one-third in the 1950s (Green and Owen 1998).

• The deformalization and deregulation of the labour market, with increasing use of flexible employment practices (Green 1996). The number of people in temporary work is growing (Howarth *et al.* 1998).

Overall, the result is an increasing division between individuals and households who are doing well in the new economy and those who are not. The distinction between employed and unemployed is only part of the story; the type of work available is also important. Those who are doing badly include not only those who are out of work but some who are in low-paid, low-skilled work, or those in insecure part-time jobs.

These are broad changes, but some neighbourhoods have suffered more than others. There are indications that during the 1980s, the most disadvantaged wards became relatively worse off. Hills (1995) showed that, nationally, while economic inactivity fell in the best tenth of wards from 16.7 per cent to 13.5 per cent, in the worst tenth it fell much less (from 29.3 per cent to 28.6 per cent), in relation to its starting point. The gap seems to be widening as the most disadvantaged areas fail to keep up with the demands of the new economy. The same pattern emerges from local studies (Noble and Smith 1996; SEU 2000).

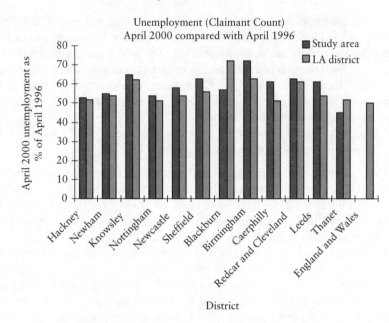

Figure 8.2. *Comparative fall in unemployment*

Our own analysis demonstrates the extent of polarization. Our study is following *areas* (typically about 20,000 people) and smaller *neighbourhoods* within them (typically the size of a large housing estate). In 1991, the average electoral ward had 27 per cent of its working-age population not working, studying, or training on a government scheme. The areas in our study averaged 42 per cent. The specific wards in which the neighbourhoods are situated typically had two or three times as many people without work as their most advantaged neighbours. In three of them, worklessness predominated, with more people of working age unemployed or inactive than working, studying, or training.

Although deprived neighbourhoods have certainly shared in economic recovery since 1991, the gap between them and the rest remains great. For example, in April 1998, the worst affected ward in Newcastle had an unemployment rate of 24.4 per cent compared with 2.6 per cent in the best, and 8.7 per cent in the city as a whole.[4] Indeed, evidence from our study suggests that, as unemployment falls, the gap between the poorest areas and the rest is growing slightly. Ten of our study areas have experienced a smaller proportionate fall in numbers claiming Jobseeker's Allowance since April 1996 than the local authority districts in which they are situated (see Figure 8.2). All bar one have had a smaller fall than the national average.

[4] Ward-level unemployment rates are not generally available because ward populations for years since 1991 are not known. Data are therefore only available for local authorities, like Newcastle, that have produced population estimates since 1991.

Thus economic restructuring seems to have produced an increasing division not only between individual winners and losers, but between winning and losing neighbourhoods:

The decline in the number of non-precarious job opportunities for those at the lower end of the occupational spectrum, in many instances exacerbated by problems of spatial mismatch, would appear to be leading to a growth in no-earner households, neighbour-hoods and labour markets, in conjunction with a growth in 'dual-career' neighbourhoods and labour markets in other locations within the urban and regional system.

(Green 1996: 290)

Both demand-side and supply-side factors are at work. On the demand side, skill mismatches and spatial mismatches are continuing to develop despite economic growth. The economic problems of the poorest neighbourhoods are not simply problems of short-term recession or of an industrial restructuring process which is now complete. Turok and Edge (1999), in their study of employment in cities, have shown that manufacturing is continuing to decline. Although service-sector jobs have grown, and there has been net job growth overall, most large cities actually have seen net job losses since 1991. For example, Manchester lost 9 per cent of its total employment between 1991 and 1996, Liverpool 12 per cent, Sheffield 6 per cent, and Birmingham 5 per cent. The biggest decline in employment has been in the inner cities. Job growth has been physically in the wrong place for inner-city residents, especially given that car ownership is typically low in poor areas. Moreover, the new jobs are of a different type. Even since 1991, the biggest decline in jobs in cities has been in unskilled manual work, and the biggest increase in professional and managerial positions. It is the least skilled who are most likely to be affected by lack of work. The House of Commons Select Committee on Education and Employment concluded in April 2000 (para. 31) that 'in certain parts of the country, a lack of appropriate jobs is one of the barriers to employment faced by unemployed people'. Thus the central problem is that the demand for labour in these areas has shifted, and is continuing to shift, because of structural changes in the economy.

Supply-side factors are also important. We argue that these also have both an individual and a neighbourhood dimension.

Certainly, deprived neighbourhoods are characterized by a high proportion of individuals with low levels of skills and qualifications. A survey for the Basic Skills Agency in 1996/7 found 15 per cent of the population with low or very low literacy.[5] In the wards matching our study neighbourhoods, the proportion was much higher; in some cases twice as high. In half of them, more than 25 per cent of the population has low or very low literacy (see Figure 8.3). This is increasingly being recognized as a major problem (see Chapter 11 by Jo Sparkes and

---

[5] Further research in 1997 estimated the figure at 19 per cent (6 per cent with very low skills and 13 per cent with low skills), but ward-level comparisons are not available for these data.

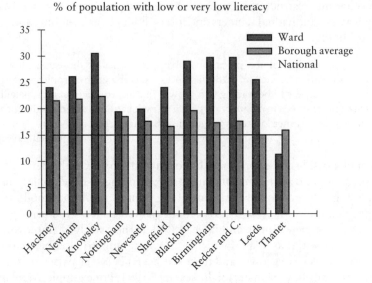

% of population with low or very low literacy

Figure 8.3. *Levels of basic literacy skills, 1995*
Source: Basic Skills Agency.

Howard Glennerster). The influential 'Moser Report' on basic skills showed that people who have entry level skills[6] can only access about 50 per cent of jobs, while those who are below entry level can only hope to access 2 per cent (Moser 1999).

Attainment at school is also low. None of the schools serving our study neighbourhoods achieves the national average GCSE pass rate (for five grades A*–C). On average, the rate for these schools is 21 per cent compared with 47.9 per cent nationally.

There are also 'softer' supply-side problems in areas where labour markets have been depressed for long periods. Our interviews with employment advisers, training providers, and community workers in deprived areas have revealed how lack of employment or learning opportunity after school and prolonged spells of unemployment reduce people's confidence to learn, train, and apply for jobs. People who have got off to a bad start in the labour market often need support, encouragement, and confidence-building as well as skills training (H. Evans 2001). Mental health or addiction problems also develop in some cases, so that people are unable to work when opportunities arise. In these circumstances, economic inactivity among people of working age can increase even if unemployment is declining nationally and locally. During the 1980s growth in

---

[6] People with entry-level skills can read simple text and extract information provided there are no other distractors. Below entry level, people struggle to read the simplest text.

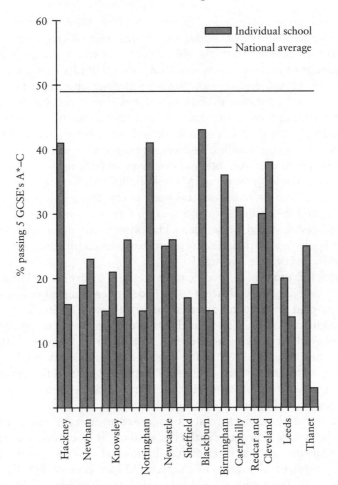

Figure 8.4. *GCSE performance in schools in study areas, 2000*
Source: DfES School Performance Tables 2000 (dfes.gov.uk/performance/schools).

non-employment in mining and industrial areas was accounted for entirely by a growth in economic inactivity (Green and Owen 1998). Rates of Incapacity Benefit claims are high in former industrial areas. In some of our study areas, twice as many people are claiming Incapacity Benefit as do so nationally. Many people claiming Incapacity Benefit can be considered as 'hidden unemployed'; a withdrawal or detachment from work being a response to a more difficult labour market (House of Commons Select Committee on Education and Employment 2000).

However, the problem is not just at an individual level. Individual labour-market problems can be compounded by 'concentration effects' in neighbourhoods where worklessness is common. Wilson (1987) has shown how in neighbourhoods where the majority of families experience spells of long-term joblessness, people become isolated from the social networks which are so important in learning about or being recommended for jobs. Attitudes to work can also be affected. Page (2000) describes an 'estate culture' which accepted low personal achievement and educational attainment, had low expectations, held estate norms that were different from those of mainstream society, and exerted strong peer pressure. Negative attitudes to work and low motivation characterized the attitude of jobless young males. And as the prospects for employment diminish, or are perceived to diminish, other alternatives, outside the formal labour market, become realistic alternatives (Macaskill 2000; McKenna 2000). Our fieldwork suggests that there are several such alternatives, which are of varying prevalence, and impossible to quantify, in the different areas. The main ones are undeclared cash-in-hand work, such as labouring, driving or restaurant work, usually irregular and varied, trading contraband goods, dealing in stolen cars or other goods, and dealing in drugs.

Although it is unusual for people to be engaged in any one of these activities on a full-time basis, they do seem to provide better financial options than the formal low-paid or insecure jobs that might otherwise be available to people with low skills, especially if combined with the security of an income from benefits. Some people of working age become detached from the formal labour market (Smith and Macnicol 1999). In some of our study areas, the Employment Service attributes part of the decline in unemployment to the disappearance from the register of people who have alternative incomes and who do not wish to participate in welfare-to-work schemes.

If worthwhile jobs in the formal economy are perceived as difficult to obtain, and there is a viable alternative in the informal or illegal economy, the perceived value of education and skills training is diminished. Schools in our study areas have high rates of absence. On average, 13 per cent of half-day sessions are missed, compared with 8.7 per cent nationally. The biggest difference is in unauthorized absence (truancy), where three times as many days are lost (3 per cent compared with 1 per cent). Headteachers in the study schools report that low attendance is one of the biggest barriers to improving attainment. Evidence from the Youth Cohort Study supports this. Thirty-eight per cent of persistent truants failed to get any GCSEs, compared with 3 per cent of non-truants. (Bosworth 1994). Lower participation continues after compulsory school-leaving age. The 1991 Census shows that just over half of 16–18 year-olds (53 per cent) are in full-time education. All of the study areas have lower participation rates—on average 41 per cent. A recent investigation of attitudes to adult education and training in one of our areas showed that many people are suspicious of the role of education in getting employment, because of their own experiences of doing work which does not require training, or of arbitrary and discriminatory employment practices. An instrumental view of education as a means to occupational enhancement is not always shared by people in areas where the job market rejects or marginalizes them (Bowman, Burden, and Konrad 2000). Thus education and training programmes, the very things which are so essential to help people compete in the modern economy, are more difficult to implement successfully in the poorest areas.

The evidence presented so far in this chapter suggests that the poorest neighbourhoods respond less well than others to economic recovery. Often there is a net loss of jobs, and where there is job growth, not all the new jobs are suited to the skills profile of the area, and many are likely to be part-time or insecure. On the supply side, unemployed workers are ill-equipped to find and compete for work. A high concentration of worklessness in an area has its own impact—reducing the number of working role models, limiting job-finding networks, creating alternative networks in the informal economy, and breaking the link between education, training, and work. As other neighbourhoods respond more readily, the poorest, even though improving, can be left relatively further behind. Rather than rising up with the tide, they may become 'beached as the tide turns' (Green and Owen 1998).

Economic decline, however, does not account for all of increasing polarization of neighbourhoods. The predominance of social housing, and changes in the tenant profile of social housing, have accentuated the problem (Lee and Murie 1997). Since the 1980s, more and more people have aspired to buy rather than rent. In a 1999 survey commissioned by IPPR, 89 per cent said they hoped their children or grandchildren would be home-owners in twenty years time (Hills 2000*b*). Aspiration to home ownership was encouraged in part by the Conservative 'Right to Buy' legislation, introduced in 1981. Under this legislation, many better-off tenants, particularly in popular areas, bought their homes. This reduced the council stock overall, and concentrated it more in the least popular stock. This had three concentrating effects. First, the remaining tenants, who could not exercise the right to buy, were more concentrated at the lower end of the income scale. The profile of the tenure changed simply because more affluent tenants left. Secondly, the remaining council stock came under more pressure, so that often only those in highest need could access it. In areas where there is strong competition for social housing, a smaller stock inevitably leads to a higher concentration of low-income tenants, because there is no room for others. Demand pressures from low-income vulnerable groups have also increased. For example, there are now greater numbers of lone parents, and the closure of long-stay institutions has meant that more vulnerable people are looking for social housing in the community. Thirdly, as a lot of the popular stock was sold, the image of council housing became less attractive. Thus social housing has become predominantly a tenure of the poor. Eighty per cent of households in social housing have a weekly income of less than £200. In 70 per cent of households in social housing the head of household is not in paid work (Howarth *et al.* 1998). Areas of concentrated social housing are, almost by definition, areas of concentrated poverty.

RESIDENTIAL SORTING AND NEIGHBOURHOOD HIERARCHIES

Despite these developments, much social housing is still popular and attractive, as are some neighbourhoods in inner-city and industrial locations. A process of residential sorting takes place, leaving those neighbourhoods at the bottom of the hierarchy extremely unpopular while others remain desirable.

Our study shows that residential sorting is occurring *within* unpopular areas as well as between these areas and the rest. Our study neighbourhoods are all located in areas which are relatively undesirable compared with the cities or boroughs in which they are located. Typically they have been unpopular for a long time because of their intrinsic characteristics; they are inner-city areas with poor housing or environment, or peripheral areas with poor access to facilities or services, or industrial areas under the shadow of steelworks or slag heaps.

Within these areas, a hierarchy of neighbourhoods has developed. Table 8.1 describes their histories. It shows that ten of the twelve have become unpopular and stigmatized; they have become neighbourhoods of least choice even within wider areas of unpopularity. In two, this has happened because of the intrinsic characteristics of the neighbourhood, such as bad design or location or economic downturn, while in others, a downturn in fortunes has happened because the population mix has changed or because of the acquired characteristics of the neighbourhoods, including crime or drug problems, or anti-social behaviour, and deteriorating neighbourhood environments. These characteristics are, in some cases, long-standing (notably a bad reputation for crime), but often they have been acquired more recently, during the 1980s or 1990s. In this period, neighbourhoods which were formerly stable underwent a change in character.

Residents and front-line workers can identify a 'trigger point' when they say the character of the neighbourhood turned; a point at which a few difficult and antisocial families moved in. Events precipitated by these families included serious criminal damage, intimidation, drug-dealing, burglary, joyriding, and excessive noise. The neighbourhoods became notorious. Some residents moved out, and were replaced by people who had little choice about where they lived. In a relatively short time, the population mix of the neighbourhoods changed, with an unsustainably large proportion of antisocial or criminal residents, young single parents, large numbers of young children with reduced adult supervision, and people with social problems such as drug and alcohol misuse. The declining reputation of the neighbourhoods, and declining conditions, made them increasingly unattractive to more well-off residents. We illustrate this 'lettings spiral' in Figure 8.5.

Although in all cases, the arrival of a few difficult families was the trigger for neighbourhood decline, different circumstances enabled this to happen in different areas. We portray these in Table 8.2.

Table 8.2 illustrates the importance of a balance between housing supply and demand. Pockets of empty housing provided the opportunity for problems to

Table 8.1. *Neighbourhood unpopularity: case histories*

Local Authority in which neighbourhood is located	Predominant tenure and type of housing	Age of housing stock	Unpopular housing area relative to city/borough	Unpopular neighbourhood relative to local area	Popularity of neighbourhood and change over time
Hackney	Council flats and maisonettes	1950s/1960s	✓	✗	Formerly white working-class estate—increasing allocations to immigrant families and refugees since early 1980s due to inner London housing pressures and fall in demand from white families after Right-to-Buy.
Newham	Council flats and maisonettes	1950s/1960s	✓	✓	Formerly white working-class estate. Tough reputation, so low demand. Growing African and Bangladeshi population since late 1980s, driven both by inner London housing pressures and low demand for estate.
Knowsley	Council family houses	1930s/1940s	✓	Was, but now typical of area	Stable population with unchanged social and economic mix. Acquired bad reputation for drug dealing and intimidation in early 1990s, and demand plummeted. Restored by modernization and tackling drug problem.
Nottingham	Council houses and flats	1970s/1980s	✓	✓	Quickly became unpopular because of design. Bad reputation for drug dealing and crime. Declining popularity since late 1980s. High concentration of single parents, young single men, ex-offenders.
Newcastle	Council family houses	1930s/1940s	✓	✓	Falling population in area generally led to empty properties since early 1990s. Allocations to single parents, ex-offenders, drug dealers. Bad reputation developed. Now difficult to let.
Sheffield	Mixed tenure, houses and flats	1970s/1980s and older stock	✓	✓	Inner city area—always magnet for newcomers and mixed ethnic population. Gradually declining. Bad reputation for drug dealing.

Table 8.1. (Cont.)

Local Authority in which neighbourhood is located	Predominant tenure and type of housing	Age of housing stock	Unpopular housing area relative to city/borough	Unpopular neighbourhood relative to local area	Popularity of neighbourhood and change over time
Blackburn	Council family houses	1970s/1980s	✓	✓	Quickly became unpopular because of design and lack of facilities. Some lettings to antisocial households. Acquired bad reputation in early 1980s for crime. Difficult to let.
Birmingham	Mixed tenure terraced houses	Pre-1919	✓	✗	In 1960s unpopular 'twilight zone' populated by immigrants—West Indians and Irish. Now popular area among Pakistani community because of social networks, mosques, and shops.
Caerphilly	Mixed tenure houses and flats	Pre-1919 and 1970s/1980s	✓	✓	Unpopular area due to inaccessibility—end of Valley. Gradual decline in services and facilities. Depopulation has produced housing surplus. Perception that 'problem families' are dumped from other areas.
Redcar & Cleveland	Mixed tenure houses	Pre-1919 and 1930s/1940s	✓	✓	Steep decline in population due to economic decline led to empty houses and increase in private renting. Rapid rise in crime, antisocial behaviour and drug dealing, leading to further depopulation.
Leeds	Council family houses	1930s/1940s	✓	✓	Estate acquired bad reputation for crime and antisocial behaviour after a few difficult households moved in 1970s. Stigma. Difficult to let.
Thanet	Private large Victorian and Edwardian conversions	Pre-1919	✓	✓	Formerly area of hotels. Decline of tourism saw conversion to bedsits and hostels. Influx of unemployed, homeless, and now asylum seekers.

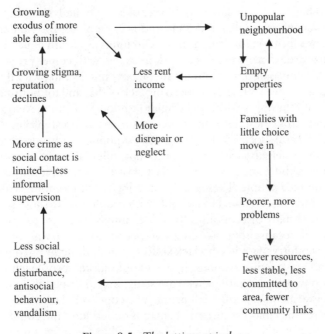

Figure 8.5. *The lettings spiral*

Source: Adapted from Power (1996).

Table 8.2. *Circumstances precipitating influx of difficult families in the six areas where a 'trigger point' was identified*

Local Authority area in which neighbourhood is situated	Reason
Knowsley	No specific reason identified.
Newcastle	Depopulation due to economic decline, and exodus to new sheltered housing schemes created pockets of empty properties on estate.
Blackburn	Insufficient social housing demand in borough as a whole. New estate lacked services and facilities and was peripheral, so pockets of empty housing appeared.
Redcar and Cleveland	Depopulation due to economic decline. Further accentuated by regeneration of neighbouring area displacing troublesome families.
Leeds	Largest family houses in area—problematic large families allocated there.
Thanet	Decline of tourist trade generated surplus property and economic incentives for owners to accept DSS clients in large numbers.

develop. They were allocated to households who had no other choice, or remained vacant, symbolizing decline and being a target for vandalism, arson, and theft, or a location for drug-dealing. Our interviews with police and residents suggest that drug dealers prefer to work in streets with empty property, because there are fewer people about and because empty homes can be used for delivery, trading, and storage. While the underlying lack of demand for housing in a city or borough is not the only reason why neighbourhood problems develop, it can have a deep and rapid destabilizing influence on the poorest places (Power and Mumford 1999). As social housing becomes less popular with more secure families, more and more neighbourhoods are becoming vulnerable to these pressures.

Once a neighbourhood becomes a 'last choice location', it attracts two types of disadvantaged people. These can be described as 'households with problems' and 'problem households'. 'Households with problems' are those which are disadvantaged socially or economically. For example, there are people who are in housing need because they escaping violence at home, or war and oppression in another country, people who lack skills or find it difficult to communicate in English and are at a disadvantage in the labour market, people who suffer from mental or physical ill health or who are struggling to bring up children on their own on a low income. Some such people will cope well. Others need more help and support. They may create extra demands on services, and could be less likely to participate in the local social networks which help to build community resources and a set of norms and rules shared by the majority of residents, but their behaviour is not necessarily problematic for others.

Ward-level data show that there are much higher concentrations of households with potential problems in the most deprived areas. In wards containing our twelve study neighbourhoods, proportions of lone-parent families are typically between twice and five times the national average, levels of long-term illness are one and a-half times the average, and rates of Income Support claim between twice and four times the average.

Concentrations of households with problems are much more marked within smaller neighbourhoods, below electoral ward level. As an example, one local authority has looked more closely at part of our study area, a 'triangle' of 95 council houses of which 88 are occupied. Table 8.3 shows the very high concentration of economic and social problems within these households. Another of our study neighbourhoods has six times as many Child Protection cases as a comparable area nearby.

'Problem households' are those whose behaviour creates problems for others, either because of deliberate acts (such as committing crime against neighbours) or because of unintentioned acts (such as noise or intimidating behaviour by people with serious mental health problems who have been discharged into the community). In half of our study areas, local GPs pointed to a higher than average proportion of people with severe and enduring mental illness—former long-stay patients or those who might have been in-patients had community-care policies not been introduced.

Table 8.3. *Concentrated deprivation in a small neighbourhood (%)*

	No.	%
Households		
containing someone with a criminal record	11	13
in receipt of income related benefit	73	83
in arrears with rent	29	33
containing no one who is working (excluding lone parents)	34	39
single parent households	20	23
not turning out to vote at last local election	74	85
Total households	88	
Proportion of primary school children:		
Below average for their age		67
Above average for their age		5

Source: City Council data, 1999.

A small number of households can create serious problems for a neighbourhood, because their behaviour can be very prominent and very difficult to manage either by residents or services. This applies particularly to those who are intentionally antisocial, because their activities tend to draw in others, from outside the neighbourhood, whose behaviour is also problematic. In most of the study neighbourhoods, police attribute a large proportion of the crime to no more than ten prolific individuals. However, where these people are acting together, for example where there are extended criminal families, a small number of households can form a very destructive antisocial network. Neighbourhoods which appear dominated by the activities of drug dealers can have no more than five to ten active dealers, but may draw in many more people who are buying drugs and sometimes committing offences while in the area. Addresses of active dealers can receive several hundred visitors in a twenty-four hour period.

Thus neighbourhood unpopularity leads to relatively large numbers of people with social and economic problems, and a small number of prominent individuals or households with extreme problems who create problems for their neighbours. Different policy approaches are needed to prevent each of these problems.

ACQUIRED NEIGHBOURHOOD CHARACTERISTICS AND NEIGHBOURHOOD DECLINE

We have shown how, through the processes of economic decline and neighbourhood sorting, the least advantaged areas become populated by the least advantaged people.

Concentrating the disadvantaged together in the least favourable circumstances brings its own consequences. Our interviews with residents and front-line workers suggest that the area concentration effect impacts on six different aspects of neighbourhood life:

- The physical environment;
- Existence of private-sector services;
- Performance of public-sector services;
- Sense of power, control, and inclusion of residents;
- Levels of social organization;
- Social order.

These are what we refer to as the acquired characteristics of neighbourhoods. We illustrate them in Table 8.4 with examples from the study neighbourhoods. Not all of these characteristics were evident in all of the neighbourhoods.

These effects are not independent of each other. High levels of neighbourhood crime and disorder impact on people's sense of control over their environment, their trust of their neighbours, and their confidence in the authorities to resolve neighbourhood problems (Geis and Ross 1998). Conscious that their neighbourhood is

Table 8.4. *Negative acquired characteristics of poor neighbourhoods*

Physical environment	Private-sector services	Public-sector services	Sense of power, control, and inclusion	Social organization	Social order
Empty housing and shops	No bank	Failing schools	Sense of area decline	Reduced social networks	High crime
Damage to empty buildings	Few shops	Poor standard of housing and repairs	Mistrust of public-service providers	Isolation	Noise
Litter	High shop prices	Ineffective environmental services	Feeling of inferiority *vis-à-vis* professionals	Divided community	Speeding cars/bikes
Dumped household rubbish and goods	'No-go' area for taxis and newspaper delivery		Low take-up rates	Mistrust of neighbours	Neighbour intimidation and aggression
Dumped cars			Sense of being 'no good' because of bad reputation of area		Drug dealing
Used needles			High levels of mental ill-health		High levels of truancy and exclusion
Burglary			More dependence		Unsupervised children and youth nuisance
Vandalized bus shelters and lights					Stray dogs
Overgrown hedges and verges					
Broken fences					
Graffiti					

Sources: Visits and interviews in 12 study neighbourhoods, 1999.

declining and no one seems to be doing anything about it, residents become less likely to interact with others in the area, and less likely to intervene themselves to resolve problems, or to call on services. Community spirit is not necessarily lost—rather it becomes more contained within smaller groups. Residents often refer to a strong sense of community within tightly knit kinship groups or long-standing friendship networks, but see this as being threatened by elements in the wider community. As social organization, participation, and confidence diminishes, so does social control, because residents are less confident of shared norms and standards that can be collectively promoted or enforced. Antisocial behaviour escalates. Litter, graffiti, and vandalism accumulate. Pockets of empty housing develop and are prone to vandalism.

This process of diminishing social capital is connected to a process of diminishing human capital. Residents who lack a sense of control over their living environment and day-to-day security, and who lose trust in others also often lack confidence in their ability to control other aspects of their lives, such as job prospects or housing choices (Geis and Ross 1998). A sense of powerless and alienation can develop, and is evidenced by high levels of depression, low levels of take-up of support services, and the need for confidence building and support for people who do follow education or training programmes.

Thus the sense of powerlessness engendered by neighbourhood disorder affects both social organization and individual trajectories. These two outcomes are themselves linked. People who engage in successful collective action to turn their neighbourhood around often gain the confidence to effect changes in their own lives, such as retraining. Likewise, the confidence gained from getting a job or qualifications can encourage people to be proactive in trying to change their neighbourhood environment either by direct action themselves or by lobbying other organizations.

There are other processes at work too. A concentration of people on low incomes can result in the withdrawal of shops and financial services (HM Treasury 1999*a*) which can no longer operate profitably. Some are also driven away by high crime. An unfavourable operating environment also impacts on public services, which struggle anyway to respond to the extra demands of many households with economic and social problems. They report difficulties in recruiting and retaining staff, higher levels of staff sickness through stress, and more budgetary pressures because of high spending on theft and vandalism. As public services decline, residents lose confidence in them. Communication and take-up diminish. A sense of powerlessness increases. Often there is also an impact on the physical environment as backlogs arise in repairs and street cleaning, or on social order, as police fail to keep up with crime problems and support services struggle to meet the needs of children with behavioural problems. Figure 8.6 shows how these six kinds of area effects are linked together.

This cycle of neighbourhood decline can develop rapidly and with serious consequences. One of the study neighbourhoods has suffered a rapid decline over a five-year period. A rapid rise in crime, drugs, vandalism, and litter has

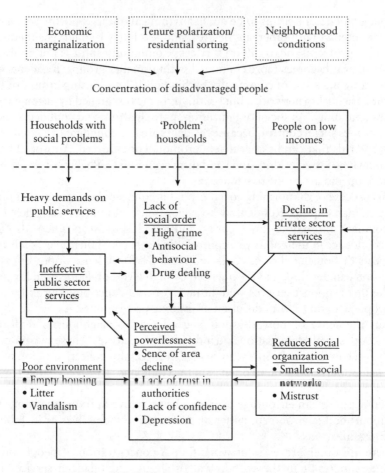

Figure 8.6. *Interlinked effects of area concentration of disadvantage*

caused extreme depopulation, plummeting house prices, and no demand for social housing. The entire viability of the neighbourhood is threatened despite the injection of extra mainstream services and investment in the housing stock, environment, and economic development via the Single Regeneration Budget.

But neighbourhood decline is neither a standard process nor an inevitable one. Tables 8.5 and 8.6 demonstrate that not all problems manifest themselves in all areas. In our interviews and meetings, some problems, such as lack of shops and services, emerged as major problems for residents in less than half of the neighbourhoods. Nearly all were troubled by drug-dealing and antisocial behaviour, but only half by empty housing. The reality of life can be quite different in areas which are ostensibly similar in terms of deprivation indicators. Areas which are intrinsically disadvantaged because of their economy, environment, and location, even those which are at the bottom of the neighbourhood hierarchy, do not

Table 8.5. *Problems identified by residents in interviews*

Problem	No. of areas where problem mentioned
Drugs	11
Antisocial residents	10
Youth nuisance/nothing for young people	9
Crime/antisocial behaviour	8
Loss of community	7
Empty homes	6
Stigma/reputation	6
Poor public services (schools, health, police)	5
Poor housing	5
No meeting place or community facility	4
Few shops	2

Sources: Interviews with residents, 1999. We interviewed residents' representatives in 11 of the 12 neighbourhoods and also attended 23 youth groups, tenants' meetings and local conferences, as well as having informal discussions with residents we met during the course of the work.

Table 8.6. *Problems with neighbourhood environment (based on field observation and interviews with residents)*

Problem	No. of areas with problem
Derelict/boarded-up houses or shops	10
Dumped rubbish or household goods	6
Extensive litter	4
Extensive graffiti	4
Poorly maintained common areas, kerbs, verges, and fences	4
Extensive vandalism	3

Sources: Visits to neighbourhoods, 1999.

necessarily acquire negative characteristics which tip them into rapid decline. Certain local factors and interventions protect neighbourhoods against the tipping process.

We interviewed about 30 residents, front-line workers and policy-makers in each area. Analysis of this data suggests that these protective factors (some of which are explored further in Chapter 12) include:

- Social organization and collective action on local issues, providing local support and identity.
- Strong social capital and a shared set of norms and values, built up either by strong family and kinship networks through community development,

provision of community facilities and meeting places, and models of local decision-making which give residents genuine control.
- High population density so that shops and services are viable.
- Mixed tenure development bringing more affluent residents to the area.
- Aspects of neighbourhood management such as proactive local housing management, caretaking, visible policing, and effective joint working between agencies to respond to problems.
- Support services for vulnerable and isolated people and families with multiple problems.

Nor is neighbourhood decline irreversible. Even when neighbourhoods have 'tipped', there is potential for protective factors to have an impact—for the development of a virtuous circle of recovery to counteract the vicious circle of neighbourhood decline. For example, one of the study neighbourhoods had a severe problem with drug-dealing, serious intimidation, and antisocial behaviour. One-third of the properties in one street were empty. A combined initiative involving concerted policing and housing investment, supported by residents, put a stop to these problems. Within a year, the area had a small waiting list. Although social and economic problems remain, neighbourhood order has been restored. Moreover, tackling the drug problem restored residents' pride in the area and feelings of efficacy. Since then they have re-established community activity such as trips away and an annual festival. Some volunteers have got involved in wider projects such as health promotion, or gone on to develop their own skills further through training or work. Stronger links have been built with service providers. The links between perceptions of power and control, social organization, social order, neighbourhood environment and services are working in a positive direction rather than the negative one established in Figure 8.6. Thus seeing the processes by which neighbourhood problems interlink enables us to identify not just reasons for decline but strategies for prevention and recovery.

IMPLICATIONS FOR POLICY

This chapter has shown that the neighbourhood problems which contribute to social exclusion can be caused by intrinsic disadvantages, residential sorting, and the acquisition of negative neighbourhood characteristics which impact on daily life and contribute to further neighbourhood unpopularity.

Intrinsic disadvantages are, by their nature, difficult to tackle. However, our evidence points to continuing economic marginalization of the poorest neighbourhoods. This needs to be addressed not just by supply-side economic initiatives, such as welfare to work programmes or skills training, but through regional and local economic development strategies to deliver appropriate employment opportunities. Site redevelopment, transport provision, business incentives, support to existing businesses, and the proactive development of strategic sectors are all likely to feature in such strategies.

Residential sorting and acquired neighbourhood characteristics are more susceptible than intrinsic features to policy interventions. Such interventions may not tackle the intrinsic disadvantages of neighbourhoods, but may prevent them slipping into acute decline.

First, we need measures to limit *economic and social polarization* of neighbourhoods:

• Limiting the release of undeveloped land on the edge of cities and in rural areas. New building is pulling people who have a choice out of cities. This increases social segregation and also undermines the least popular parts of cities, which are left with housing surpluses, problems of abandonment and crime, and insufficient population density to sustain services. It also extends the problems of sprawl, road congestion, and environmental degradation. Urban policy needs to limit land releases and incentivize inner city redevelopment (Rogers and Power 2000).

• Measures to attract more middle-income, working residents to poorer neighbourhoods, by providing housing for sale and investing in the physical environment and services.

• Changes to the way that social housing is allocated so that the poorest and most vulnerable are not persistently concentrated in the same places. For example, attracting young professionals to inner-city areas, allowing a proportion of lettings to be determined on the basis of better social mix, and improving information-sharing about prospective new tenants so that sensitive allocations can be made.

Second, measures are needed to *limit the impact on neighbourhoods of concentrating many disadvantaged people together*. These will include policies directed at those people individually and those which aim to manage the problem and bolster protective factors.

The range of individual policies must include generic programmes to address social exclusion, tackling social and economic issues. While there is a case for targeting such programmes at the poorest areas (G. Smith 1999), they do not only apply to individuals in poor areas, but those who are at risk of social exclusion anywhere. For example:

• Programmes to improve the skills and qualifications of the unemployed and to help them with finding and keeping jobs.
• Programmes directly aimed at alleviating poverty, such as increased benefits levels or schemes to reduce costs such as free childcare or energy efficiency programmes.
• Social programmes such as family-support services, health promotion, and school improvement programmes, and more responsive and better resourced public services.

Special measures are required for those whose needs are beyond generic programmes. For example, supported housing for ex-offenders, improved community care for people with severe and enduring mental health problems, multi-agency support for at-risk young people, introductory tenancies and tenancy enforcement when people are known to be disruptive neighbours. They may also involve measures to avoid concentrating people who are difficult to live next door to in neighbourhoods where there are already concentrations of people who are vulnerable. For example, in one of our study areas, the council is looking at ways of changing the design and allocation of a block of bedsits, attracting mainly young single men, some of whom are ex-offenders or substance misusers, because of its location on an estate with many young lone mothers and opposite a hostel for women fleeing domestic violence.

In addition to individual-centred policies, we need measures to manage the problem in the short term. These will include:

- Better resourcing of direct public services (e.g. education, housing management, primary health care) or different models of service delivery.
- Providing more locally based services and ground-level supervision, such as detached youth work, neighbourhood wardens, and local housing management.
- Giving local residents a real say in the decisions which affect their lives.
- Tapping the skills and resources within these neighbourhoods and building the capacity of the community to self-manage; enhancing social control by providing locally needed services through the community and voluntary sector, bringing in funding, restoring a sense of pride and optimism.
- Managing neighbourhoods in an integrated way, so that services work to a common agenda.

Many of these issues are beginning to emerge in New Labour's policies, both in the National Strategy for Neighbourhood Renewal (Social Exclusion Unit 2000) and in the broader policy arena; for example, in welfare-to-work policies, the recommendations of the Urban Task Force (DETR 2000a) and the Housing Green Paper (DETR 2000b). It is becoming clearer that, while targeted area regeneration policies, such as the New Deal for Communities and Single Regeneration Budget, can be the vehicle to kick-start regeneration, they are only part of the answer. The deep problems of poor areas need to be tackled by addressing society's economic, social, and spatial polarization over the long term as well as by more immediate neighbourhood-level interventions.

Poor neighbourhoods are, in a sense, a barometer for social exclusion. They illustrate sharply the more general problems of social division, inequality, and lack of opportunity in society. The difficulties of poor neighbourhoods can only be understood and tackled when seen in this broader context. However, their study also reveals another dimension; illuminating the processes and consequences of spatial segregation, demonstrating how the concentration of the most disadvantaged people in the areas with the worst intrinsic problems compounds the difficulties that individuals already face, promoting exclusion and inhibiting inclusion.

9

Child Poverty

DAVID PIACHAUD AND HOLLY SUTHERLAND

INTRODUCTION

Poverty in childhood is important for social exclusion not only because of its immediate effect in constraining children's lives but also because it is a cause of social exclusion in later life. Chapters in this volume on inter-generational associations (Hobcraft, Chapter 5), on how experience in childhood is linked with teenage pregnancy and relationship breakdown (Kiernan, Chapter 6), and on educational performance (Sparkes and Glennerster, Chapter 11) all show the significance of child poverty. It is therefore important in analysing the determinants of social exclusion to examine the determinants of child poverty. This is what this chapter attempts to do.

In seeking causes of child poverty we must inevitably consider causes of the poverty of parents. Parents may be poor because of unemployment, disability, low pay, or for other reasons. In addition, parents' circumstances are in many ways affected by children: for example, labour-market participation, particularly of women, is affected by the number and particularly the ages of children. Children are not merely a money cost to families, they also involve time costs which either result in forgone earnings or the cost of alternative child care.

This chapter examines the extent of child poverty in Britain—first considering how it has changed over the last twenty years and then analysing its relationship to demographic and economic characteristics. A comparison is made between the industrialized nations to consider whether child poverty is a common feature among them all or whether the experience of children in Britain is markedly different. The next section examines the response of government to child poverty, in particular describing and evaluating the New Labour Government's attempt to tackle child poverty, taking account of measures announced up to March 2001. Finally the extent to which tackling child poverty will or will not end social exclusion is discussed.

THE EXTENT AND CAUSES OF CHILD POVERTY

The definition of poverty has been subject to extensive discussion. During the years of Conservative government (1979–97) there was no official concession

Table 9.1. *Children in poverty, by economic status of the family, 1979 and 1998/9*

	No. in poverty (millions)				% in poverty			
	AHC		BHC		AHC		BHC	
	1979	1998/9	1979	1998/9	1979	1998/9	1979	1998/9
One or more full-time workers	0.5	1.6	0.5	1.1	4	18	4	13
Others:								
single parents	0.3	1.8	0.2	1.2	28	73	24	49
couples with children	0.6	1.2	0.6	1.1	45	74	40	66
All	1.4	4.5	1.2	3.4	10	35	9	26

Notes: Poverty = Below 50% of mean equivalized income level, after housing costs (AHC) and before housing costs (BHC).

Sources: 1979—Department of Social Security (1998*b*); 1998/9—Department of Social Security (2000*b*). Figures for the two years are not fully comparable because they use different data sources.

that poverty existed and no definition of it was accepted (although statistics relevant to poverty continued to be published). Now Labour ministers talk openly about poverty, for the most part concentrating on income poverty. They use statistics often based on a poverty line of a proportion of mean or median equivalized disposable income. While many different measures of poverty are used and debated, such a relative definition of poverty has continued to be used by most of the academic community and follows practice in most other countries. In this paper we shall follow this approach using 60 per cent of median equivalized disposable income as the poverty standard wherever possible. This is increasingly used by the British government and is recommended by Eurostat. (Details of the methodology are discussed further in Department of Social Security 2000*b*).

This definition of poverty is applied for each child but it is based on the family's income. Within families resources may be unequally distributed. Some children in poor families may be protected from some of the effects by their parents taking less than their 'share'. The reverse may also be true with some children being seriously deprived in families that are by no means poor. Given that income is generally pooled within families, there is little alternative in practice to considering the income of the whole family. But it should not be suggested that child poverty is being fully assessed.

The changing extent or incidence of child poverty is shown in Table 9.1. To make comparisons over time we consider here the number of children living in families that were below half mean income level (after housing costs).[1] On this

[1] At the end of the period, half of mean income and 60 per cent of median income were roughly the same.

basis one-third of children were living in poverty in 1998/9. The extent of child poverty in 1998/9 was three times as high as in 1979, with a sixfold increase in poor children in single-parent families with no full-time worker. Looking at incomes before adjusting for housing costs, the increase in the rate of child poverty was less steep, from 9 to 26 per cent.

The incidence of poverty among children in different family circumstances is shown in Table 9.2. This and subsequent tables define poverty as being below 60 per cent of *median* income level *before* housing costs. The 'before housing costs' definition is used since it permits more accurate simulation of policy changes. We do not make any adjustment to the median income level resulting from the policy changes that are analysed. On this basis some 3.4 million children were in poverty under the policy prevailing in 1997 when the Labour Government came to power. The incidence of poverty was twice as high for children in one-parent families as for those in two-parent families. Overall, the younger the mother at the birth of the oldest child the higher was the incidence of poverty.

Table 9.2. *Child poverty rates by family characteristics (%)*

	Two-parent families	One-parent families	All
All	21.5	41.9	25.9
Age combination of children in family:			
All under 5	17.2	19.5	17.6
Some under, some over 5	29.1	55.4	34.4
Youngest 5–10	21.5	47.8	28.1
Youngest 11+	15.2	30.0	18.2
Age of mother (at birth of oldest child)*:			
Up to 17	59.1	50.2	55.5
18–21	37.8	47.8	41.4
22–29	18.5	38.9	22.1
30+	13.3	34.7	16.6
No. of children:			
1	14.6	22.5	16.7
2	15.8	33.5	19.3
3	26.1	64.3	33.0
4+	51.2	78.7	58.1
Children with parent(s) in work	10.8	14.8	11.2
Children with no parent in work	58.6	54.9	56.9

*Oldest child is taken to be oldest child that is currently dependent.

Note: Poverty = Below 60% of median equivalized income level before housing costs in 2001/2 prices.

Source: POLIMOD (see text).

Where the child has no parent in paid work the incidence of poverty is over five times that in families with one or more paid workers. The importance of worklessness for child poverty is clear from the data. (The relationship between child poverty and low pay is discussed further by Abigail McKnight in Chapter 7.)

The composition of child poverty is shown in Table 9.3. While the incidence of poverty is far higher in one-parent families, such families only contain about one-third of the poor children. Children with very young mothers make up only a small proportion of poor children. Children in two-parent families with a paid worker make up one-quarter of all poor children.

Britain had the third highest proportion of children in relative poverty overall and the highest of any European country except Italy (UNICEF 2000). As shown in Table 9.4, the rate (on a more severe poverty line of 50 per cent of national median income) was more than twice that in France or the Netherlands and over five times that in the Nordic countries. The proportion of children with lone mothers in Britain was the highest of any country and the poverty rate of such children among the highest. While most of the countries studied had child poverty rates that changed little in the last decade or so, Britain and Italy of the EU countries had a fast growing poverty rate.

Table 9.3. *Composition of child poverty by family characteristics (%)*

	Two-parent families	One-parent families	All
All	65.2	34.8	100.0
Age combination of children in family:			
All under 5	9.7	2.4	12.1
Some under, some over 5	24.9	11.9	36.9
Youngest 5–10	20.8	15.4	36.2
Youngest 11+	9.8	5.1	14.9
Age of mother (at birth of oldest child)*:			
Up to 17	2.5	4.3	6.7
18–21	13.4	19.3	32.7
22–29	14.4	32.1	46.5
30+	4.5	9.5	14.1
No. of children:			
1	9.2	5.1	14.4
2	21.9	11.5	33.4
3	18.5	10.2	28.6
4+	15.6	8.0	23.7
Children with parent(s) in work	25.4	4.0	29.4
Children with no parent in work	39.8	30.8	70.6

*Oldest child is taken to be oldest child that is currently dependent.

Note: Poverty = Below 60% of median equivalized income level before housing costs in 2001/2 prices.

Source: POLIMOD (see text).

Table 9.4. *International comparison of child poverty (%)*

	Proportion in poverty[1]	Proportion of two PFs workless[2]	Proportion in one PF[3]	Proportion of one PF in poverty[4]	Effect on poverty of transfers[5]
Sweden	2.6		21.3	6.7	−20.8
Norway	3.9		15.0	13.1	−12.0
Finland	4.3	7.8	11.8	7.1	−12.1
Belgium	4.4	6.3	8.2	13.5	−13.4
Luxembourg	4.5	2.1	5.8	30.4	−17.7
Denmark	5.1		15.2	13.8	−12.3
Netherlands	7.7	5.7	7.4	23.6	−8.3
France	7.9	5.9	7.7	26.1	−20.8
Germany	10.7	5.5	9.8	51.2	−6.1
Spain	12.3	9.0	2.3	31.6	−9.1
Greece	12.3	3.1	3.7	24.9	na
Ireland	16.8		8.0	46.4	na
UK	19.8	10.7	20.0	45.6	−16.3
Italy	20.5	6.6	2.8	22.2	−4.1
USA	22.4	5.7	16.6	55.4	−4.1

[1] Percentage of children with income below 50% of national median. (*Source*: UNICEF (2000), Fig. 1.)

[2] Percentage of two-parent families with no worker. (*Source*: OECD (1998), table 1.7.)

[3] Percentage of children in one-parent families. (*Source*: UNICEF (2000), fig. 3.)

[4] Percentage of children in one-parent families below 50 per cent of national median. (*Source*: UNICEF (2000), fig. 3.)

[5] Child poverty post-taxes and transfers minus child poverty pre-taxes and transfers. (*Source*: UNICEF (2000), fig. 9.)

GOVERNMENT RESPONSE

Until the twentieth century, concern with child poverty in Britain was very largely a private matter. Families had to deal with the causes and consequences of child poverty as best they could. From Elizabethan times, in cases of destitution, Poor Law institutions might become involved, but the price to pay for this was often the permanent separation of the child from his or her relatives. The work of Rowntree (1901) showed how poverty was a feature of the life-cycle of many families. Instead of preaching about moral inadequacy, Rowntree urged redistribution to families with children. Eventually concern about child poverty and other pressures led in 1946 to the institution of Family Allowances, cash benefits for second and subsequent children, which were part of Beveridge's overall plan to end 'want'.

When Abel-Smith and Townsend (1965) showed that poverty had not been abolished, and in relative terms was growing, this led to pressure—notably from the newly formed Child Poverty Action Group—to increase Family Allowances. This pressure did lead to a doubling in rates of Family Allowances in 1967, but this was accompanied by a reduction of child tax allowances which effectively targeted the increase on poorer families.

A new departure occurred in 1971 with the introduction of means-tested support for working families in the form of Family Income Supplement, the precursor to Family Credit and more recently the Working Families Tax Credit. In 1976 Family Allowances and child tax allowances were merged and extended with the introduction of Child Benefit, a non-means-tested cash benefit for all children.

Thus the response of successive governments to child poverty had been largely through the benefit and tax system, emphasizing redistribution either to all children or redistribution targeted on poor children. Yet, despite this redistribution, child poverty had increased dramatically, as discussed earlier. The main reasons for this—the growth in workless and lone-parent families and the escalating inequality in earnings—were not directly addressed by raising universal or selective cash benefits.

The New Labour Government elected in 1997 has given child poverty a higher priority than any previous government. In March 1999 Tony Blair said, 'Our historic aim will be for ours to be the first generation to end child poverty... It is a 20-year mission' (Walker 1999). The Chancellor of the Exchequer has called child poverty 'a scar on the nation's soul' (Brown 1999). While the government has not set out any one official definition of child poverty, a plethora of policy initiatives and a series of review documents show the priority that the government now gives to reforming and modernizing the welfare state in general and to tackling child poverty in particular.

The overall strategy of welfare reform has the aim of ensuring '[paid] work for those who can, security for those who cannot'. The principal measures to reduce child poverty may be conveniently divided into three categories:

• Policies to alter income levels directly through the tax and benefit system. The aim is to provide direct financial support to all families, recognizing the extra costs of children, while targeting extra resources on those who need it most.

• Policies to promote paid work. The aim is to ensure that parents have the help and incentives they need to find work. Paid work is seen as the best long-term route to financial independence for families. The Government aims to reduce the number of working-age people in families claiming Income Support or income-based Jobseeker's Allowance for long periods of time.

• Measures to tackle long-term disadvantage.

Taxes and Benefits

By April 2001 the main changes to the system of taxes and benefits for children introduced or planned by the new Labour Government were the following:

1. Working Families' Tax Credit (WFTC) was introduced in October 1999. This tax credit, normally to be paid through the pay packet, replaces Family Credit which was a means-tested benefit paid direct to families. The tax credit,

like Family Credit, is withdrawn according to income. WFTC is substantially more generous with a higher maximum payment and a lower taper. To qualify a person must work 16 hours a week or more, have a dependent child and not have capital of more than £8,000. The credit is larger if a parent does paid work for 30 hours a week or more. The WFTC not only redistributes income to poorer working families, it is also intended to encourage paid work.

2. Child Benefit is a universal benefit paid for each eligible child without any test of means and not subject to income tax. Between 1997 and 2001 it was increased in real terms by 26 per cent for the first child and 4 per cent for second and subsequent children.

3. Children's Tax Credit was introduced from April 2001. This tax credit, which is a replacement for the Married Couple's Tax Allowance and the corresponding tax allowance for lone parents, is to be paid to a parent in all families that pay income tax and have children aged under 16, except that it will be withdrawn from higher-rate tax payers. It will be worth up to £520 a year in 2001. From 2002 it will be worth twice this amount in the year of a child's birth.

4. Income Support (IS) is the means-tested safety net available to unemployed, sick or disabled families, and to lone-parent families. This and other associated means-tested benefits have been increased for families with children, particularly for those with children under 11.

Other general measures, such as changes to income tax and the introduction of a National Minimum Wage, also affect families with children. Other decisions, such as that to abolish special benefits for lone parents and the tax relief on mortgage interest will tend to reduce incomes of some families with children.

The effects of all the tax and benefit policies in Labour's five Budgets up to and including 2001 and of the minimum wage have been analysed for this chapter using the Cambridge University Microsimulation Unit's tax–benefit model POLIMOD based on Family Expenditure Survey data updated to 2001/2 prices and incomes. This extends earlier analysis in Piachaud and Sutherland (2000 and 2001). For more details of the precise policy changes that are included, see Sutherland (2001). Table 9.5 shows the effects on children as a whole and in one- and two-parent families separately.

Overall the tax and benefit measures in Labour's five Budgets have the effect of reducing child poverty from 25.9 per cent by 10.1 percentage points to 15.8 per cent, assuming other things remain unchanged.[2] This would remove two-fifths of child poverty. The largest absolute fall is among children with no parent in work—from 58.4 to 36.2 per cent—but the biggest proportionate fall is among those with a parent in work—from 11.5 to 6.8 per cent.

---

[2] As well as general changes in the level and distribution of pre-tax and benefit incomes, median household disposable incomes will shift upwards by about 4 per cent simply because of the policy changes that have been introduced. No account of this is taken here.

David Piachaud and Holly Sutherland

Table 9.5. *Poverty rates before and after Labour's policies (in Budgets up to March 2001)*

	All persons	Children		
		All	One parent	Two parents
All households:				
Poverty rate, April 1997 policy (%)	19.4	25.9	41.9	21.5
Poverty rate, Labour policy (%)	14.0	15.8	18.8	15.0
% point difference	5.4	10.1	23.1	6.5
Net number removed from poverty	3,090,000	1,330,000	650,000	670,000
Moved out	3,170,000	1,350,000	660,000	680,000
Moved in	80,000	20,000	10,000	10,000
Households with paid worker(s):				
Poverty rate, April 1997 policy (%)	7.4	11.5	15.8	11.0
Poverty rate, Labour policy (%)	4.9	6.8	8.8	6.6
% point difference	2.5	4.7	7.0	4.4
Net number removed from poverty	900,000	430,000	80,000	360,000
Moved out	930,000	440,000	80,000	360,000
Moved in	30,000	10,000	~	~
Workless households:				
Poverty rate, April 1997 policy (%)	40.4	58.4	56.4	60.1
Poverty rate, Labour policy (%)	29.9	36.2	24.6	45.7
% point difference	10.5	22.2	31.8	14.4
Net number removed from poverty	2,200,000	900,000	580,000	320,000
Moved out	2,240,000	910,000	590,000	320,000
Moved in	40,000	10,000	10,000	~

Notes: Poverty = Below 60% of median equivalized income level before housing costs in 2001/2 prices. Numbers of people are given to the nearest 10,000. Rows and columns may not add due to rounding. ~ indicates less than 5,000.

Source: POLIMOD (see text).

As we have seen (Table 9.3), children in one-parent families are over-represented among the poor and make up 35 per cent of poor children; the policy changes reduce the proportions of children in poverty in one-parent families by considerably more than in two-parent families, both absolutely and relatively. Poverty reduction is greater among children in families where there are young children, due to the larger increases in means-tested benefit and credit levels for children aged under 11.

Paid Work

The second component of the government's approach has been to promote paid work:

Our strategy is to tackle the causes of poverty and social exclusion by helping people find work. A proactive welfare system is at the heart of tackling worklessness. Our ambition is to deliver a change of culture among benefit claimants, employers and public servants, with rights and responsibilities on all sides. Those making the shift from welfare into work are being provided with positive assistance, not just a benefit payment. We are shifting the focus to include all groups—partners of the unemployed, lone parents, carers, people with a long-term illness or disability—not just the claimant unemployed. (DSS 1999*a*: 84)

The strategy rests on two key components: making work pay and helping people return to or find paid work. One of the aims of the Working Families Tax Credit (and the associated Childcare Tax Credit) is to 'make work pay'.

The policy changes are designed to push or pull people not doing paid work into the labour market. Whether or not these policies will have the desired effect and how large it will be depends on many factors and is difficult to forecast. We have simulated *possible* changes to analyse their impact on child poverty, exploring the implications for poverty measures of two scenarios of changed work patterns. In broad terms:

Work scenario A: puts parents with children aged 11 or over into paid work.
Work scenario B: puts parents with children aged 5 or over into paid work.

More precisely, for lone parents we assume that changes in paid work will not occur when the youngest child is aged under 11 (or under 5). For couples we assume changes in paid work if the youngest child is aged at least 11 (or 5) or if the other parent is not in paid work. In addition we assume that work-entry occurs only if:

- the parent is under pension age;
- the parent is not currently employed or a full-time student;
- the parent is not receiving benefits that indicate they would not/could not accept paid work (disability benefits, maternity benefit, etc.).

Thus it is possible in some couples for both parents to enter paid work on these scenarios. In our simulations we put *all* people in our target groups into work. This is to illustrate the maximum potential impact of part-time work-entry.

For all those entering paid work we assume they work for 16 hours at the minimum wage of £4.10 per hour (£65.60 per week), 16 hours being the minimum required to qualify for Working Families Tax Credit.

The impact of these scenarios for children in families where work entry occurs is shown in Table 9.6. Most of those affected were poor (pre-Labour); the

Table 9.6. *The effect of parental work entry on the numbers of children in poverty*

	All with parents entering work (000s)	Of which:		Mean weekly change in:	
		Poor, pre-Labour	Poor, post-Labour and work entry	Gross earnings (£)*	Disposable income (£)*
Scenario A:					
All children	1,700	1,170	790	67.64	48.57
Children in one-parent families	140	90	30	66.14	47.71
Children in two-parent families	1,560	1,080	760	67.85	48.69
Scenario B:					
All children	2,720	1,690	860	69.72	55.83
Children in one-parent families	640	460	80	66.16	54.00
Children in two-parent families	2,080	1,240	780	70.87	56.42

*For the whole household (there can be more than one family per household as well as more than one extra employee per couple).

Notes: Poverty = Below 60% of median equivalized income level before housing costs in 2001/2 prices. Numbers of people are given to the nearest 10,000. Only children in families affected by work entry are included in this table.

Source: POLIMOD (see text).

combination of tax/benefit and work entry reduces the extent of poverty particularly in one-parent families. While mean gross earnings increase by about £70 per week, the average change in disposable income lies around £50 per week. This is the combined effect of many factors but the Working Families Tax Credit in particular serves to enhance the net gain in disposable income.

The impact of these work scenarios is shown in Table 9.7. In two-parent families most already had a paid worker, including those with very young children; neither of the two work scenarios that were simulated had a large impact on the prevalence of paid work (although this table does not indicate the entry of a second paid worker). For lone parents the impact is much more marked. Work scenario A would result in 910,000 entrants into paid work and work scenario B 1,420,000 entrants. For children in families affected by work entry under scenario B, poverty would be halved.

The overall impact of these scenarios is that the total number of children removed from poverty is estimated at:

Benefit/tax policies alone	1,330,000
Benefit/tax policies plus Work scenario A	1,450,000
Benefit/tax policies plus Work scenario B	1,680,000

Table 9.7. *Poverty rates before and after Labour's policy with higher work entry*

	All persons	Children		
		All	One parent	Two parents
% poor, April 1997 policy	19.4	25.9	41.9	21.5
Benefit/tax policies				
% poor	14.0	15.8	18.8	15.0
% point difference	5.4	10.1	23.1	6.5
Net no. removed from poverty	3,090,000	1,330,000	650,000	670,000
Benefit/tax policies plus work entry, Scenario A				
% poor	13.6	14.9	16.8	14.4
% point difference	5.8	11.0	25.1	7.1
Net no. removed from poverty	3,330,000	1,450,000	720,000	740,000
Benefit/tax policies plus work entry, Scenario B				
% poor	13.0	13.2	15.5	13.6
% point difference	6.4	12.7	30.4	7.9
Net no. removed from poverty	3,710,000	1,680,000	860,000	820,000

Notes: Poverty = Below 60% of median equivalized income level before housing costs in 2001/2 prices. Numbers of people are given to the nearest 10,000. Rows and columns may not add due to rounding.

Source: POLIMOD (see text).

Interestingly, entry into employment is generally more effective at reducing child poverty in lone-parent families than in two-parent families.

It should be noted that both work scenarios involve a major expansion of employment, on scenario B by nearly 1.5 million jobs; this contributes by taking about 350,000 extra children out of poverty. Even then, overall child poverty is reduced by 1,680,000: roughly halved, not reduced to zero. The explanation mainly lies in the fact that not all children have a parent that is available to enter work. Those that remain workless are the sick and disabled, parents of very young children, and people already working for low earnings. These families may be helped by tax and benefit policy, but not—at least in the short term—by employment strategies.

Another constraint on paid employment for parents of young children is the availability of childcare. The new National Childcare Strategy is starting to increase the amount of available childcare but, as yet, provision remains patchy so that its impact on employment will, for the next few years, be limited.

Tackling Long-Term Disadvantage

The third component of the government's approach was to break the cycle of disadvantage. One of the objectives of many reforms in education, healthcare, employment, and environmental policy is to provide a better start for vulnerable families and children. There has been a focus on children in the pre-school period, who in the past have been treated as almost entirely a private family responsibility. In addition to the National Childcare Strategy, the Sure Start strategy is offering help to families with children from birth up to the age of 4 in areas where children are most at risk from poverty and social exclusion. It works with parents to promote the development of young children so that they are ready to take full advantage when they start school.

A number of initiatives are being taken to make sure that all children benefit from increased opportunities. For example, following an investigation by the Social Exclusion Unit (SEU 1998c), £500 million is being invested to reduce exclusion and truancy in schools and to raise the attainment levels of children at risk of social exclusion. Measures are also being taken aimed at halving the rate of teenage conception (SEU 1999a). The UK has the highest teenage birth rate in Western Europe with the highest rates in the poorest areas and among the most vulnerable young people, especially those in care and those excluded from school (for further discussion, see Chapter 6).

These and other measures to tackle long-term disadvantage lie at the heart of the government's attempt to tackle the causes of future child poverty. How far they will be successful remains to be seen—indeed in many cases it is beyond the range of any social science knowledge to forecast their effects.

The Prospect for Child Poverty

The results of microsimulation of the policy changes indicated that on current and already announced policies (at the time of writing in March 2001) the number of children in poverty will by 2002 fall by about 1.3 million—a reduction of about two-fifths. If paid work increases substantially, by 1.5 million jobs on scenario B, then child poverty would fall by a total of 1.7 million—a reduction of one-half. But this is an illustration of what *could* happen, not a forecast.

It is important to stress that, while child poverty should be substantially reduced, the extent of child poverty that will remain in 2002 is extremely high by post-war Britain standards and by European standards. Child poverty will still be over twice as high as when a Labour government was last in office. Moreover, this forecast depends on unemployment being kept down. As was stated in *The Changing Welfare State*:

Sharp economic downturns and structural change lead to high unemployment and economic inactivity. This in turn can increase benefit caseloads dramatically. Such changes are not automatically reversed as the economy improves. If no action is taken, high levels of worklessness can persist for long periods. And persistent worklessness leads to poverty and social exclusion. (DSS 2000a: 67)

Table 9.8. *Income support and poverty levels, 2001/02 (£)*

	Income support (IS)	Poverty level (PL)	IS as percentage of PL
Couple with one child aged 6	129.95	192.06	67.7%
Couple with two children aged 4, 8	162.15	223.81	72.4%
Couple with three children aged 3, 8, 11	194.35	265.08	73.3%
Lone parent with one child aged 6	101.15	120.63	83.9%

Notes: Income Support level is mean of rates applying April–September 2001 and October 2001–March 2002. Poverty level for 2001–2 is 50% mean AHC income for 1998–9 (Department of Social Security, 2000*b*) adjusted for actual and forecast rise in real household disposable income and Retail Price Index set out in Pre-Budget Report, 2000 and Budget Report, 2001 (HM Treasury 2000 and 2001).

Ending child poverty for those not in paid work requires an adequate minimum income. For those in Britain who will continue to depend on social security, the minimum income, or safety net, is the Income Support system. The levels of Income Support are shown in Table 9.8 in comparison with the after housing costs poverty level. It will be seen that for those who do not have employment, the minimum income is far below the poverty level. The reduction of poverty, and the achievement of the goal of security for those who cannot work, depends on reducing those deficits.

CONCLUSIONS

Child poverty in Britain remains, despite the reductions being achieved by the New Labour Government policies, much higher than it was twenty years ago and much higher than in most industrialized countries. Further reductions are central to improving the life chances of poor children and reducing the extent of social exclusion. At the same time, policies to reduce social exclusion are also likely in the long run to reduce income poverty generally and child poverty in particular.

The Labour Government has adopted redistributive tax/benefit policies and active labour market policies that should by 2002 reduce the number of children in poverty by over one million. This will be a substantial achievement. Yet, even if the promotion of paid work were successful, this would still leave over one and a-half million children in poverty. The promotion of paid work is not only a matter of financial incentives: it also involves childcare, transport, and working hours. The difficulties and stress—impinging on both parents and children—that result from combining paid work and the care and upbringing of children will only be marginally affected by measures taken thus far to promote family-friendly employment.

Poverty in childhood reduces opportunities for children to consume and opportunities for investment in children. Reduced consumption by children may affect children's social isolation, but it is less important than reduced investment in children which can have lifetime effects. Separating consumption by children and investment in children is not easy: buying and reading a book may be both consumption and investment. But some forms of expenditure on children—on junk food, stultifying toys, and designer clothes, for example—may be socially inclusive in the short term but yield little or no benefit in the long run. Pressures to consume rather than invest in children serve to exacerbate the long-term damage caused by child poverty.

Poverty is only one of many influences on child development—although certainly an extremely important influence. The opportunities of children also depend crucially on their family environment, on the local community, and on the wider economic and social environment. Ending income poverty is important but it is not on its own enough to ensure decent opportunities for all children. If, as the Secretary of State for Social Security wrote, 'Children born in run-down estates should have the same opportunities as those born in leafy suburbs, the same good health, the same decent education and the same hope for the future' (Darling 1999), then a more fundamental rethink about public and private responsibilities for children and the role of childhood in society will be needed. Since children are shaped by the society into which they are born—with all its inequalities and divisions—the goal of equal opportunities for all children is more radical than is often realized.

10

Response and Prevention in the British Welfare State

PHIL AGULNIK, TANIA BURCHARDT, AND
MARTIN EVANS

Social policies are designed to tackle social exclusion in a number of ways. They can intervene through preventive approaches to make exclusionary events (for example, unemployment) less likely, or respond to events that occur to lessen the exclusionary impact. John Hills develops a typology of policy approaches in Chapter 13, and shows that the distinction between prevention and response is more complicated both in principle and in practice than is commonly assumed. Once a dynamic framework is introduced, 'responsive' policies may seek not only to ameliorate current circumstances, but also to promote escape from an undesirable state, while 'prevention' may involve reinforcing the benefits of exit to make a return less likely. The implementation of preventive and responsive policies inevitably overlaps. Indeed, one of the hallmarks of the current Labour Government approach is a recognition that separate policy actors may not formulate a 'joined-up' solution. Social exclusion can, in part, result from inconsistent or incomplete strategies from the different 'silos' of government programmes, some oriented more towards prevention and others towards response.

This chapter analyses three areas of potential social exclusion: due to *unemployment, disability during working life*, and *the loss of income in retirement*. We concentrate on three main questions. How far are these areas served by preventive and responsive policies, in all their various forms? What profiles of social exclusion arise from these forms of intervention? How successful are they in combating social exclusion?

UNEMPLOYMENT

Unemployment is not synonymous with social exclusion. Sacked chief executives of large companies may experience unemployment but would rarely experience social exclusion. Their jobs would have given them an income sufficient to build up resources to cover brief periods of need and their skills and experience would make them attractive to alternative employers. However, for many, unemployment is the opposite: a combination of poverty-level income and a constrained ability to enter or re-enter the labour market, and once there to command a wage that could build up resources to lessen the risk of future unemployment. Once unemployed, long-term unemployment also increases the risks of social exclusion and is strongly associated with ill health, especially mental health, to living in workless households, and hence to the experience of multiple deprivation.

The Risks of Unemployment

The post-war heyday of the British welfare state was founded on full employment. Unemployment was a risk that was rare—around 2.5 per cent of the workforce—and was largely short term. The economy at that time was run with a commitment to full employment, a factor that, in international comparison, has been shown to be a strong predictor of national experience of unemployment (Therborn 1986). The oil shocks of the early 1970s caused huge pressures on jobs and created both a U-turn in unemployment and in the British policy commitment to full employment.

Since the late 1970s, the factors that caused the U-turn have disappeared but unemployment has not yet returned to the low levels which prevailed before the 1970s. The overall average risk of unemployment has increased only by one-fifth since then (Nickell 1999), but the risk is now far more unequally shared. Understanding the change in risk profile is thus central to combating unemployment. We know that part of the reason for this new profile is to do with the characteristics of the unemployed and the changing demand for high- and low-level skills. Another part is the result of macroeconomic policy, and a further part is the unintended effect of social policy—paying benefits will necessarily have an effect at the margins on rates and durations of unemployment. However, drawing together a cogent analysis of just how far each element of the overall risk profile contributes to unemployment is hotly debated by economists and policy-makers.

Current economic orthodoxy lays most responsibility on the supply-side characteristics of the unemployed and on the policies that assist them. However, it is worth pointing out that current macroeconomic orthodoxy accepts the efficacy of a level of unemployment that does not result in inflation and such a rate is estimated far higher than the old 2.5 per cent. Non-inflationary employment policy thus hopes to reduce unemployment *and* increase skills in order to increase productivity.

Turning to the characteristics of the unemployed, what do we know about who is at greatest risk? First, the risk is not so much unemployment per se, but long-term unemployment. Today's unemployed remain so for three times as long on average as before the mid-1970s. Second, the demand for unskilled and skilled work has changed since the 1970s to mean that unemployment and earnings have been skewed in opposite directions. The low-skilled and/or poorly educated are far more likely to be unemployed and when they work they do so

Table 10.1. *Unemployment rates and changing risk of unemployment by level of qualification, 1979 and 1998*

Qualification level	Unemployment rate (%)		% change in risk
	1979	1998	1979–98
Degree holders	2.1	3.0	+43
Higher intermediate	3.2	4.2	+31
Lower intermediate	4.0	7.1	+78
Unqualified	7.1	12.2	+72
All	4.8	6.2	+29
Difference in risk to the unqualified compared to average risk	+48%	+97%	

Source: Authors' calculations from Nickell (1999).

for earnings that have fallen hugely in *relative* terms over the past 25 years (see Figure 7.4 in McKnight, this volume).

Table 10.1 shows that the difference in risk of unemployment between the unqualified and the average risk doubled between 1979 and 1998—from 48 to 97 per cent. Unemployment between 1979 and 1998 has grown for all but the change in risk over time has grown fastest for those with low or no qualifications.

Third, men are more likely to be unemployed than women. The growth of female participation in employment, and higher education, and the growth of part-time work have helped to widen a gendered experience of unemployment that disfavours men, while continued discrimination in work disfavours equal remuneration for women, who are over-represented in low-paid and part-time work.

Fourth, age affects risk of unemployment. Young people aged 16–24 are twice as likely to be unemployed as the average. Older workers within ten years of retirement are also more likely not to work, but high numbers of such older workers are classified as inactive due to long-term sickness, rather than as unemployed.

Fifth, the geographical distribution of unemployment is unequal. Changes in industrial structure and differential economic growth over the 1980s and 1990s have meant that the highest concentrations of long-term unemployment still mostly exist in the once manufacturing-rich North and the centre of large cities (Turok and Edge 1999). In 1997, 28 per cent of all unemployment was in 9 per cent of areas where the vacancy to unemployment ratio was over 4 to 1 (EPI 1998). However, this unequal distribution of unemployment and area concentrations does not alter the fact that current economic growth is producing jobs in all areas. It merely means that the queue for jobs is far longer in some parts, and that many in the queue are not adequately skilled or experienced to take many of the jobs that arise.

Sixth, unemployment has increasingly been concentrated in workless house-holds. This means that other forms of non-participation in work—inactivity due to long-term sickness, caring for children and disabled relatives, and early retire-ment have become concentrated at the household level. Britain has become a nation of households where both adults work and households where no-one does (Gregg, Hansen, and Wadsworth 1999).

Prevention through Redefinition

How have these risks been mediated by policy? The legacy of unemployment handed to the 1997 Labour government from the Conservative years 1979–97 was mixed. The healthy economy with good prospects for further growth meant that unemployment was falling rapidly but from high overall levels of unem-ployment and inactivity. Unemployment claimant numbers grew rapidly in the early 1980s and early 1990s to reach very high levels at each trough of economic activity, as shown in Figure 10.1. Meanwhile the numbers of long-term sick and disabled and lone-parent claimants grew rapidly over the period, even at the boom points of the economic cycle.

However, what was *counted* as unemployment changed dramatically over the same time because the Conservatives adopted a claimant count approach and changed the basis of claiming many times. The 1980s saw numerous changes in definition and changes in benefit rules that meant that the claimant unem-ployed total under-reported unemployment (Atkinson and Micklewright 1989)

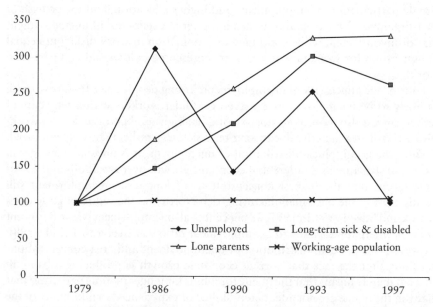

Figure 10.1. *Working-age welfare, Great Britain, 1979–1997 (index 1979 = 100)*

However, the significance of such changes is greater than mere statistical definitions. There was a combined effect from changes to unemployment, active employment, and benefit policy that sorted people into different status groups. Those labelled as unemployed have had to establish active labour-market involvement through tests that have got progressively tougher over the period. Put simply, the obligations of 'signing on' became more onerous and required greater proof of active search for work and availability for employment. Running alongside such changes were also changes in definition of other categories of benefit claimant. For instance, men aged 60 and above were excused from signing on and encouraged not to do so by higher rates of social assistance. Other social assistance claimants became more rigidly defined in ways that meant they were not 'unemployed' but lone parents or long-term sick. Indeed, for a significant period in the 1980s those unemployed with chronic health problems were actively encouraged to redefine themselves as long-term sick. They received higher benefits and less hassle for doing so.

The other fixation of Conservative policy was on improving incentives to work. However, this commendable aim meant that unemployment benefits fell relative to entry-level wages but at the same time fell relative to benefits for the non-unemployed. Thus the unemployed were far better off claiming social insurance benefits for long-term sickness if they could—not only because they were more generous, but also because their partners could continue to work without benefit withdrawal. For those who had no right to social insurance benefits, the status of lone-parenthood, early-retired, sick, or disabled provided higher income and fewer hassles.

Public-sector administrative changes also reinforced the process. The soaring social assistance populations of the 1970s and 1980s made discretionary individualized assessment of benefits untenable. Simple but rigid definitions made sense if the mass means testing of 16 per cent of the British population was to be efficiently computerized. The civil service also had pressures to become more efficient. The benefit payment and employment exchange functions were devolved to independent Next Step agencies, that were given targets and performance indicators. Training and active employment programmes were increasingly provided under quasi-market conditions with private providers. These changes introduced a set of organizational incentives that reinforced rigidity and categorization. The Benefit Agency's performance was measured solely on administering benefits—whether they were accurate, paid on time, and so on. The Employment Service was encouraged to get claimants off the unemployment count—both by providing access to active employment measures, but also by defining claimants as 'not unemployed' and hence the sole responsibility of the Benefits Agency. At the same time, the training providers were given performance indicators that encouraged cream-skimming, and were under no obligation to provide childcare or other services for non-priority groups. Education providers—mainly Further Education Colleges—had to match different funding streams with perverse rules that restricted access to high-quality education for those defined as unemployed.

The net result of this system was that 'the unemployed' were narrowly defined as those on Unemployment Benefit (later Jobseeker's Allowance), but had access to active employment programmes that could be seen to perform optimally, in part because of systematic sorting and creaming. Other claimants of working age had little or no access to such programmes. The only major programme to encourage work for these groups was the boosting of in-work incomes through benefits for families with children (called Family Credit and now replaced by Working Families Tax Credit, described below).[1] These benefits significantly increased the incomes of a growing number of mostly part-time women workers who were either the partners of unemployed or lone parents.

Response through Welfare-to-Work and the New Deals

Programmes to train and place the unemployed in work ('active' labour-market programmes) have been a core part of the British policy response to unemployment since the 1970s. European Union and OECD policies have also moved towards a more active role in moving the unemployed into work rather than allegedly passive programmes of providing out-of-work transfers. There are several potential responses. The first question is at what point to intervene. Most British unemployment spells have only short durations of six months or less. A policy that sought to prevent long-term unemployment can thus either 'wait and see' who fails to find work after a short period of signing or can try to catch the potentially long-term unemployed early and target extra help on them. While US experiments have shown that unemployment profiling can identify some of the potential 'hard-core' long-term unemployed, the British approach tends to have set time thresholds—at six months, twelve months, and two years—which trigger different forms of intervention. The difficulty for policy is that early identification wastes high-cost interventions on those who would have entered employment in any case, while late interventions may exacerbate the difficulty of assisting returns to work.

There are four main kinds of intervention: (1) in-depth one-to-one assessment of individual needs, behaviour, and barriers to work; (2) job-search activity; (3) training and education programmes; and (4) work-based programmes—either subsidies delivered to employers/employees or the provision of work experience. The essence of post-1997 government policy is to improve access to, and levels of provision of, all four. However, such improvements are not comprehensive: there is still significant rationing of welfare-to-work programmes.

For the unemployed, all four areas have been enhanced but most of the focus is on the 18–24 age group. This focus reflects the increased risk of young people being unemployed (see above) and the risk of such unemployment seriously affecting subsequent employment and life chances (Gregg 2000). In these terms it can thus be seen as both a responsive and a preventive policy. However, the

---

[1] A similar benefit for disabled people—Disability Working Allowance—also existed but had very low take up (10,000 claimants by the end of 1998) (DSS 1999*b*).

disproportional funding bias towards the under 25s is mostly the result of manifesto promises prior to the 1997 election, to raise funds from a windfall tax on privatized utilities to pay for specific youth unemployment programmes.

These programmes, called the 'New Deal for Young People', consist of a huge investment in individual counselling and mentoring from personal employment advisers (called the 'Gateway'), which leads either to employment or to one of four options in active labour market programmes: (1) an employer-subsidized six-month job placement with training; (2) full-time education/training to a minimum standard for up to twelve months; (3) employment in a voluntary organization; or (4) work in an Environmental Task Force (a public works programme at benefit rates of pay). For the older unemployed their New Deal began after two years of unemployment and comprises a compulsory activation programme followed by two non-mandatory options: (1) an employer-subsidized six-month job placement; or (2) full-time education/training to a minimum standard for up to twelve months. Both the New Deals for the unemployed are mandatory and have been implemented nationally.

For a wider group of over-50s (unemployed and those on other benefits), there is a voluntary scheme offering a personal advisory, in-work benefits and training grants. Additionally there is a New Deal for the partners of unemployed, offering a personal adviser and job-search assistance.

Most radically, other New Deals have been introduced that recognize the needs of the non-unemployed. Lone parents and long-term sick and disabled people can voluntarily participate and obtain individual counselling and mentoring from personal employment advisers. However, these New Deals will being overtaken by policy moves to extend employment advice to all claimants of bene-fits across the board—through what has been termed a 'single work-focused gateway' but is now branded as 'ONE'. This approach is currently being piloted but will be compulsory for all new claimants of benefits—the unemployed, sick, disabled, lone parents, and other carers. The extent to which other elements of active labour-market programmes—especially work-based training—are open to non-unemployed is not clear.

New policy initiatives have also tried to trade across the boundaries of benefits, employment, and training by creating 'Employment Zones' in areas of high unemployment, where hypothetical future benefits can be rolled forward to long-term claimants to pay for education, job subsidies, and other active employment measures by broker organizations acting as intermediaries.

Measures to improve in-work incomes have also been introduced. Tax rates at low incomes have been reduced and an improved in-work benefit for families with children has been introduced—Working Families Tax Credit (WFTC), with additional tax credits to help pay for childcare. A minimum wage has been introduced ensuring that all the costs of making work pay do not fall solely on government. This package of in-work help means that incentives to work are improved greatly, although the WFTC will go to many who are currently in work and can be seen as an anti-poverty measure in the main.

Evaluation: Will these Policies Combat Social Exclusion?

Long-term benefit dependency is seen as a central cause of social and economic exclusion. This view takes much from the US analysis of their public assistance programmes and the associated views that allege 'culture of dependency' and the creation of an underclass.[2] The increased conditionality of benefits and of compulsory training and work programmes in Britain echoes mainstream US practice and a move towards paternalistic styles of administration advocated by Mead (1997). Moving from reliance on out-of-work benefits and into work is also likely to increase income and the likelihood of further income.

A second and linked view of social exclusion is that it is a result of poor education and skills. The high priority given to providing minimum levels of qualifications as part of welfare-to-work programmes, distinguishes Britain from the current US approach, in which entry into work is the overriding priority (the so called 'Work First' approach).

Welfare-to-work programmes are thus both preventive and responsive. Those out of work with no or low skills can have access to training, which, especially if they are young, should improve medium- to long-term employability and earnings capacity, and reduce the risk of future unemployment. However, compulsory rules and increased conditionality of benefits have also raised the likelihood of many falling or opting out of the system, thereby losing all benefits—relying instead on family, friends, begging, crime, or the illegal economy for income.

Pulling in the opposite direction is a commitment to a better appreciation of individual needs. This gives a third dimension to the view of social exclusion adopted by these programmes. Responding to and preventing social exclusion is said to require a holistic approach—a coordinated response to the whole individual, rather than rigid demarcated policy programmes each responding to different and partial assessments of needs. The possibility that the process of exclusion can be an unintended outcome of the implementation of government programmes has been recognized. However, how far the New Deals do this in practice—especially with young people at risk and difficult to serve—is not yet clear, despite massive investment by government in evaluation of the New Deal programmes.[3]

A further question of policy also remains largely unanswered. Is welfare-to-work merely interested in getting people into jobs or in improving independence and incomes through work? Many unemployed have cycled though the system before and require a more dynamic approach that not only focuses on a transition but also steps in to raise skills in the hope of improving their trajectory and stability in the labour market.

---

[2] Indeed, the American welfare reforms of the 1980s and 1990s have been a major source of policy, as well as giving the new British programmes the prejudicial labels of *welfare* reform and *welfare*-to-work.

[3] Evaluations of the New Deal programmes are too numerous to list. Millar (2000) provides a summary.

DISABILITY DURING WORKING LIFE

Estimates of the proportion of the working-age population who are disabled at any one time vary from 12 to 20 per cent, depending on the definition used. About one-third of these will have been disabled since childhood; the remainder become ill or acquire an impairment later in life. Looking over the life cycle, an even higher proportion will experience disability at some point during their working life. Disability is thus a major source of risk with which the welfare state is concerned.

Individual or Social Risk?

That there is no consistency across the welfare state in definitions of disability will come as no surprise to anyone familiar with the piecemeal way in which provision for disabled people has developed. Beveridge put 'cripples' along with 'the deformed . . . and moral weaklings' in the category of people who could not be expected to provide for themselves through work and National Insurance, and hence would have to rely on means-tested assistance (quoted in Glennerster and Evans 1994). Contemporaneously, but apparently independently, employment protection for disabled people was enacted through a quota system, reserving 3 per cent of jobs in any workforce of over 20 employees for people registered as disabled—clearly not the same people Beveridge had in mind (Hyde 1996). Meanwhile social services developed their own assessments of need on an individual, case-work basis, which were unrelated to employability. In education, it was not until the Warnock report in 1978 that the tide began to turn against segregating disabled children. The institutions which they attended often did not regard education, let alone preparation for an active role in the labour market, as the highest priority (Humphries and Gordon 1992).

Despite this lack of consistency, there was a recognition from the outset that being or becoming disabled was a risk with which the state should concern itself. In the first place, disability, like illness, was seen as a misfortune that might befall anyone, and for which the individual was not to blame. Secondly, disability was, in some cases, regarded as an injustice; hence the compensation schemes for those injured at work or on military service. Thirdly, the risk of being or becoming disabled was perceived to carry certain consequences: low or reduced income through limited earning potential, additional expense on aids and adaptations, and the need for support services.

The concept of disability as a personal misfortune or injustice leading to unemployability and financial dependence is at odds with the social model of disability developed by organizations of disabled people (Barnes, Mercer, and Shakespeare 1999). The social model distinguishes 'impairment', which refers to the loss of bodily or mental function, from 'disability', which is the disadvantage arising from society's failure to accommodate the needs of impaired people. The key differences in policy terms between this definition and the so-called individual model are, firstly, that economic and social disadvantage are not seen as an inevitable consequence of impairment, and, secondly, that breaking the link between impairment and disability is seen as requiring change at the level of social institutions, rather than changing the individual. We return to these differences later in evaluating the welfare state's success in preventing and responding to the risk of disability.

Prevention and Prevalence Rates of Disability

The welfare state's efforts to minimize the likelihood of disability have focused on health care and health and safety regulation. (In social model terms, they have therefore focused on preventing impairment). Vaccination and public health campaigns, road safety and drink-driving legislation, were all specific (and often successful) attempts to reduce illness and accident. But arguably the most important influences on the prevalence of impairment have been broader social changes, rather than targeted government initiatives. There were fewer war casualties in the second half of the twentieth century; better standards of living have been instrumental in improving health generally and especially in reducing the prevalence of crippling childhood diseases like rickets, polio, tuber- culosis, and malnutrition; medical advance has meant that more conditions can be treated. Some trends have worked in the opposite direction: medical advance has also meant that more people survive illness and accident, but with impair- ment; and there has been greater recognition (and possibly higher incidence) of mental illness and stress-related conditions. Finally, a more 'flexible' and service- sector orientated labour market, the blurring of gender roles and a greater emphasis on leisure activities have all contributed to changes in expectations of what it takes to be a fully functioning member of society—with the result that some impairments may now be more disabling than they were 20 or 30 years ago.

The combined effect of all these factors seems to have been a gradual rise in the prevalence of disability over the last few decades, even after taking account of the changing age structure of the population. Figure 10.2, based on the General Household Survey, shows that the proportion of working-age people with 'limiting long-standing illness or disability' has been slowly rising since the mid-1970s. Other sources confirm this impression. According to the Labour Force Survey series, the number of working-age people who say they have a 'health problem or disability that would affect any kind of paid work' they might do, rose from 3.3 million in 1984 to 5.7 in 1996 (Cousins, Jenkins, and Laux 1998). A follow-up to the 1996/7 Family Resources Survey, specifically designed to be comparable to the 1985 OPCS Survey of Disabled Adults in Private Households, reports increases in prevalence rates of disability among all adult age groups below 60 (Grundy *et al.* 1999).

Responses to survey questions such as these are sometimes regarded as too subjective. There has been no 'real' increase in disability, the argument goes,

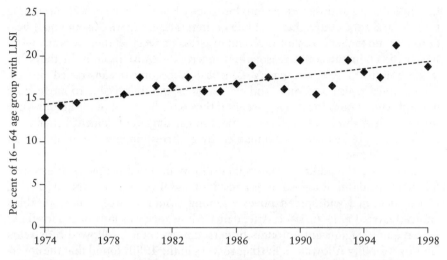

Figure 10.2. *Prevalence of limiting long-standing illness or disability (LLSI) among working-age population*

Source: General Household Survey.

simply an increase in the proportion of people who see themselves as disabled. Changes in the labour market and in eligibility rules for benefits may have knock-on effects on who regards themselves as disabled, as discussed in the first part of this chapter. It is difficult to support or counter this subjectivity charge, since 'objective' indicators of impairment have not been collected on a consistent basis over time. Arguably, subjective assessments of disability are in any case more useful than more rigid measures in terms of reflecting individuals' actual experience, predicting their behaviour and their use of services.

Response through Benefits and Employment Policy

The recognition of disabled people as a distinct group in need of financial assistance came in 1971 with the introduction of Invalidity Benefit (IVB), a National Insurance benefit for those unable to work due to sickness or disability.[4] In addition to the basic benefit, IVB had age-related and earnings-related components, and hence served both to provide an out-of-work income and to protect—to a limited extent—accustomed standards of living. A corresponding non-contributory flat-rate benefit followed in 1975, though its restrictive nature brought criticism that it discriminated against women, and it was overhauled nine years later. Under a decade after its introduction, IVB began to be cut back. First, in common with all long-term benefits, up-rating became linked to price inflation rather than average earnings; then the earnings-related allowance was

---

[4] A more detailed account of the development of disability benefits can be found in Burchardt (1999).

lost. In 1995 it was transformed into Incapacity Benefit, in the process becoming taxable, and subject to tighter eligibility criteria. Age, experience, and qualifications were no longer taken into account in assessing whether there was any work which the claimant could reasonably undertake. Most recently in the 1999 Welfare Reform Act, Incapacity Benefit has become means-tested against occupational pension income, and claimants are no longer able to move from unemployment onto Incapacity Benefit if they have been out of the labour force for more than three years. Retrenchment in earnings-replacement benefits for disabled people has been accompanied by a corresponding rise in receipt of means-tested benefits.

Response to the additional costs incurred by disabled people—for example for aids and adaptations—came as a result of an OPCS survey in the late 1960s, which identified widespread poverty among Britain's three million disabled adults (Harris 1971). In 1971, Attendance Allowance was introduced for those who required significant amounts of personal assistance, followed four years later by Mobility Allowance. Further surveys in the 1980s found that the coverage of these 'extra costs' benefits was inadequate, and they were replaced in 1992 with Disability Living Allowance. Additional payments for disability as part of means-tested benefits were regularized when Supplementary Benefit was replaced by Income Support in 1988, and this too had the effect of increasing payments to claimants classified as disabled (Evans, Piachaud, and Sutherland 1994). Extra costs benefits have steadily increased in generosity and comprehensiveness, but at the same time, the practice of charging for social services on a means-tested basis has become more widespread. This has created a new form of benefits trap: the more income a disabled person receives, the more he or she is asked to pay towards support services, resulting in no overall improvement in his or her living standard (Kestenbaum 1997).

Overall, benefit expenditure on disabled people trebled between 1974 and 1997. Reasons for the growth are complex (Berthoud 1998), but if part of the explanation is increasing effectiveness of social security's response to the risk of disability, we would expect to see disabled people's position in the income distribution improve, and their living standards approach more closely those of the general population. Two surveys just over a decade apart, the 1985 OPCS Survey of Disabled Adults in Private Households, and the 1996/7 Family Resources Survey Disability Follow-Up, used the same set of questions to identify disabled people, and therefore should provide the ideal basis for comparisons.[5]

Table 10.2 compares the position of disabled people in the overall income distribution, according to the two surveys. Figures in columns 2 and 3 use a definition of income based on net current family income, equivalized to allow

---

[5] The two surveys did however differ in sampling methodology. This appears to have affected overall estimates of prevalence, but not the distribution across severity categories or age groups below retirement age. For a discussion see Grundy et al. (1999). For details of the income calculations, see Burchardt (2000b).

Table 10.2. *Position of disabled people in the overall income distribution*
(adults in non-pensioner households)

Fifths of the population by income	Percentage in each income group of general population			
	Unadjusted income		Income adjusted for extra costs	
	1985	1996/7	1985	1996/7
Bottom	29	26	46	38
2nd	33	33	27	27
3rd	20	19	15	16
4th	12	14	8	12
Top	6	8	4	7
All	100	100	100	100

Notes: Quintile groups based on all adults in non-pensioner family units.

Sources: Author's calculations using 1985 OPCS Survey of Disabled Adults in Private Households, 1996/7 Family Resources Survey Disability Follow-Up, and 1996/7 Households Below Average Income dataset; Martin and White (1988).

for differences in family size, while columns 4 and 5 make an additional adjustment for the extra costs disabled people face in maintaining a standard of living (for example, on heating or transport).[6] In both cases the distribution is defined over all adults in non-pensioner families.

Looking first at unadjusted income, we see that over one-quarter of disabled people are in the bottom fifth of the income distribution, with a further one-third in the second group from bottom, and that the distribution has changed little since 1985. Taking account of extra costs increases the proportion of disabled people in the lowest fifth of the distribution—to nearly one-half in 1985—but reveals a significant improvement between the two years. It appears that widening eligibility for extra-costs benefits has succeeded in lifting some disabled people out of poverty, although the concentration in the bottom fifth of the distribution remains pronounced.

The second principal strand of policy response to the risk of disability has been through measures to promote employment, and has developed largely independently of benefits policy. The 1944 quota system was widely ignored or circumvented by employers and there were only a handful of prosecutions for non-compliance during its 50-year history. It was supplemented with various forms of sheltered employment, but these were criticized for stigmatizing disabled workers and providing little opportunity for individuals to progress (Townsend 1981). Supported employment, where disabled workers are placed by a sponsor organization in open employment, is now the preferred alternative. In 1995, the quota scheme was replaced by the Disability Discrimination Act,

---

[6] The extra costs adjustment is based on Berthoud, Lakey, and McKay (1993).

which, among other provisions, requires employers to make 'reasonable adjustments' to accommodate disabled employees or prospective employees. One limitation is that prosecutions can only be brought on behalf of specific individuals who feel they have been discriminated against, but the idea that it is primarily the responsibility of the employer to adjust to the individual, not vice versa, is a new direction for policy. Another recent development is the New Deal for Disabled People (mentioned in the first part of this chapter), a rare attempt to cross the boundary between employment and benefits policy. The first tranche of funding in 1998 was for 'innovative schemes' to help disabled people get jobs and for a pilot scheme of personal advisers for new claimants of Incapacity Benefit. The welfare-to-work philosophy focuses attention on those who have recently exited the labour market, leaving aside the needs of those who have been excluded long-term, and its effectiveness over the course of the economic cycle remains to be seen.

How successful have these policies been in promoting employment of disabled people? According to the Labour Force Survey, the number of disabled people in employment in Britain rose from 1.4 million in 1985 to 2.3 million in 1996 (Cousins *et al.* 1998), but the number of disabled people overall was also rising over the same period, with the result that the proportion of disabled people of working age in employment has remained more or less constant at 40 per cent (varying slightly with the economic cycle). There have been changes in the type of employment: the proportion of disabled men and of disabled women who are employed in managerial occupations has grown. However, changes in type of employment have also been occurring in the general population, such that the proportion of disabled men in unskilled occupations has actually increased relative to the general population over this period. The same is true of disabled women in partly skilled occupations.

Evaluation: Mis-specification of the Problem?

Despite a number of government campaigns to improve health and reduce accidents, age-specific prevalence rates of disability appear to have increased over the last few decades. In response, benefits designed to maintain the incomes of disabled people were extended in the 1970s, but contracted again by a series of rule changes through the 1980s and 1990s. Means-tested benefits have picked up the tab for the worst-off, but leave employees who do not qualify for insurance benefits facing large drops in income when they become unable to work through disability. There is evidence of improvement in the incomes of the worst-off disabled people, relative to the rest of the population, over the last decade, but the concentration of disabled people at the bottom of the income distribution remains. Employment policy has developed slowly from providing segregated, low-paid, and low-status jobs to providing support in finding and retaining work in the mainstream labour market, but the proportion of disabled people in employment remains static. The impact of the most radical reforms, the New Deal for Disabled People and the Disability Discrimination Act, has yet to become apparent. Recognition of the extra costs of disability has gradually increased, and the corresponding benefits now form an important component of disabled people's incomes, but a higher proportion is now clawed back through increased charging for social services. More general issues of exclusion have only recently made it on to the policy agenda, and measures to combat it are underdeveloped.

The mixed success of the welfare state in preventing and responding to the risk of disability can be attributed to three causes. Firstly, there has been a lack of coordination between the two main strands of responsive policy: the benefits system and employment support. Broadly speaking, the income-replacement function of social security requires the disabled person to demonstrate that they are incapable of working, while employment support depends on the individual showing that they can be (nearly) as productive as a non-disabled employee. This artificial choice does not reflect most people's circumstances and creates an unnecessarily high barrier between being in or out of work. The introduction of Disability Working Allowance for disabled employees was intended to smooth the transition between benefit receipt and work but it remains to be seen whether the replacement, Disabled Persons Tax Credit, will overcome the problems of low take-up and poor targeting which plagued its predecessor.

The second reason is the tendency of policies implemented in response to one problem to create another. Greater reliance on means-testing has increased the benefits trap. Higher rates of benefit for incapacity than for unemployment— designed to reflect expected long duration of spells on incapacity benefit—may have encouraged disabled people to opt out of 'unemployment' and hence cease to receive job-search advice and assistance. The 1999 Welfare Reform Act aimed to block this route but may in turn have unwanted effects: those losing their jobs who have a health problem or disability may opt straight for Incapacity Benefit without an intervening spell of job-seeking.

The third and most fundamental reason for the welfare state's lack of success in managing the risk of disability is mis-specification of the problem. The idea of disability as personal misfortune, the inevitable consequences of which are lack of earnings capability and dependency, has focused attention on responding to the individual's plight. The outcome is a continual struggle for state benefits and services to pick up the pieces where other institutional structures have failed. By contrast, a social model of disability points to breaking the link between impairment (loss of physical or mental function) and disability (economic and social disadvantage) through examining the intervening institutions. Why does becoming impaired lead to job loss in so many cases? Why do such a high proportion of disabled children leave school with low or no qualifications? If policy were directed not towards preventing impairment, but to preventing impairment leading to disability, progress might begin to be made in these areas. Responsive strategies can then be reserved for special cases and to provide transitional protection. The 1995 Disability Discrimination Act, requiring employers and service providers to make 'reasonable adjustments' to accommodate the needs of impaired people, and the establishment of a Disability Rights Commission, were first, tentative, steps in this direction. They will need to be supplemented and reinforced if they are to overcome the entrenched disadvantage of disability.

RETIREMENT AND INCOME RISK IN LATER LIFE

Over the last one hundred years or so retirement has become the norm in developed countries and pensions are now a major concern of the welfare state. This section looks at how public policy has attempted to counter the income risks associated with this stage of the life cycle.

Defining the Risk: Old Age, Retirement or Poverty?

Historically men and women faced very different income risks as they grew older. For women the risk was that the male breadwinner would no longer be there to provide for the household's needs and that her own earning power would be insufficient to make ends meet. The risk which increased with age was therefore of widowhood. In contrast, the income risk faced by males as they grew older was connected with their position in the labour market—until as late as the 1920s the majority of men over 65 (the current state retirement age for males) were in work and employment might thus be considered their standard source of income (Macnicol 1998). The risk which increased with age was therefore that earnings would unexpectedly cease, for instance because of ill health or unemployment.

The situation today is rather different. First, the growth in female labour-force participation means the risks faced by men and women have become more closely aligned. In both cases it is loss of earned income in later life which is now the problem.[7] Second, as employment rates among older workers (particularly men) have fallen, a period of worklessness at the end of life has become more of a certainty and less of a contingency. Hence in modern society retirement in itself is not a risk—almost everyone now reaches old age and almost everyone now retires. Rather, the concern today is that retirement brings with it a number of associated risks which, to a greater or lesser extent, require the state to become involved in this part of the life cycle.

The starting point for economic analyses of retirement is that if people expect their income from employment to fall at some point towards the end of their life they will take some form of action to build up alternative means of financing consumption during these years. In other words, they will attempt to smooth

---

[7] Issues connected with spouses' (and divorcees') pension rights are, of course, still important. However, as women's lifetime earnings converge on those of men such transfers will become more gender-neutral, though it is doubtful whether they will ever be completely neutral.

consumption over their life cycle. However, as discussed by Barr (1998), such consumption smoothing is unlikely to take place simply through individuals accumulating assets during working years and then gradually selling these off during retirement. Rather, people will seek ways of pooling risk through insurance arrangements of one kind and another.

Two risks are particularly important in this life-cycle model of pension provision. First there is *investment risk*—the risk that the assets purchased during working life will not go up in value as much as expected (or, at the extreme, will go down in value). Second, there is *information risk*—the risk that through ignorance or misinformation an individual will not save 'enough' for their old age (even assuming average longevity and investment returns).

In theory, a competitive market should naturally evolve financial products capable of dealing with investment risk. However, in practice, though the market can reduce this risk through various devices (such as with-profit policies), there will always be some variation in returns to individual savings pots, with variations in charges adding a further element of risk (see Cook and Johnson 2000). Eliminating investment risk requires that saving is collectivized in some way, with either employers or the state offering a guarantee of benefits (Barr 1998); this is also likely to minimize administration costs.[8] Investment risk therefore provides a rationale for government regulation of private pensions and (potentially) for state provision of retirement saving vehicles. Taken to the extreme, the comprehensive earnings-related social insurance systems commonplace in continental Europe might also be justified in this way. However, the real rationale for this kind of approach must be found in the second risk—that people will not save enough for retirement due to information problems.

As discussed by Le Grand (1995), people may not only decide to save in the wrong way but may also make incorrect decisions about how much to save. If individuals have a tendency to be myopic (short-sighted) in their financial planning, the bias of these incorrect decisions will be for them not to save enough, so that in retirement they experience a bigger drop in their income than they would have wished (if planning their life-cycle finances with perfect foresight and knowledge). State intervention to ensure that workers always receive a pension worth a particular fraction of their (lifetime or final) earnings can set a minimum earnings-replacement rate, thus limiting (or, if the replacement rate is high, eliminating) information risk.

If lifetime earnings were narrowly dispersed and economic growth low or nil, this would be the end of the income risks connected with retirement. However, in reality neither of these assumptions hold (at least in Britain). Some individuals have such low lifetime earnings that—even if they distribute their lifetime

---

[8] Note that investment risk can never be reduced to zero. If there is a severe economic downturn it may prove impossible to meet promised pension pay-outs whether this promise is made by the state or by employers. In other words, if national income falls then pensioners' living standards can only be protected by them receiving a larger slice of the cake, which for economic and political reasons may not be desirable (or feasible).

income 'correctly' (through voluntary or compulsory saving during working years)—they will end up with a retirement income which is below an acceptable level. Particularly if the minimum income standard is higher for older people (as is implicit in Income Support), the 'natural' fall in income between working and retired years may well be sufficient to push some people into poverty. Moreover, the fact that (at best) real income remains static during retirement, while definitions of (relative) poverty rise in line with earnings, means that better-off members of older cohorts can also fall into poverty as they grow older, even if they initially retired with an income above the minimum. While these two effects are analytically distinct, in looking at how the welfare state has acted to protect incomes in later life it is simplest to consider the two together as *poverty risk*.

Three Tiers of Prevention and Response

The policy response to income risk in retirement takes a number of forms. The World Bank (1994) provides a useful classification, distinguishing between three 'pillars' or 'tiers' of pension provision: a first tier of means-tested or flat-rate state benefits, a second tier of compulsory earnings-related benefits, and a third tier of voluntary pension contributions by individuals and employers. As shown in Table 10.3, all three tiers exist in Britain. We look below at how each of these tiers helps to reduce the various income risks described above (for convenience the tiers are discussed in reverse order).

Third-tier provision can help to reduce both investment and information risk, regulation influencing the nature of voluntary provision (thereby reducing investment risk), and tax reliefs influencing the level of voluntary provision (and so information risk). Given the problems associated with personal pension schemes, in particular their high and variable charges, the assertion that third-tier provision reduces investment risk may seem somewhat peculiar. However, the government's proposed Stakeholder Pensions give a better idea of the potential for regulation to reduce this risk: as charges will be capped at one per cent (and will fall wholly on investment returns without an annual fee) the risk of low

Table 10.3. *Pension provision in the UK*

First tier (compulsory flat-rate or means-tested)	Second tier (compulsory earnings-related)	Third tier (voluntary)
Basic pension	State Earnings-Related Pension Scheme (SERPS)	Voluntary contributions to and payments from private pension schemes
Income Support (Minimum Income Guarantee)	NIC rebates for private pension schemes and consequent benefit payments	Tax relief on voluntary contributions and on investment income

returns due to excessive costs will be smaller. This said, Stakeholder schemes need not have any mechanism for evening-out returns (though such financial products would be possible) and so are likely to remain subject to a substantial degree of investment risk. Nevertheless, the fact that the majority of voluntary pension saving in Britain occurs via occupational pension schemes, which are normally defined-benefit (i.e. the employer offers a guarantee of pension benefits), means that most third-tier provision does not suffer from investment risk.

The effect of tax reliefs is to reduce the cost of buying retirement income, hence they act to increase the amount people save in the form of a pension. Such reliefs therefore reduce information risk, albeit in a rather haphazard way. While myopia (if it exists) tends to reduce pension saving, tax reliefs will have the opposite effect; the hope is that in combination something like an optimal level of saving will be achieved.[9] However, it should be noted that rather than leading to a higher pension income (and so less of a fall in consumption on retirement), such reliefs might equally be used to finance a longer (rather than a richer) retirement. In other words, tax reliefs necessarily subsidize early retirement as well as retirement income itself.

In its current form *second-tier provision* is concerned predominantly with information risk, which it reduces by imposing a compulsory earnings-replacement rate of a fifth of lifetime earnings (between the National Insurance earning limits). However, when second-tier provision was first introduced in 1978 its aims were more extensive. Not only was the earnings-replacement rate higher but, as only occupational schemes were allowed to 'contract-out', all benefits produced by the scheme were defined-benefit. In addition, the original scheme also helped to inflation proof occupational pensions through the system of 'guaranteed minimum pensions'. Though both these aspects of the scheme were abolished under the 1986 and 1995 Pension Acts, the importance of investment risk as a factor behind the introduction of a second tier should be borne in mind.[10]

What neither of the above tiers do is to reduce poverty risk. This is the job of *first-tier provision*. However, the two elements of this tier—Income Support (or 'Minimum Income Guarantee') and the basic pension—do not manage to ensure that all pensioners receive a minimum income, and hence poverty risk is not completely eliminated. In the case of the basic pension gaps in entitlement reflect the design of National Insurance, which excludes workers earning below the lower limit (£66 per week in 1999/2000) and non-workers who are ineligible for credits.[11] In the case of Income Support the gaps reflect more fundamental

[9] This presentation of pension tax relief as a rational response to the problem of myopia is not historically accurate; as shown by Hannah (1986), the current system reflects a series of ad hoc decisions. There was never any grand design.

[10] It is perhaps no coincidence that SERPS was introduced in the aftermath of the 1974 oil crisis, when inflation was higher and stock markets less bullish than today.

[11] Around 17% of the working-age population are currently not in employment and not receiving basic pension credits (Kumar 1999).

problems: means-tested benefits are always likely to have less than complete take-up due to the difficulty of identifying eligible individuals and, more arguably, because of the social stigma attached to claiming such benefits.

The level of benefits offered by the first tier also affects the extent of poverty risk. Though it is currently government policy to increase Income Support for pensioners (though not the basic pension) in line with earnings, the previous Conservative administration indexed all benefits to prices. If an absolute poverty standard is used, or if poverty is itself defined by the level of means-tested benefits, this policy will not have affected the number of pensioners defined as poor. But if a relative standard is used, as the Government is now proposing, and as is used in the Households Below Average Income statistics (for example, DSS 2000b), then the level of the minimum income very directly affects poverty risk.

Evaluation: Trends in Retirement Incomes

In some respects the British welfare state seems to have dealt reasonably well with the income risks associated with retirement. As a group, pensioners are much better-off today than in the past (both absolutely and relatively) and many pensioners now have an occupational pension offering a secure guarantee of benefits. Despite the fact that benefit rates were linked to prices throughout the Conservatives' time in office (see Figure 10.3 below), mean pensioner income increased by 64 per cent in real terms between 1979 and 1997/8 (averaging between single and couple households and after tax), nearly twice as fast as the 38 per cent real growth in average earnings (DSS 2000c: 22). Consequently the gap between pensioners' and workers' living standards narrowed, with mean pensioner income rising from 49 to 57 per cent of average earnings over this period. Moreover, the most important contribution to pensioners' above-earnings income growth came from occupational pensions, which grew by 162 per cent in real terms between 1979 and 1996/7 (DSS 1999c). Both investment and information risk have therefore been reduced, largely through the widespread provision of occupational pensions.

In contrast, the risk of poverty in retirement has worsened since 1979. Though the proportion of the poorest fifth of the population accounted for by pensioners fell from 37 per cent in 1979 to 20 per cent in 1998/9, so that in the most recent estimates pensioners are only barely over-represented among the poorest (DSS 1995 and 2000b, table D1), this phenomenon largely reflects the declining fortunes of other household types (in particular lone parents and workless households under pension age). Rather than looking at the composition of the poorest, the real question is what proportion of pensioners have an income below an acceptable level. Using half mean household income as the poverty standard, the estimates in DSS (1995 and 2000b, table F1) show that there were over one and a-half times as many poor pensioners in 1998/9 as in 1979, the proportion of single and couple pensioners with incomes below this

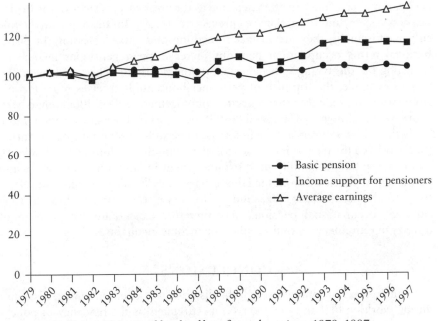

Figure 10.3. *Real levels of benefits and earnings, 1979–1997*
Source: DSS (2000*d*).

threshold growing from 16 per cent in both cases in 1979 to 26 and 25 per cent respectively in 1998/9.

The main reason for this increase in pensioner poverty is that throughout this period, government policy was to uprate benefits in line with prices. As shown in Figure 10.3, this meant that the value of the basic pension and Income Support for pensioners fell substantially behind earnings. Indeed, Figure 10.3 overstates the increase in the real value of Income Support, as changes in the structure of benefits in the late 1980s explain much of the 17 per cent increase in the headline rate (see Evans, Piachaud, and Sutherland 1994).

A further important development in pensioner incomes should also be noted. As well as increased poverty, the period since 1979 has also been marked by widening inequality among pensioners, with the Gini co-efficient rising from 0.2 in 1979 to 0.26 in 1996/7 for single households and from 0.24 to 0.3 for couples (DSS 2000*c*, chart 1.6). Though this is not one of the income risks described earlier (it affects society rather than individuals) it is, or should be, of concern to government. However, while the government has stated that it wants, 'all pensioners to share fairly in rising national prosperity' (DSS 1998*c*: 12), the goals of increasing pensioner incomes in aggregate and ensuring a more equal distribution of incomes among pensioners may not be compatible.

As well as boosting mean pensioner income, occupational pensions are also largely responsible for the increase in pensioner inequality. Accordingly, though occupational pensions are often depicted as the great success story of the British pension system, and the archetypal preventive strategy for dealing with income risk in retirement, they are in fact something of a mixed blessing. In distributional terms occupational pensions increase mean pensioner income by 'dragging-up' the average—benefits go predominantly to richer pensioners. (By way of example, the top fifth of pensioner households receives more income from this source than the other four-fifths put together; see DSS 2000c, chart 3.2). Moreover, as shown by Campbell (1999), occupational pensions make it more likely that older workers are the first to go in periods of economic restructuring (or are offered the biggest incentive to make themselves voluntarily redundant), and increase the probability that unemployment in late middle age will cause permanent withdrawal from the labour market. By helping to reduce the effective length of working life, and hence raise the risk of low lifetime earnings, occupational pensions may therefore exacerbate the problem of poverty in retirement, as well as enlarging income inequalities.

CONCLUSIONS

A common theme running through the discussion of unemployment, disability during working life, and income risk in retirement, is the tendency of policy-makers to redefine the problem in such a way as to make it more amenable to resolution. In the case of unemployment, for example, part of the strategy has been to prevent claimants becoming classified as unemployed in the first place an approach taken to the extreme in some American Work First schemes, where potential claimants are diverted at the door. On disability, policy-makers have found it easier to develop health and safety-type preventive strategies, rather than grasp the nettle of anti-discrimination policies which would help to prevent impairment leading to social and economic disadvantage. With respect to pensions, attention has been focused on longevity and investment risk, to the detriment of addressing the risk of poverty in old age.

Frequently, redefinition merely shifts the problem elsewhere—into the domain of other branches of government. Keeping the claimant unemployment count low through the 1980s contributed to the rise in numbers classified as long-term sick and disabled, a group who are only now beginning to be reached by active labour-market policies. Lack of coordination between benefits and employment policy has been especially apparent, and has begun to be addressed by the reorganization of the Benefits Agency and Employment Service into a combined Working Age Agency. But the need to join up is not restricted to social security and employment departments. Compulsory participation in back-to-work programmes like the New Deal for young unemployed ensures they reach more people, but early evidence suggests it may also lead to worryingly high numbers disappearing from the system altogether: around 5 per cent of first-year claimants left the New Deal for Young People to 'unknown destinations' that were not work (Hales and Collins 1999). To take another example, occupational pensions have been highly successful in raising the retirement incomes of certain sections of the workforce but are also implicated in the trend towards early retirement, a phenomenon which is now causing concern to the government.

The current concentration on paid work as the solution to all social problems could fall into the same trap: a preventive strategy, successful in its own terms, but creating problems elsewhere. For those unable to work, or unable to work for a sufficient proportion of their working life—whether through disability or a lack of demand or some other reason—the emphasis on paid work could lead to a deepening of social exclusion, particularly if it is accompanied by the emasculation of mechanisms for amelioration of poverty. Very little has been announced by the Labour Government to implement the 'security' side of its welfare reform mantra, 'work for those who can, security for those who cannot', yet it is an essential part of the equation.

When it comes to thinking about social exclusion, response cannot be easily disentangled from prevention. This interdependence appears to have been recognized in the case of child poverty: responding to the plight of families with children by ensuring that they receive sufficient income through employment or social security or a combination of both, is seen as a way of preventing the next generation from experiencing such high levels of deprivation (Piachaud and Sutherland, Chapter 9, this volume). A similar argument can be made with respect to other vulnerable groups. Adequate levels of benefit and support in the present (traditionally considered a 'response')—whether for the unemployed, disabled people, or pensioners—may be the most effective way to prevent a slide into deeper social exclusion in the future.

11

Preventing Social Exclusion: Education's Contribution

JO SPARKES AND HOWARD GLENNERSTER

EDUCATION MAKES A DIFFERENCE

Several strands of CASE's work have reinforced the conclusion that educational failure is strongly associated with the process of social exclusion (see for instance, John Hobcraft's chapter in this volume, and Hobcraft 2000). Moreover, there is growing evidence that this is more than an association. The relationship is causal and can be reversed. But it is a long and difficult process to do so. And we still know too little about what works and what does not. Particularly disturbing is some evidence that the reforms of the 1990s in the UK did indeed boost the performance of average and above-average children and schools but did not work for the most deprived. More recent evidence is more encouraging. We are beginning to raise the achievements of the lowest performing schools and pupils in primary schools. However, the gaps at 14—Key Stage 3 and beyond— are yawning. In this chapter we first set out the evidence and then discuss what we can do to narrow the gap further.

EDUCATIONAL ATTAINMENT, EMPLOYMENT, AND EARNINGS

John Hobcraft's analysis of National Child Development Study (NCDS) data, presented in Chapter 5 identifies educational test scores during compulsory schooling as 'the most powerful of any childhood precursor' of negative adult outcomes. This and other research suggests that individuals who leave school with low levels of educational attainment are at a higher risk of experiencing social exclusion as adults, with those who lack basic literacy and numeracy skills at particular risk.

Educational attainment is strongly related to unemployment and earnings across the developed world. In general unemployment rates decrease as the educational attainment of workers increases (OECD 2000). This trend is apparent across countries with widely different dispersions of educational attainment in their populations and labour-market profiles. Basic literacy and numeracy attainment have a particularly profound effect on labour-market participation and unemployment. Evidence (Bynner and Parsons 1997; Moser 1999) suggests that the experience of those with poor literacy and very poor numeracy skills is particularly marked. In terms of labour-market access only one in every 50 jobs is open to those without Basic Skills Agency 'entry-level skill' and only 50 per cent of jobs are open to those with skills at only entry-level (Moser 1999).[1] Subsequently adults with poor skills are up to five times more likely to be unemployed, compared with those with average skills (Bynner and Parsons 1997; Ekinsymth and Bynner 1994). The labour-market difficulties associated with poor basic skills emerge during the early stages of working life. Analysis of the 1970 British Birth Cohort Study (Ekinsmyth and Bynner 1994) revealed that at the age of 21, poorly skilled male school leavers were more likely to be unemployed, and had experienced twice as many months of unemployment, as their counterparts with average basic skills. Poor literacy and numeracy skills were found to be of equal importance in explaining the higher levels of unemployment. However other work on basic skills has suggested that mathematical attainment is of particular importance in terms of maintaining employment in the modern economy (Bynner and Parsons 1997). Poorly skilled female school leavers experienced less unemployment than their male counterparts, tending to follow mixed trajectories, experiencing a variety of jobs, training and education; interspersed with unemployment or early family formation. By the age of 21, one-third of females with poor literacy defined themselves as engaged in house care.

When making judgements on the value of employing individuals, employers require easily accessible and comparable data—educational qualifications most commonly fulfil this requirement. Hence there is a link between qualifications, labour-market participation, and earnings. There is strong evidence that a lack of qualifications is associated with an increased risk of unemployment (Dolton and O'Neil 1996). Individuals increasingly require some form of qualifications to access the modern labour market. In 1986, only 62 per cent of jobs required some form of qualifications; by 1997 the proportion had risen to 69 per cent (Green *et al.* 1998). The importance of qualifications as an explanatory factor in unemployment is known to be increasing over time (Arulampamlam and Stewart 1995). In terms of attainment at 16, Robinson and Oppenheim (1998) suggest that,

possession of five or more lower grade GCSEs significantly reduces the chances of exclusion post 16. Possession of one or more higher grade GCSEs has a further positive effect.

They suggest that the proportion of 16-year-olds failing to gain at least 20 GCSE points in a maximum of seven subjects is a key indicator of educational exclusion. On the basis of Youth Cohort Study analysis, they claim that this is the clearest cut-off point in terms of the relationship between GCSE attainment and participation

---

[1] The Basic Skills Agency entry-level skill is broadly equivalent to level two in the National Curriculum in schools, BSA level one is approximately equivalent to National Curriculum level 4 (the expected level for 11-year-olds) and BSA level two is equivalent to GCSE Grade A–C (Moser 1999).

Table 11.1. *Labour market position (at age 16) and qualifications, 1996*

	F/T Ed	Gov. train	F/T job	Excluded*
5+GCSE A–C	92	3	2	3
1–4 GCSE A–C	68	13	9	10
5+ lower grades	49	24	12	15
1–4 lower grade	34	22	13	30
No grades	26	20	17	38
Total	71	11	7	9

*Excluded includes those out of work/unemployed and inactive but also a small number (1–2%) who are in part-time work.

Source: Robinson and Oppenheim (1998), YCS cohort 8, sweep 1.

in education, training, or employment during young people's post-school careers. In addition, attainment at this level has been associated with progression to Level Two vocational qualifications or above.

Basic skills attainment has a profound effect on earnings. Low earnings are far more likely if one has poor basic skills than if one has good skills. In a follow-up of the sample of children born in 1958, Bynner and Parsons (1997) show that twice as many men with very low numeracy skill levels earned a low wage as men in the highest numeracy group. Forty-two per cent of those with very low or low literacy had low incomes in comparison to 24 per cent of those with good literacy. Numeracy skill has a particularly powerful effect on the likelihood of low adult annual earnings.

Poor basic skills are associated with a range of other adult outcomes. Bynner and Parsons (1997) show that by the age of 37, one-third of those with very low skill levels did not own their own home, compared with under 10 per cent of men and women with good skills. Large numbers with poor basic skills do not vote in general elections. Literacy skill is more powerful than numeracy in this respect— 32 per cent of men and 30 per cent of women with low literacy skill failed to vote in the 1987 General Election compared with 22 per cent of men and 17 per cent of women across the 1958 NCDS sample. In addition educational attainment is inversely related to poor reported general health and depression as measured by the Malaise Inventory (Whitty *et al.* 1999; Bynner and Parsons 1997). Given these findings it is particularly worrying that Britain's record on basic skills is so poor. Numbers with very low literacy and numeracy standards are three times those in Germany or Sweden—a fifth of the population (Moser 1999).

OTHER EDUCATIONAL OUTCOMES ARE IMPORTANT TOO

Success in formal examinations and tests only measure one type of skill. Non-cognitive educational attainments are also significant in relation to later adult outcomes. Recent research on employability (Kleinman *et al.* 1998; Moss and Tiley 1995) has emphasized the importance of individuals' personal qualities and 'softer skills' in accessing the labour market. Moss and Tiley (1995) identify two clusters of soft skills;

The first, interaction, has to do with ability to interact with customers, and co-workers. This cluster includes friendliness, teamwork, ability to fit in, spoken communication skills, and appearance and attire. A second cluster we call motivation, taking in characteristics such as enthusiasm, positive work attitude, commitment, dependability and willingness to learn.

According to the authors, soft skills are measured neither by educational attainment nor standardized test scores. In Moss and Tiley's sample of American employers, 86 per cent included soft skills in their list of most important hiring criteria and almost half put soft skills first in that list. Surveys of employers in the UK have also stressed the importance of soft skills. Employers are evidently dissatisfied with the responses of the education system in these respects (Kleinman *et al.* 1998). However soft skills have yet to be adequately defined and their importance, relative to formal qualifications, for different groups of people and at different stages in the life cycle is unknown.

Evidence also suggests that school attendance is an important factor with small but significant independent effects on early adult outcomes. Early research (Gray *et al.* 1980) suggested that the difficulties encountered by truants, particularly in the labour market were a result of their depressed examination performance and lack of qualifications at the end of their schooling; and that thereafter their problems were no greater than others with similarly poor qualifications. However, more recent research (Hibbert *et al.* 1990) has demonstrated that the occupational outcomes of former truants are distinct from other poor achievers:

Truancy is a predictor of employment problems and of a more severe kind than will be experienced by others who share the disadvantaged backgrounds and low attainment, which typify the truant.

At the age of 23, truants have lower-status occupations, less stable career patterns and are up to twice as likely to be unemployed as non-truants. Interestingly, when in work former truants' income is no lower, but if the number of children in the household is taken into account they are considerably less well-off. These differences remained statistically significant after controlling for the effects of social background, educational ability, poor attendance due to other reasons (e.g. sickness) and qualifications on leaving school. Preliminary analysis indicates the independent effect of truancy on adult outcomes is even more marked for those individuals who also reported truanting at the age of 11, in addition to truanting at age 16.

Hibbert and Fogelman (1990) suggest that by the age of 23, truants are up to three times more likely to have experienced marital breakdown, up to ten and a-half times more likely to smoke heavily (over thirty cigarettes a day) and up to three times as likely to suffer depression as non-truants of similar background, ability, and educational attainment. Interestingly, holding these factors constant, truancy has no statistically significant impact on age of the first child or patterns of alcohol consumption. Truancy has also been linked with offending behaviour. Home Office research findings of self-reported offending amongst 14–25 year olds in England and Wales found that the odds of offending were almost three times as high among truants as those not truanting (SEU 1998c). These findings suggest that schools contribute to individuals' human capital formation, and reduce their vulnerability to social exclusion as adults, in ways which are not reflected in traditional examinations.

EDUCATIONAL ATTAINMENT AND OUTCOMES: THE CURRENT STATE OF PLAY

Although Britain does reasonably well in overall school achievement, it has a very worrying history of a wide dispersion in achievement levels, although not as bad as some other advanced economies (Keys *et al.* 1996; OECD 2001). Although general levels of attainment have been rising, a significant number of young people truant from school and leave school without attaining qualifications or basic and personal skills. In terms of GCSE attainment, there have been year-on-year improvements in the proportion of young people attaining five GCSEs at grades A–C. At present around 45 per cent of young people obtain qualifications at this level. However the proportion leaving with no GCSE passes has remained stable in the 1980s and 1990s at approximately 1 in 12 young people. In 1996/7 the figure was 7.7 per cent. Over three-quarters of this group were not entered for any examinations (DfEE 1997). In terms of average GCSE point score, there was a national improvement of 2.8 points in the period from 1993 to 1997. Improvements have not been evenly distributed across the ability range. In this period, the top decile group improved by 4.4 points whilst the bottom 10 per cent experienced a *deterioration* of 0.1 points (West and Pennell 2000). This polarization has been attributed, at least in part, to the introduction of league tables focusing on high attainers as performance indicators (West and Pennell 2000; Pearce and Hillman 1998). This created powerful incentives, which have encouraged some schools to focus attention and resources on pupils who are on the borderline of achieving five GCSEs at grades A–C, as these are published in the DfEE's examination performance tables, at the expense of lower attainers (Kleinman *et al.* 1998).

Since 1997 more attention has been directed to failing schools. Education Action Zones and Sure Start have focused on poor areas. Of most significance, primary schools have been required to devote an hour a day to literacy and to numeracy. The idea began as a way of ensuring that children in poorer neighbourhoods gained the basics. It was then generalized. David Blunkett set schools targets to raise the scores children attained in the national tests at ages, 7, 11, and 14.

There have been some striking improvements and some more modest ones. Achievements at age seven have been modest but at age eleven there have been significant improvements in the percentage of pupils reaching the expected levels. The exception has been in science at age 14 where performance seems to have dipped. However, these averages do not tell us anything about the performance of those at the bottom. Here there is a little good news. Between 1996/7 and 1998/9 GCSE points scores rose on average from 35.9 to 38.1. The scores achieved by the bottom 10 per cent rose from 0.7 to 1.6 (West and Pennell 2000). Still a terrible difference, but at least a larger proportionate gain by those at the bottom.

Of much more significance have been the gains made by schools in the national attainment tests from 1995–2000 (Glennerster 2001). At Key Stage 1 (expected for 7-year-olds) the gains made by the schools in the lowest quartile rose more than in the average and the best schools. In maths the lowest performing quarter of schools raised their scores by 11 points—from 71 per cent gaining the expected level to 86 per cent. The top schools raised theirs from 92 to 98 and the median school from 83 to 93 per cent. The bottom schools were closing the gap. At Key Stage 2 (age 11) the gap between the top and bottom schools narrowed in each subject. At Key Stage 3 (age 14) the gap narrowed in every subject except science. Clearly there is a ceiling effect here. The top schools find it more difficult to improve. But that does not take away from the fact that there has been a catching-up. If we look at the poorest schools—those with 40 per cent or more children having free school meals—we find them catching up on the richest schools—those with only 5 per cent on free school meals or less.

In maths at Key Stage 2, for example, the rich schools improved their performance. Seventy-nine per cent of their pupils reached the expected levels in 1997. By 2000 this was 86 per cent. The poorest schools raised their level of achievement from 37 to 53 per cent. In science the gap closing was bigger still, from 45 per cent to 70 per cent. The gaps in achievement at Key Stage 3 remain vast. Eighty-three per cent of pupils in rich schools at this point reached their English target in 2000, whereas *none* of those in the poorest schools did! None of those in the poorest schools had done so in 1997 either.

VARIATIONS IN COMPULSORY EDUCATIONAL ATTAINMENT

Despite these gains we must recognize that factors beyond the school remain dominant in explaining the differences in pupil performance. Research suggests that non-school factors are a more important source of variation in educational attainment than differences in the quality of education that students receive. Thomas and Mortimore (1996) reported that between 70 and 75 per cent of school variation in 16-year-old attainment in GCSEs is explained by pupil-intake factors. However, there is broad consensus that schools can make a difference, which is both educationally and statistically significant. Reynolds *et al.*

(1996) conclude from their review of school effectiveness research that schools have an independent effect of approximately 8–15 per cent on student attainment, with the effect of primary schools being greater than that of secondary schools. Non-school and school factors are known to vary in their pattern of relationship with achievement in different subject areas. Background factors are far more important determinants of English than mathematics attainment and are of relatively little importance in accounting for variations in science results. The proportion of total variance accounted for by correlation with background factors (age, free school meals eligibility, fluency in English, and gender) ranged from 13 per cent in English, 7.5 per cent in maths and only 2.4 per cent in science attainment. Concurrently, the percentage of variation attributable to schools ranged from 5.3 per cent for English, 13.8 per cent for mathematics, and 20 per cent for science (Sammons *et al.* 1997).

NON-SCHOOL FACTORS AND EDUCATIONAL ATTAINMENT

Strong associations between non-school factors and low levels of educational attainment have long been recognized in the sociological and education literature. However the recent research focused on the 'school effect' has diverted attention from these links. In order to isolate the value added by schools, 'appropriate' allowance is made for socio-economic variables and/or prior attainment to control for differential school intakes. As a result, inequalities in final educational outcomes arising from background factors may be at risk of becoming acceptable and even regarded as inevitable. Although the associations between different non-school factors and educational attainment are well documented, the factors that are causal, and not simply associated with attainment, have yet to be identified. A number of key background/non-school variables are associated with educational attainment in the literature. These include:

- pupils' personal characteristics: prior attainment, gender, health;
- socio-economic: low income (eligibility for free school meals), parental unemployment, social class (father's occupation), and housing (e.g. overcrowding);
- educational: parents' educational attainment—qualifications and basic skills;
- family structure: family size, lone parent status, institutional care;
- ethnicity/language: ethnic group, fluency in English;
- other: parental interest/involvement/practice, locally based factors.

The evidence is reviewed under these headings below.

It is widely accepted that there is high level of interdependence between many of the factors highlighted above and that the cumulative impact of risk factors may be greater than the simple sum of separate factors. Older educational priority studies showed that multiple disadvantage has devastating implications for educational attainment (Table 11.2). As the number of risk factors experienced by the pupil increases, so too does the risk of falling into the bottom 25 per cent

Table 11.2. *Percentage of secondary pupils experiencing different numbers of educational priority criteria by measures of educational outcomes and behaviour*

Numbers of factors	% of pupils in verbal reasoning Band Three	% of pupils with disturbed behaviour
0	10.8	5.6
1	16.7	9.4
2	25.5	14.7
3	32.2	20.4
4	38.6	25.1
5	49.1	28.6
6	61.5	32.7
7	91.7	42.3

Source: Sammons *et al.* (1981).

of the age group at age 11 (verbal reasoning band 3) and the chance of being rated as having some kind of disturbed behaviour. We now examine non-school factors and their interactions.

Pupils' Personal Characteristics

Prior Attainment

At the pupil level, prior attainment explains the greatest proportion of variance in educational attainment. This is thought to explain up to 59 per cent of total variance in pupils' academic test scores (Thomas and Smees 1997)—more than social economic background variables. However, there is a high correlation between socio-economic variables and prior attainment; the former is used as a proxy for prior attainment when prior attainment is not available (Levacic and Hardman 1999).

Even at the earliest stages of educational assessment when pupils are aged seven, prior attainment accounts for 26–43 per cent of variance in national assessment results (Sammons and Smees 1998). Prior attainment on the sub-scale of 'sound' may provide the best predictor of Key Stage One results, highlighting 'the value of developing children's phonological knowledge at a young age' (Sammons and Smees 1998). Variations in cognitive development/ attainment are evident during early infancy. Analysis of BCS70 data (Feinstein 1998a) demonstrates a social-class gradient in cognitive development at 22 months which increases by 42 months and at 5 years. The proportion of individual variance in educational attainment accounted for by variations in genetic intelligence at birth is unknown and has been the subject of vigorous academic debate. Environmental factors are known to affect cognitive development prior to birth. Maternal smoking and poor nutrition during pregnancy, for example, have been associated with low levels of latter educational attainment among children. Regardless of their origins, innate variations fail to offer a sufficient explanation of poor educational attainment, as high proportions of children with normal IQ achieve only low levels of educational attainment (Rutter and Madge 1976).

There is a broad consensus that intervention in the early years is among the most effective means of improving educational performance and outcomes. Such interventions are likely to be an important facet of strategies that help to lift children out of cycles of deprivation and onto positive trajectories. Waldfogel (1998) provides a useful summary of the effectiveness of early childhood interventions in the USA. The evidence is promising and suggests that well-designed programmes are successful at raising educational attainment and other positive adult outcomes. The most successful programmes involve early and intensive intervention, and include a follow-through component in the later stages of the child's development. In the UK, evidence of the effects of pre-school provision is mixed, particularly for children who participate in day-care programmes before their first birthday. In general, research studies suggest that in comparison to no experience, all forms of pre-school experience have a positive impact on attainment in national assessment tests, taken at age 7 (Sammons and Smees 1998; Daniel 1995). In addition, pre-school attendance has been found to improve 'school commitment', reducing the risk of disaffection during the latter stages of schooling and delinquency (Sylva 1994; Shepard and Farrington 1995). However, the quality of provision appears to be a crucial determinant of the effects on educational attainment. Definitions of high-quality provision are subject to debate, but frequently refer to small group size, high adult–child ratios, a balanced curriculum, and trained staff.

If pupils do fall behind, they have few opportunities to make up lost ground in the current education system. Such pupils tend to fall further behind their peers and may give up altogether the attempt to catch up (Mortimore *et al.* 1988). Subsequently, transient events in a pupil's life may have an unnecessarily high impact in the longer term. Specific intervention projects, which offer pupils opportunities to accelerate their educational development, allowing children to catch up may be beneficial. One such project is the reading recovery programme. This involves training teachers to recognize reading problems among young disadvantaged children, and has been positively evaluated using controlled experimental methodology (Sylva and Hurry 1995).

Gender

In national curriculum tests and at higher-level GCSE grades, girls outperform boys. For example, in 1997 49 per cent of girls achieved five or more higher grade GCSEs compared with 40 per cent of boys (DfEE 1997). However, at the lower levels of GCSE attainment, the gender gap is smaller in percentage point terms. In 1997, 8.8 per cent of boys and 6.5 per cent of girls failed to gain any GCSE qualifications (DfEE 1997). Evidence of a gender effect on the propensity to truant is mixed. Some evidence suggests that boys are slightly more likely to truant than girls, whilst other results have shown that there no differences

(Bosworth 1994; O' Keefe 1993). These findings have significant implications. If truancy is not a male-dominated phenomenon whilst juvenile crime is, the notion of a causal link between the two needs to be treated with considerable caution. As Pearce and Hillman (1998) suggest, 'factors other than gender are more important in explaining disaffection and underachievement'.

Health

Physical illness is associated with high levels of absence and low levels of educational attainment (Rutter and Madge 1976). As poor health is correlated with low-income and poor housing conditions, this is likely to explain, in part, the strength of correlation between disadvantage and attainment. In a review of urban education, the Office for Standards in Education (1993) noted a prevalence of dental problems, speech disorders, ear, nose, and throat disorders that did not always receive prompt treatment, as parents were unable to access the appropriate health services due to poor transport links for example. Hence, lack of access to one public service inhibits access to the human capital which is developed by the education service. Recent school-based health interventions such as the healthy schools initiative and breakfast clubs explicitly recognize the link between health and educational attainment. Findings from a local study of such an intervention have shown positive effects on attainment, attendance, and bullying (McInnes and Toft 1998). Despite the mantra of joined-up thinking for joined-up problems, health and education action zones have proved difficult to connect (Whitty *et al.* 1999). Health improvement plans are meant to be a way of linking local agencies but health inequalities are deep and difficult to change (see Ruth Lupton's chapter in this volume).

Socio-Economic

Growing up Dependent on Income Support/Eligible for Free School Meals

Low income, as indicated by free school meal eligibility, is strongly correlated with low levels of educational attainment at all levels, from the age of 7 upwards. West *et al.* (1999) show that the proportion of children dependent on Income Support recipients (at a local authority level) is very strongly correlated with levels of educational attainment. This indicator of need accounted for approximately 66 per cent of variance in educational attainment at a local authority level. The strong correlation between low income and GCSE attainment is reiterated in analysis undertaken at school level (Levacic and Hardman 1999). Low income is frequently conceptualized as an undifferentiated experience, but as Tabberer (1998) has highlighted, the effect of temporary, or recurrent, compared to persistent, poverty on educational attainment is little understood.

Dearden *et al.* (1997) also found household income had no effect on truancy levels. In contrast, the correlation between free meals and absence levels is much stronger, accounting for 42 per cent of school-level variance. This would include *authorized* and *unauthorized* absence. It is important to note that the decision not to attend may not be one taken independently by the child. Surveys suggest in some cases families/parents are aware of pupils' absence from school, and often condone it in order for children to take on caring responsibilities or to engage in illegal employment in order to maintain family incomes (O'Keefe 1993; Galloway 1985). This is likely to reflect lack of access to money and to affordable childcare structures among such families. Fox (1995) suggests that 10 per cent of all school absence results from children undertaking duties associated with their home. Research on truancy and part-time work post-16 has shown that participation in part-time work significantly increases the probability of truancy for both males and females (Dustmann *et al.* 1997).

Parental Unemployment/Employment
The relationship between parental unemployment and education is difficult to disentangle as adults are only eligible for Income Support (and hence their children eligible for free school meals) if they are unemployed and available to work. Some evidence suggests that it is the loss of income which is important. Gregg and Machin (1997) report that in the absence of financial difficulties, the association between low educational attainment and paternal unemployment is significant, but small, for boys and non-significant for girls. The impact of maternal employment on educational success varies with the age of the child, and type of employment and different types of outcome. In terms of reading, maths, and behaviour, maternal employment when a child is under the age of 1 year is associated with problems in at least one of these areas in later life. At other ages under 5 there is no evidence of a negative effect and there maybe a positive effect if the mother undertakes work when her child is aged between 5 and 17 (Joshi and Verropoulou 1999). Once again the actual relationships and the strength of them varies for different types of attainment. Maths attainment for example was not significantly affected by mothers employment at any stage. Part-time work appears to be particularly beneficial. One study found that a child in a household where the mother works part-time alongside a working father is 70 per cent less likely to attain low GCSE grades (all D–G grades of nil passes at GCSE) than a child in a household where the father is the sole earner (O'Brien and Jones 1999).

Evidence of the effects of growing up in a workless households is mixed. This has a negative impact on maths attainment and anxiety levels but no impact on reading attainment and aggressive behaviour (Joshi and Varropoulou 1999). Qualitative evidence, for example, suggests that household employment may be particularly important for the acquisition of personal softer skills. Findings suggest that many pupils who grow up in workless households are not exposed to working role models, and as a result fail to learn in the home about the behavioural aspects of work (Kleinman *et al.* 1998). Research is needed which differentiates unemployment in terms of its duration, the presence of other workers in the household or neighbourhood, and type of work undertaken. Studies of educational attainment and different types of employment and unemployment may be useful in disentangling the processes through which low attainment is linked to unemployment.

Housing Tenure and Conditions

The associations between housing tenure, conditions, and educational attainment are well established. Individuals living in council housing are less likely to attain qualifications and are more likely to report playing truant than those living in other forms of accommodation (Bosworth 1994). As earlier chapters have discussed, it is important to recognize that this does not necessarily suggest causality—it is unclear whether council housing residency exerts an independent effect. Poor housing, in particular overcrowding, access to basic amenities, and temporary accommodation are also associated with lower educational attainment. Such conditions adversely effect a child's health, development, and access to friends and social networks, which are likely to affect school attendance and performance. Exploring the processes which translate homelessness into poor educational outcomes, Whitty *et al*. (1999) highlight that 'the nature and organisation of current services and professional responses . . . were often as much part of the problem as the solution.' The authors highlight a lack of formal policy mechanisms, to ensure the priority of the education of homeless children. Data derived from a survey of LEAs on the administrative arrangements relating to the education of homeless children, revealed high levels of confusion, inconsistency and a lack of clear lines of communication and responsibility. For example, homeless parents who elect to continue their child's education at their existing school may incur additional financial costs for transport.

Parent's Educational Attainment

Parental education attainment has long been recognized as an important predictor of a child's educational attainment. The mother's level of educational attainment is particularly important in this respect. Dearden (1998) for example found that the probability of a woman undertaking a degree increases by 1.1 percentage point for every extra year of education undertaken by her mother. The association is particularly strong in terms of literacy attainment. Research at City University (Moser 1999) has shown that 60 per cent of children in the lowest reading attainment group at age 10 had parents with low literacy levels, whilst only 2 per cent had parents with high literacy scores. In contrast parental education is only weakly related to the likelihood of truancy from school (Bosworth 1994). The means by which better-educated parents confer advantage to their children remains open to question. Research has highlighted the importance of parents' human, and social capital. Clearly if parents are unable to read, they are unable to assist their child's learning in this respect. Policy interventions which have increased parent's human capital, for example family literacy projects, have been favourably evaluated.

Family Structure

Growing up in a Lone-Parent Family

Controlling for other variables, lone parenthood is non-significantly or only weakly associated with educational attainment (Gregg and Machin 1997). However some evidence has suggested the effect depends on the sex of the parent, and that living with a lone father has a slight negative effect on attainment (Bosworth 1994). When experienced in combination with other risk factors, notably low income, lone parenthood does increase the probability of low educational achievement (Mortimore and Mortimore 1983). The circumstances of family disruption are also relevant. The children of widows, for example, seem to experience fewer negative effects than do divorcees. Similarly the addition of a step-parent into a family also appears to have negative effects (Kiernan 1992). Parental circumstances are strongly associated with truancy and absence. Holding other factors constant, Youth Cohort Study analysis demonstrates that family structure is significantly related to the likelihood of truancy. Individuals in two-parent families were the least likely to truant, followed by those who live with the mother, those who live with the father, and those living away from parents (Bosworth 1994; Casey and Smith 1995). Other studies have also found that behaviour such as school lateness and negative teacher evaluation appear to reflect family structure/disruption effects and not just economic factors (Featherstone *et al.* 1992). Hence the link between disadvantage and educational attainment may involve a link between family relationships and educational outcomes as well as between resource availability and learning performance.

Growing up in an Institutional Care Placement or Multiple Foster Places

Surveys show that over 75 per cent of those who have been in local authority care gain no qualifications on leaving school—compared with 11 per cent in the general school population within the same geographical areas. Furthermore over 80 per cent of care leavers remain unemployed two and a-half years after leaving school compared with 9–16 per cent within the general population (Biehal *et al.* 1992; Garnett 1992). Young people who experience multiple care placements are at an especially high risk of low attainment (Biehal *et al.* 1992). The low levels of educational attainment among in-care children are primarily, though not entirely, accounted for by their traumatic backgrounds (Osbourne and St Claire 1987). However, studies show that the experience of care tends to compound the educational difficulties experienced by children in care. Contributing factors in this respect have been found to be: inadequate liaison between carers and schools, the prioritization of welfare above educational concerns, disruption caused by placement moves, lack of transport to school, low priority given to education by social workers, low expectations, and stigmatizing treatment by teachers and bullying by peers (Carleen *et al.* 1992; Fletcher-Campbell and Hall 1990).

Growing up in a Large Family

Individuals with large numbers of siblings have a slightly higher probability of failing to gain qualifications at the age of 16 than others. In addition if they succeed in gaining qualifications they are likely to attain lower test scores (Bosworth 1994). The association between large family size and low attainment is strongest in respect to reading and verbal intelligence, moderate in terms of mathematics ability, and far weaker in respect of other forms of non-verbal intelligence, suggesting that lack of verbal interaction with adults may be the key factor. Wedge and Prosser (1973), for example, found that in the middle classes, only those children from a family with four or more siblings were adversely affected, whilst in working-class families children were progressively disadvantaged by each additional sibling. Birth order, the sex, and ages of other siblings have also been associated with educational attainment. Dearden (1998) found that boys with fewer older siblings had better levels of attainment than boys further down the birth order. In addition, women with only brothers were found to have significantly higher levels of attainment. Males are more likely to truant when there are older siblings in the household, but the presence of younger siblings has no effect. For females the presence of older siblings has no effect whereas there is a weak but significant effect where young siblings are present (Dustmann *et al.* 1997).

Ethnic Background

There are no comprehensive national data on the attainment of pupils from different ethnic backgrounds (DfEE 1997). However Gipps and Gillborn (1996) suggest that on average the attainment of Afro-Caribbean pupils, and particularly boys, is low relative to other ethnic groups. Asian pupils attain almost as well, or better, than whites of the same class and gender. There are however substantial differences among Asian groups. Pupils of Indian origin consistently attain high levels whilst Bangladeshi and Pakistani pupils' average attainments are lower, and they are more likely to leave school without having acquired any qualifications. Patterns of attainment vary considerably at LEA level. For example, in the London borough of Tower Hamlets, Bangladeshi pupils now achieve higher average GCSE point scores than white and Afro-Caribbean pupils. Summarizing the research on progress Gipps and Gillborn (1996) indicate that the gap between ethnic minorities and white students widens during primary school years. However at secondary school this trend reverses for students from Asian and Chinese backgrounds, who tend to make better progress than their white counterparts. Differences between the progress of black and white pupils remains smaller and less consistent. Hence as pupils proceed through secondary schooling, some ethnic minorities narrow the attainment gap, but in general (with the exception of some inner London areas) fail to close it completely. The Social Exclusion Unit report (1998*c*) concludes ethnicity is not associated with the propensity to truant persistently.

Parental Interest/Involvement/Practice

Recent analysis of NCDS data has identified parental interest in education as one of the factors most strongly related to educational attainment and adult outcomes (Feinstein and Symons 1997; Hobcraft 1998, and this volume). Feinstein and Symons (1997) found parental interest in schooling had a massive direct effect on children's attainment at 16, far greater than the direct effects of social-class variables. Their results showed that in mathematics tests, the improvement of children between the ages of 11 and 16 whose parents exhibited high levels of interest was 15 per cent greater than that of pupils whose parents exhibited no interest. In terms of reading attainment the difference was 17 per cent. Other NCDS analysis has shown that the father's interest has a crucial and sizeable effect on the attainment of educational qualifications (Hobcraft 1998). Findings must be treated with caution as analysis is based on teachers' assessments of parental interest in education, and hence on perceptions rather than objective measures. Sammons (1998) suggests,

this variable is likely to reflect teacher perceptions, which may well be coloured by cultural factors . . . it may well be an indicator of socio-economic disadvantage . . . measurement problems are compounded by the decision to set the mother's or father's interest at zero where the parent is absent. This means that this variable may well be picking up the impact of one parent family status.

Direct evidence from parents suggests that very high proportions are interested in their child's education (Tizard *et al.* 1981; West *et al.* 1997; Lareau 1997).

Several studies have highlighted the significance of parental involvement in their child's education and learning. Indeed parental involvement is the only non-school factor that is widely cited in the school effectiveness literature (Mortimore *et al.* 1988). Despite the current enthusiasm for increasing parental involvement (DfEE 1997) research findings as to its efficacy are somewhat mixed. Little is known of the ways in which parents are involved in their children's education—particularly outside the formal school setting. Numerous studies have focused on one measure of parental involvement yet this is unhelpful as parents can display their involvement in different ways. Differentiation is crucial as some types of involvement, such as use of parental helpers in the classroom have been found to be non-significant or negatively correlated with educational attainment (Sammons *et al.* 1997).

Past research concerned with parental involvement has focused on a number of different issues. Some research has focused on parents' involvement as consumers/decision-makers in education. This would include parents' choice of school in the education 'quasi market' and participation on school governing bodies. Other studies have focused on home–school communication, for example newsletters, and parents' evenings/meetings. High levels of contact and trust between parents and the school are associated with beneficial outcomes in the school improvement literature (Mortimore *et al.* 1988).

Other research has tended to focus on parents' role as educators—usually in specific curriculum areas such as reading and to a lesser extent mathematics. Studies have shown the amount of direct teaching or 'intellectual stimulation in the home' is highly correlated with children's attainment, particularly during early school years (Parkinson 1982). Considerable optimism about the efficacy of this form of involvement as a means of raising reading/educational attainment among disadvantaged pupils, was first generated by the experimental study known as the 'Haringey project' (Tizard *et al.* 1982). The project took place over two years, during which time parents were encouraged by their child's teacher and home visitors to hear their child read. After the two-year intervention there were considerable differences in reading-test scores. In the control classes, very few children scored at or above the test norm for the age group, whilst in the experimental class over 50 per cent of the children scored above average. Subsequent research has however failed to confirm the efficacy of increasing this type of involvement as a means of improving attainment (e.g. Hannon 1987). The success of the Haringey project may be attributable to the home-visiting component of the programme (Hannon 1987). Home visits were frequent and involved specific advice on good practice, and prescribed what parents should do. This draws attention to the issue of what parents actually do when listening to their children read. The type of parental input may be a crucial factor. Studies which have examined this issue suggest that the way in which parents interact with their children whilst listening to them read is significantly differentiated by the level of the parents' education (Greenhough and Hughes 1998). This is in line with direct evidence from parents, which suggests that the majority recognize the importance of family support for educational attainment, but lack the confidence, and crucially the knowledge as to what they should do to help their child. When combined with time and family pressures, Tizard *et al.* (1981) noted that working-class parents who lacked confidence found it particularly difficult to sustain involvement in their child's reading. Many parents report willingness to spend more time on learning activities with their children if teachers gave them more guidance as to what they should actually do. However contact with parents is given remarkably low status and little or no time allocation in a teacher's day and the training which teachers receive provides limited preparation for collaboration with parents (Hanock 1997).

Other research has focused on parents' involvement as facilitators of education. This involves the provision of support for children's education through encouragement and an environment within which pupils can become good learners and benefit fully from teaching. Examples of this type of involvement include the provision of space and time for education within the family home life, positive parent–child relationships and lack of conflict within the home. One US study on variations in literacy attainment among pupils from low-income families, found that emotional and organizational dimensions of family life were strongly correlated with writing capacity. However these factors were negligible in terms of their relationship with other components of literacy—vocabulary, word recognition, and reading (Snow *et al.* 1991). This suggests that different forms of parental involvement are differentially related to different areas of educational attainment. Parents' own behaviour and attitudes impact on the educational attainment of the child.

One study of both formal and informal parental involvement found no statistical differences in terms of social class as defined by father's occupation (West *et al.* 1997). Differences were found in relation to mother's level of educational qualifications in terms of attendance of parents' evenings, informal contact with teachers, use of work books at home, and private tuition. However parental education does not differentiate other forms of parental involvement. This suggests that the stereotype of the less-involved, less-educated parent may not hold true for all types of involvement. Hence differences in parental involvement in low-income families/households may be an important facet of explanations as to why some children from disadvantaged circumstances succeed educationally whilst others do not. It is therefore important for research to clarify exactly how parents are involved and the relative importance of different types of involvement of mothers and fathers, for different areas of attainment, and at different stages of their children's lives. In addition more needs to be known of the involvement of different groups of parents and of the key factors which inhibit or foster involvement.

The literature has also highlighted the influence of parents' and pupils' wider social networks in their educational attainment. Research suggests that informal teachers, group leaders, and mentors fulfil important roles when young people begin to negotiate independence from their parents (Hendry *et al.* 1992). Interestingly, a high level of personal support from a trusted adult has been identified as a key success factor in a number of highly successful projects, which prevent exclusion among high-risk groups (Pearce and Hillman 1998; Sparkes and West 2000). Other work has drawn attention to the considerable influence of peer groups as young people are establishing their own identities (Cullinford and Morris 1997). Studies show that parental influence sharply decreases during adolescence due to the rising counter-influence of peers. Peer groups emerge as 'surrogate families', and their influence is known to be more significant when the counter-influences of the family are weak. Harris (1999) has controversially argued that parents have relatively little influence over their child's behaviour outside the home, and emphasizes peer group relationships, focusing on ways in which children socialize each other collectively. A greater understanding of the significance of peer groups and of how and why they are important would be beneficial.

Area-based Factors

The literature suggests that local factors such as limited work opportunities in the local labour market, racial tensions, and local violence may impact negatively upon educational attainment and outcomes. Recent analysis of Youth Cohort Study (YCS) data (Bosworth 1994) found that holding other factors constant, 'travel-to-work' area types did not play any consistent, significant role in creating different pupil attitudes to school. In addition, controlling for other factors, the probability of truancy was found to be highest in *high*-wage and manufacturing areas. In contrast 'travel-to-work' area 'type' was related to examination performance. Individuals whose travel-to-work area types were in some sense disadvantaged were, however, less likely to gain a examination score. The ranking running from highest to lowest performing areas was:

(1) high-status growth areas;
(2) high-wage areas;
(3) northern and midland metropolitan areas;
(4) high-unemployment areas;
(5) service-dominated areas;
(6) low-wage, low-growth areas;
(7) manufacturing-dominated areas.

Differences in absolute scores across the regions were not large but smaller areas with very poor opportunities may have large effects. Similar effects have been noted in the USA (William Julius Wilson, in Halsey *et al.* 1997).

SCHOOL FACTORS ACCOUNTING FOR VARIANCE IN EDUCATIONAL ATTAINMENT

Studies have highlighted the possibility of improvement in schools with disadvantaged pupils (DfEE 1997). Case studies of schools with below average intakes who *succeed against the odds* emphasize the importance of leadership built on a team approach, a vision of success, careful use of targets, improved physical environment, common expectations about pupils' behaviour and success, and investment in good parent and community relations (National Commission on Education 1996). However we must be careful in assuming that school improvement is a remedy for social exclusion. Mortimore and Whitty (1997) argue, 'it cannot be assumed that such strategies will contribute to greater social inclusiveness.' Reiterating the conclusions of Rutter in the *Fifteen Thousand Hours* study, the authors suggest,

If all schools performed as well as the best schools, the stratification of attainment of achievement by social class would be even more stark than it is now. This would happen because socially advantaged children in highly effective schools would achieve even more than they do now in less conducive environments and the gap between them and their less advantaged peers would increase.

It is what happens to all pupils within schools that matters not the average performance of children.

Exclusion

Exclusion is the ultimate sanction a school can employ against a pupil who is persistently disobedient, disruptive, or violent. Exclusion may be permanent or fixed term (whereby a pupil is excluded for not more than fifteen days in any one term). At individual-pupil level the longer-term consequences of school exclusion are often profound. For example, students who are excluded from school in the final two years of compulsory education are two and a-half times as likely not to participate in education, training, or employment between the ages of 16 and 18, than those not excluded (SEU 1999b). Of those who are excluded on a permanent basis, only 27 per cent of primary-age pupils and 15 per cent of secondary pupils return to mainstream education (Parsons 1996). Those not returning to school lose their right to full-time education and receive what is legally defined as 'education otherwise'. The nature of this provision is determined by the LEA. However, in the majority of cases young people attend Pupil Referral Units (PRU), receive home tuition, or attend further education colleges. The quality of education received by pupils in Pupil Referral Units has been seriously criticized in OFSTED Inspection reports (1995). Criticisms draw attention to the low standard of educational attainment, low expectations of pupils, poor quality of teaching and an absence of clear objectives in many PRUs. Consequently:

Permanently excluded pupils and children who for other reasons do not have a school place are therefore at risk of educational failure, leading to unemployability and long term dependency on benefits; in short from a whole range of vocational, cultural and social opportunities.   (OFSTED 1995)

However, for children in Pupil Referral Units in 1994/5 the cost per pupil was £4,300 compared to £2,500 for mainstream education; this amounted to nearly double the cost for under 10 per cent of the teaching time they would receive in school (Parsons 1996).

Exclusion grew rapidly in the early 1990s. There were 12,700 permanent exclusions in 1996/7 (DfEE 1998). This compared with 2,910 in 1990/1. Actual figures may be even higher (SEU 1998c). Although the majority are from secondary schools, rates of exclusion from primary schools also rose rapidly—by over 500 per cent during the 1990–6 period (Parsons 1998). In addition estimates from OFSTED (1996) suggested that there were approximately 100,000 fixed-term exclusions from secondary schools annually. The rapid increase in rates of exclusion has been attributed to a number of factors including the publication of league tables as performance indicators. In a competitive climate with intense pressure on schools to meet demanding standards, schools may exclude less-able students or those who disrupt other pupils learning in order to improve their league table position. The importance of institutional factors in explaining the increasing use of the exclusion sanction is reiterated in a survey of LEA Directors of Education; 8 per cent thought that the increase in exclusions was due to poorer discipline, whilst 42 per cent attributed increases to levels of competition between schools (Gillborn 1996).

Boys represent 83 per cent of those permanently excluded (DfEE 1998). Evidence on the background of those excluded indicates that 61 per cent come from unemployed households (SEU 1998*c*). High proportions are from disturbed or disrupted home contexts including family break-up, bereavement, illness, alcoholism, and abuse (OFSTED 1996). Young people in care are on average 10 per cent more likely to be excluded than their peers (SEU 1998*c*). Exclusion has particularly significant implications for this group of young people, as this frequently triggers a breakdown in their care placement (Pearce and Hillman 1998). For those with special educational needs the risk of exclusion is roughly 6 per cent higher than others. This has been attributed at least in part to the funding systems for special educational needs. Stirling (1992) suggests that from the school's perspective, the process of exclusion is a speedier and more predictable process than the implementation of the lengthier assessment procedures leading ultimately to a 'statement' of Special Educational Needs (which results in additional resources to help meet the pupil's needs) under the 1981 Education Act. In addition he suggests that schools may be using the process of exclusion to speed up the allocation of additional Special Educational Needs (SEN) funding as in many cases the act of exclusion triggers the statementing process. Afro-Caribbean and black pupils are three to six times as likely to be permanently excluded as their white peers (OFSTED 1996). Although the reasons for this are little understood research has highlighted tension and conflict in relations between white teachers and Afro-Caribbean pupils as a plausible explanation (Gipps and Gillborn 1996). Although the majority of excluded pupils are evenly divided between average and below-average ability, Afro-Caribbean pupils who are excluded are likely to have above or average ability but were generally described as underperforming. They do not usually show disruptive behaviour from early in their school careers and show less evidence of deep-seated trauma. In addition, OFSTED (1996) found that exclusion is consistently associated with limited aspirations and expectations, poor relationships with other pupils, parents, and teachers, and pressure from other pupils to perform in ways that lead to conflict with authority.

Resources

LEA and School-Level Expenditure

The debate on the effect of resources on student attainment and labour-market outcomes is ongoing. This is reflected in the oft-cited US evidence. On the basis of a large-scale meta-analysis Hanushek (1986) concluded that, 'there is no strong or consistent relationship between school resources and student performance.' Hanushek's methodology has been severely criticized and re-analysis of his sample of studies undertaken by Hedges *et al.* (1994) found a consistent and positive relationship between inputs and outcomes. Card and Kreuger (1996) also conclude that increased per pupil expenditure results in higher earnings. (For a discussion of all their work see Burtless (1996).)

In the UK there has been comparatively little research into the effects of financial resources on educational outcomes. Work that has been undertaken suggests there is no consistent relationship between LEA expenditure and pupils' learning outcomes, nor their subsequent earnings (Dolton and Vignoles 1996). However West *et al.* (1999) argue that expenditure per pupil and examination results are confounded, as local authorities with higher proportions of children from disadvantaged backgrounds are allocated additional funding by central government and therefore spend more on education. Having controlled for the confounding effect of poverty West *et al.* demonstrate that educational spending per pupil is positively associated with educational attainment at the LEA level. Interestingly analysis undertaken by Dearden (1998) found that the effect of per pupil expenditure in secondary schools on female wages at age 23 is significant and quite large: 'a 10% increase in this budget leads to a 3.1% increase in wages.'

Class Size

Econometric literature on class size has failed to find consistently positive effects. Large classes are frequently associated with better results reflecting the tendency for low-attaining pupils to be placed in smaller classes (Dolton and Vignoles 1996). However, more recent small-scale experiments in the USA and longitudinal studies have begun to tell a different story. Analysis of cohort data suggests that reduced pupil–teacher ratios increase educational attainment but are also associated with subsequent adult earnings (Dolton and Vignoles 1996). The authors summarize:

The findings suggest that additional school resources do lead to better labour market outcomes but that the effect is very diffuse. Attending a school with lower pupil teacher ratio may increase a child's human capital and consequently their labour market prospects but this effect will not be a direct one, nor will it solely be via educational attainment.

Dearden *et al.* (1997) have also found that lower student–teacher ratios enhance both the ultimate educational and labour-market performance of women in the bottom half of the ability distribution.

Teacher Effects

On the basis of NCDS analysis, Dearden *et al.* (1997) conclude that teacher quality as reflected by teachers' salary, is an important factor in determining labour market outcomes among male sample members. Controlling for educational achievement, teachers' salary at secondary school level is associated with increased wages among men at ages 23 and 33:

Teachers paid 10 per cent extra given the cost of living, produce pupils who earn 7% more at 23 . . . better quality teachers offer knowledge and skills that are important to the labour market but are not relevant for obtaining formal qualifications.

As teachers' salaries primarily reflect experience, the findings suggest that more experienced teachers may be more effective in developing students' soft or personal skills. There are also observable teacher effects on truancy levels (Casey and Smith 1995). The likelihood of truancy is reduced in schools with higher proportions of graduate teachers and low rates of staff turnover. These factors are thought to affect the level of teacher expectations and the quality of interactions with pupils. Poor relationship with teachers was the second most-cited factor identified by pupils seeking to explain their truancy (Kinder *et al*. 1996).

Market Mechanisms

Research suggests that the development of a quasi-market in education created a powerful set of institutional processes and incentives which work against the goal of an inclusive education system. Key aspects of the reform include the right of parents to express a preference for a school of their choice. In the education quasi-market-place, school funding is largely determined by the schools ability to attract pupils, and schools compete with one another for pupils on the basis of published performance indicators (league tables). West *et al*. (1997) show that many parents find the league tables difficult to understand. Such difficulties are concentrated among parents with lower levels of educational attainment. Where the mother was educated to GCE A level, 67 per cent of respondents reported that they understood the league tables; this compared with 31 per cent of respondents where mothers had GCE O level or below. This has significant implications for the equity of informed choice. Noden *et al*. (1998) examined patterns of parental choice at the secondary-transfer stage in London and found that middle-class parents' first choice schools scored more highly in the DfEE's performance tables. Middle-class parents identified first-choice schools averaging 53 per cent five or more A*–C at GCSE, whilst working-class parents chose schools averaging 40 per cent. The realization of choice is also differentiated by family socio-economic status. Fitz, Halpin, and Power's (1993) study of two LEAs found that households in which the father was not in paid employment were the least likely to gain access to their preferred school choice. In contrast those in professional occupations were the most successful.

Critics of the educational market have suggested that the publication of league tables create incentives which encourage cream-skimming, whereby schools take actions to maximize their league-table position and consequently their market advantage. Work on admissions in the UK suggested cream-skimming may have been taking place in some grant maintained and voluntary schools, that have more flexible admissions policies (West and Pennell 1998). Evidence suggests that some such schools have been covertly or informally selecting pupils who are academically or socially advantaged (West *et al*. 1998; West and Pennell 1997; Gerwitz *et al*. 1995). In addition it has been suggested that the additional application procedures in some of these schools, which may involve application forms and/or interviews, may in themselves operate against particular groups of parents (Gerwitz *et al*. 1995). However, recent work by Gorard and Fitz (1998) has suggested that social polarization of schools has *reduced* in recent years (see also Fitz and Gorard 2000).

Evidence also suggests that the introduction of devolved budgets without adequate compensation for schools with specific problems such as high levels of pupil mobility or turbulence disadvantaged them. Devolved budgets for example provide less scope for LEAs to provide additional funds to schools who have particularly difficult intakes. In their analysis of education and homelessness, Whitty *et al.* (1999) highlight the way in which some LMS budgetary formula handicap schools in turbulent areas. The authors explain that some funding formulas are based on a single headcount, which is readjusted on the basis of another headcount later in the year. As a result the school rolls of schools in turbulent areas may be underestimated, leading to significant budgetary shortfalls.

On the other hand there are powerful reasons for giving schools control of their own budgets and local management of schools has been popular with heads (Glennerster *et al.* 2000). For devolved budgets to work in deprived areas there has to be heavy weighting in the formulas to compensate schools for difficult and deprived pupils.

WHAT TO DO?

• The evidence we have reviewed confirms that intervention in a child's early years is among the most effective means of improving educational performance later and the likelihood of escaping social exclusion. The Government's Sure Start programme was heavily influenced by the American evidence of the kind Waldfogel (1998) reviewed. The aim is to work with parents and children to promote the physical, intellectual and social development of pre-school children— particularly the disadvantaged—to ensure they are ready to thrive when they go to school 'so breaking the cycle of disadvantage' (HM Treasury 2000*c*). There will be 250 local programmes in England by 2001–2. They are targeted on poorer areas. Each local group working with local parents must come up with their own ideas. Those interviewed in the twelve areas being studied by CASE (see Chapter 8) were mostly enthusiastic about Sure Start. It is, however, a long way from the tightly targeted strategies in the USA with their strong emphasis on quite expensive cognitive development of a few vulnerable children. Unless we are prepared to invest the same kind of effort in this country we cannot expect the same results.

• The education of homeless children and those in care is, we have seen, a particular problem. This is a neglected area, falling as it does between education and social services departments.

• Parental involvement has long been seen as important. Taking time to achieve this in the poorest schools takes large amounts of teachers' time. As with so much else, this is not recognized in the formulas that distribute resources to schools.

• The importance of peer groups also emerged as an increasingly key variable. We know too little about this in the UK especially in areas of social exclusion.

• Knowledge of local labour-market opportunities and the nature of the local labour market affects school performance. Employment policy and work experience are particularly important in poor areas.

• What goes on inside the school still matters. A fascinating study of schools in Auckland, New Zealand, demonstrates how differently schools operate in inner-city as compared to more-advantaged areas (Thrupp 1999). The social mix of pupils had a crucial effect on the way teachers spent their time in the classroom, on the way time and resources were spent and, in the end, on the goals the school set for themselves. There was little difference in the cash spent on the schools but the nature of the education process was quite different. This is borne out in intensive interviews Ruth Lupton has carried out with head teachers in the twelve areas discussed in Chapter 8. If a head teacher spends half her day dealing with a few disruptive children, the local police, and social services departments, it is half a day she cannot spend on the tasks OFSTED might put top of her list. These pressures are not sufficiently recognized in the measures that get resources to schools.

• School exclusion has been a target of the present government. It is committed to reduce it by a third by 2002. Yet again, the costs to the school of not excluding a very troublesome child are extraordinary.

• Finally, adults and their needs. We have mentioned the Moser (1999) report before. It set out a series of proposals that have been largely accepted by the Government. It has set up a programme to implement them. It is not an easy task. Reaching those in need who are stigmatized and fearful of admitting a difficulty is a sensitive task. Relatively few who are reached complete a course. This is perhaps the most important and difficult task we face.

What stands out above all, however, from our dissection of the research evidence is how closely educational achievement, early life experiences, and schooling impact on one another.

12

Community, Neighbourhood, and Social Infrastructure

LIZ RICHARDSON AND KATHARINE MUMFORD

In this chapter we look at a definition of 'community', describe processes of community breakdown, and examine the role of community participation in regenerating low-income neighbourhoods. This chapter is based on two pieces of work undertaken by LSE Housing (now part of CASE) between 1996 and 1999. The first is a study for the Joseph Rowntree Foundation of four neighbourhoods in Manchester and Newcastle that faced problems of incipient abandonment. The second piece of research is an action research project, called the Trafford Hall/LSE Gatsby Project. The Gatsby Project is a UK-wide community training and small grants programme, with linked research and evaluation. The Project aims to stimulate and encourage community self-help action by residents in low income neighbourhoods to tackle practical problems relating to social exclusion.

WHY DOES 'COMMUNITY' MATTER?

There is a long-standing and ongoing debate about whether geographical communities or neighbourhoods are of particular interest as a unit of analysis (Glennerster *et al.* 1999). Some commentators argue that neighbourhoods are collections of individuals with no special features or independent area effects. They argue that life outcomes for individuals, such as health or employment outcomes, are not affected by whether the individual lives in an area of concentrated disadvantage. Others argue that concentration effects exacerbate individual difficulties and that the presence of additional factors in particular low-income areas, such as service failure, means that neighbourhoods do matter. There is a well-established literature of area-focused work, such as Forrest and Kearns (1999). Chapter 8 by Lupton and Power in this book discusses the importance of area effects in social exclusion. In this chapter, we take geographical communities as our basis for analysis. We focus on geographical communities, rather than communities of interest such as ethnic communities.

Neighbourhoods have special features for the individuals who live or work there as potential sites for the consumption of goods and services, as well as the locus for some of people's social relationships. These social relationships and social systems may involve high or low degrees of direct contact between people. They may involve weak or strong attachments, or be supportive or challenging of conventional morality. However, the common thread is that the behaviour of individuals does impact on others, either via direct social contact or via signals, to create standards of behaviour and a set of social controls. These relationships make neighbourhoods into social systems, and it is these social systems that mean that people sometimes refer to particular small geographical areas as 'communities', even where there do not appear to be significant amounts of attachment to an area or lots of social contact. People also use the term 'community' to refer to those aspects of neighbourhoods that relate to the consumption of goods and services, with no reference to the social systems of an area, although the two are linked. Both the operation (or not) of social controls, and the provision or access to services and facilities affect the viability of a neighbourhood. We use the concept of *social infrastructure* in this chapter as our definition of 'community', as it encompasses both aspects of the special features of a neighbourhood—people and place. Figure 12.1 illustrates our definition of social infrastructure.

Social infrastructure is made up of two elements:

1. Services and facilities, such as housing, access to credit, goods, education, leisure activities, childcare, a well-maintained physical environment, and transport. In areas of rented housing, there is also the need for management of the homes and communal areas. There is good evidence that most people need quality accessible services and facilities and that a lack of these can be damaging for an area and its residents.

2. Social organization, such as friendship networks or group activity like residents' associations. There is more controversy about whether an area's viability hangs on the existence of social organization. We can clarify this by looking more closely at the different forms that social organization takes, in particular the following three distinct aspects:

• friendship networks and informal mutual aid;
• informal small voluntary groups, clubs, and societies;
• informal social controls operated via a set of commonly agreed norms and rules.

Not all neighbourhoods have all three aspects. Some people have argued that some highly sought-after neighbourhoods demonstrate little social contact between residents, and are characterized instead by high degrees of atomization and fragmentation (Baumgartner 1988). Therefore, it is argued that 'community' is not important to neighbourhood viability. However, this argument is based on too narrow a definition of 'community'. It presumes that social organization is solely or primarily about geographically based friendship networks. There are several reasons why strong geographically based friendship networks are not the key factor in social organization. First, some criminal family

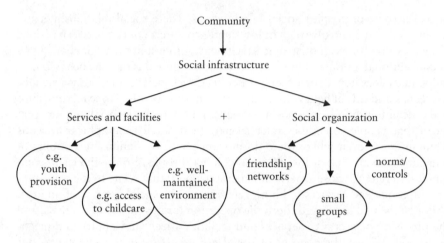

Figure 12.1. *A definition of 'community'*

networks damage an area rather than protect it by condoning illegal or antisocial activity. Secondly, some neighbourhoods work primarily on looser friendship networks outside of the locality, across other spheres of people's lives. Local
social contacts are not the key aspect of social organization, although they can
and do play a positive role.

Regardless of whether residents of an area have high or low levels of direct
social contact, the one part of social organization that appears to be critical to
area success is informal social control based on the existence of a commonly
agreed and respected set of rules and standards (norms). There may be communities where a majority agrees with illegal and conventionally unacceptable
behaviours, and where informal social controls support this. However, in the
neighbourhoods covered in our research, both residents and locally based workers stressed that only a minority of residents rejected conventionally accepted
values and standards of behaviour. Two-thirds of the community groups we
discuss later in this chapter had been provoked into taking action to reassert
responsible and law-abiding behaviours in their neighbourhoods. Further
evidence in the chapter by Lupton and Power in this book from another twelve
areas studied by CASE also suggests that a majority of residents in low-income
communities support societally acceptable value systems. We have predicated
our case for the importance of 'community' and the role of informal social
controls on this.

There are links between the three aspects of social organization, illustrated in
Figure 12.2. For example, being a member of a group can help create, articulate,
and enforce a set of shared values between members. The existence of a set of
shared values may facilitate the growth of a small group. But, the links do not
apply in all areas. It is possible for people to operate and respect informal social
controls in a particular location without having much direct contact. This is

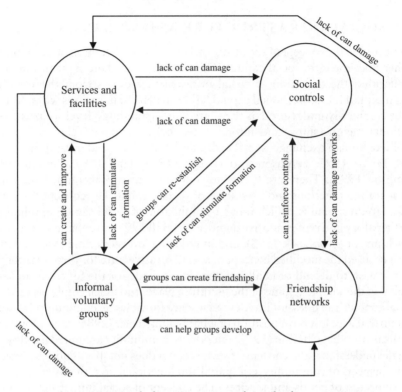

Figure 12.2. *Links between aspects of social infrastructure*

particularly true where there are fewer additional stresses such as low incomes, and other social problems such as worklessness, mental health problems, and family break-up (Wilson 1987). Informal social controls are not predicated on direct social contact, although direct social contact can be of benefit to the operation of social controls and norms.

Some feel that a discussion of rules and standards suggests an overly prescriptive approach to lifestyle issues, may even further exclude those who are 'different', or put the blame on minorities for area decline. There are some grey and contested areas. Common examples of these include whether children should be allowed to play near cars and houses, how tolerant people should be of noise levels, whether and to what extent people should participate in the informal economy, or whether people should run businesses from their homes. It is difficult to define what is acceptable behaviour in all cases. However, there are some basic minimum rules that help create and maintain workable social infrastructure, which include respect for differences where these are not harmful to others. Indeed, on some of the social housing estates we visited residents felt so strongly that acceptable standards of behaviour had broken down that they had developed estate manifestos to re-establish what these normally unspoken rules should be.

SOCIAL INFRASTRUCTURE AND SOCIAL CAPITAL

We have used the concept of social infrastructure as our definition of 'community', rather than the term social capital. The two concepts share a great number of similarities; the definition of social infrastructure draws from the wealth of social capital literature. Social capital has been defined in various ways. It seems to be commonly understood as the shared understandings, levels of trust, associational memberships, and informal networks of human relationships that facilitate human exchange, social order, and underpin social institutions (Burns and Taylor 1997; Ferguson and Dickens 1999; Hall 1997; Putnam 1993; Sampson 1999). There are divergent, but not mutually incompatible, claims made for the functions and usefulness of social capital. The concept is strongly linked to these claims, which range from the role of social capital in rebuilding participatory and representative democracy (Hall 1997), in enhancing economic development (Woolcock 1998), and in reducing levels of crime (Moore 1999). We have used the modified concept of social infrastructure for three reasons. We do not wish to defend or challenge the claims made for the functions of social capital in this chapter. Some of the literature places too much emphasis on direct social contact and does not leave enough space for views of 'community' as social system that are closer to a position of what Baumgartner (1988) calls 'moral minimalism', or what Chaskin (1997) refers to as 'community of limited liability'. As usually understood, the concept of social capital does not place enough emphasis on the aspects of community as a spatial and functional unit, that is, a site for the consumption of goods and services. The concept of social infrastructure builds on the concept of social capital, and overcomes some of these difficulties.

ILLUSTRATION OF BREAKDOWN

We can see how important social infrastructure is when we look at examples of where it has broken down.

At the most extreme end of social breakdown, people live in fear of leaving their homes. Nuisance and harassment, even by very young children, is rife. People who can leave, do so, leaving behind increasingly deprived populations. Local services find themselves trying to respond to one crisis after another.

How does such a situation arise? What is the process of breakdown? Our study of four neighbourhoods in Manchester and Newcastle (Power and Mumford 1999) found that a combination of historical, external, and local factors were at work. Breakdown had happened as a result of various polarizing forces:

• The large-scale building of public housing on the back of slum clearance, accompanied by allocations policies which came to exclude all but the most needy, created stigmatized areas of last resort.

• The industrial restructuring from the early 1970s decimated the manual jobs that so many residents of the inner city relied upon. This restructuring of the labour market pushed out the more ambitious and more skilled.

• Suburbanization and increasing ease of access to owner-occupation encouraged the better-off to flee from cities, while the release of green-field land outside cities created a ready supply of relatively cheap housing.

• City-wide depopulation resulted in extremely high turnover and rate of exodus from the poorest areas.

At the local level, continuing depopulation and exodus of those with higher incomes and skills reinforced the poor reputation of these neighbourhoods. Levels of empty property rose, becoming increasingly visible and sending out a strong signal about the low value of the area. Landlords found it increasingly difficult to attract anyone but the most desperate.

The outward movement of population broke up communities. People were less likely to know their neighbours, and they had fewer relatives and friends around. This was exacerbated by very high rates of population turnover. Knowing that their areas were unpopular made people suspicious of those who did come to live in them. This reduced the possibility of mutual aid and local friendship networks. As fear and mistrust grew, these networks were even harder to re-establish.

The formal social infrastructure was depleted as banks moved away, and shops and leisure centres closed, in response to the reduced spending power of the population. Local institutions came under growing pressure as a result of serving an increasingly needy population. Depopulation and high turnover impacted negatively on school budgets and performance, putting extra pressure on staff, children, and parents. Empty properties could be targets for vandalism and arson. Police and remaining residents were often distrustful of each other. Housing staff were under pressure to fill empty properties, and resident dissatisfaction with their service was often high. Long-term planning became a luxury and staff felt forced to focus on the immediate, serious problems they faced on a daily basis.

Residents were wary of authority both because they feared the consequences of cooperating and being seen to take a stand, and because of past experience of the inflexible response they got from embattled services. This made it even harder for the formal social infrastructure to function, because services like policing rely on local people cooperating with them.

As both informal social networks broke down, and social institutions lost respect and control, crime and anti-social behaviour escalated. Longer-term residents who had moved away tended to be replaced by people with less commitment to the area. The strong signals of neglect and unpopularity sent out by poor physical conditions, poor local economy, and boarded-up homes contributed to the remaining population feeling demoralized and isolated. People were scared to challenge even young children because of potential retaliation. Even when significant reductions in actual crime were achieved, fear of crime remained high. The areas were too empty of people to feel secure. One local authority housing manager commented, 'There is a lack of social control. You've got young men going around doing very anti-social things. You've got families that intimidate other people. It's unsurprising that it's emptying out.'

This vacuum in social control meant that problems worsened alarmingly rapidly. In one of the four neighbourhoods, one drug dealer moved in, attracted by the ready availability of properties and the weakness of social controls. This triggered the emptying of a whole street in a matter of months. The behaviour of a few can have an impact out of all proportion to their numbers.

In the four neighbourhoods we studied, the vast majority of residents shared rules of behaviour that are commonly accepted. The difference between these neighbourhoods and those where a healthy social infrastructure exists, was in the ability of the majority to enforce those rules. The more that a minority were able to flout them, the more the majority felt defeated and unable to challenge the breach, particularly when the resources of that majority had already been depleted by selective out-migration. Moving away was the most straightforward response for many, especially if their friends and relatives had already made the move.

As the impact of the minority became stronger, an alternative set of 'accepted' behaviours arose. A kind of 'negative social infrastructure' made car-smashing by children, openly injecting drugs in stairwells, disposing of dirty nappies by chucking them out of the window, hostility towards your neighbours, seem like the 'norm', even when many people in the neighbourhood were still quietly rejecting those ways of behaving. Negative social networks arose for the distribution of drugs and stolen goods, again even when the majority took no part in them.

All aspects of social infrastructure were threatened: facilities, services, and social organization. The threat could not be lifted by community action alone. But the formal services—such as police, housing, education—could not do it on their own either. Conditions were being held, and in some cases improved upon, by the formal infrastructure reconnecting with and supporting the rebuilding of informal social networks. Equally, residents' informal support of the various social institutions in the areas was crucial to improving conditions. In all four areas, there was a core group of residents committed to their neighbourhood who stayed, and fought to challenge the downward spiral.

REGENERATION AND THE 'FISHING TRIPS PROBLEM'

If 'community' is crucial to the viability of neighbourhoods, then can the 'community' itself be part of the rebuilding and maintenance of neighbourhoods?

In most low-income neighbourhoods across the UK, including the four referred to in the study of breakdown above, there are some residents who will join together to take action to make their areas better places to live in and to enrich people's lives. These groups of residents organize activities like homework clubs for children, bowling clubs for older people, parenting workshops, and sports for young people. They manage small organizations and businesses, like community cafés, credit unions, community venues, and resource centres. They work together to alter the physical environment through the creation of community gardens, and communal allotments to grow and sell vegetables. As well as taking this direct action, they lobby service providers for improved service delivery in their neighbourhoods. They seek a voice within the partnership structures that are taking decisions about their areas and that are implementing special initiatives. The quality, effectiveness, legitimacy, patterns, and levels of community activity vary from area to area.

This informal, collective organizing by residents happens spontaneously. Policy-makers have also latched on to community action as a way forward in tackling social exclusion. Community activity is a central plank in the Social Exclusion Unit's proposed National Strategy for Neighbourhood Renewal (2000), which confidently states that '[community] self help is a vital ingredient in sustainable change in a deprived neighbourhood'. In the UK and abroad, 'community', in all its forms, is seen as 'the modern elixir', with 'ubiquitous' appeal (Sampson 1999) for tackling the bundle of problems wrapped up in the term 'social exclusion'. The idea is being pushed forward in the energetic writings of veteran community-action champions such as Gibson (1996) who describe the 'world shaking' possibilities of ordinary people doing 'extraordinary things' to salvage and repair the 'fabric of society'. It has found its way into the more measured prose of UK Government guidance to regeneration partnerships that 'experience shows that solutions which are imposed on a community, rather than developed with them, won't deliver lasting change' (DETR 1998). There is currently a high level of general acceptance, in policy and practice, of the principle of resident empowerment and involvement. This can be seen in UK regeneration policy, via the Single Regeneration Budget and New Deal for Communities, in policies to reinvigorate local government such as the Best Value framework, in the work of the Active Communities Unit at the Home Office. It is also found in European policy, for example through the European Social Fund.

However, there are those who question this new-found enthusiasm for community self-help. Proponents of community action are greeted with scepticism about its value, and its potential to make significant positive impacts on the causes and symptoms of social exclusion. Some feel that the social inclusion of deprived areas will not be helped by the addition of self-help groups, voluntary organizations, and community businesses, 'normal Britain ... doesn't have community centres' (Kleinman 1998). The consensus even among the faithful is that 'community involvement attracts passionate advocates but has failed, so far, to convince its cautious sceptics' (Hastings, McArthur, and McGregor 1996). And the passionate advocates are all too aware of the nub of the problem, that small-scale community activity 'may not appear at first sight to be relevant to regeneration' (Chanan *et al.* 1999).

The debate over the value of community action was typified in our research of community self-help by the 'fishing trips problem'. One of the first projects in the study was a couple of fathers taking a group of ten children to go sea-fishing in Colwyn Bay. The response from some policy-makers and many academics working in the field of social exclusion was: 'so what?' As a tool to rejuvenate deeply disadvantaged neighbourhoods, it can be difficult to match up the rhet-oric of community self-help with the reality. How do we reconcile the claims made for the importance of community activity with the modest undertakings of groups of five committed individuals?

Finding answers to these questions is made more difficult by the slipperiness of the evidence and the thorny methodological problems. Much of the know-ledge base for the impact of community work is anecdotal, 'grey' research, and descriptions of work by practitioners. History is another compounding prob-lem. The politically radical community development approaches of the 1960s and 1970s failed to effect equally radical lasting change in deprived areas. This failure is something that still taints the current rediscovery of community development. It can be seen in the impatience of some practitioners, often ex-community workers themselves, with small-scale incremental approaches, and their enthusiasm for quick hit, testable, and proven solutions (Utting 1999).

TOWARDS SOME ANSWERS

We now look at two issues that contribute to an understanding of the role and value of small-scale community activity: the different functions of community groups; and the problem of measurement.

The Different Functions of Community Groups—Community Involvement or Community Self Help?

Many community groups, such as residents' groups on social housing estates, have a dual role. They are representatives of the wider community, providing a voice for the expression of other residents' problems, issues, and priorities to service providers and agencies working in neighbourhoods. Community repre-sentatives try to persuade others to take action to solve neighbourhood prob-lems. They act as brokers between statutory services and residents, particularly where trust has been damaged. Community groups can also be organizers of their own projects, providing services and tackling problems directly themselves.

In practice, these roles blend together as different elements in tackling the same issues. The two roles complement each other in solving area problems such as youth disaffection. A community group's ability to tackle area problems is enhanced by being able to take both forms of action. This means both, 'things we can do on our own', or 'with a little help', and actions 'we can't do, but we can tell other agencies what needs to be done' (Neighbourhood Initiatives Foundation 1999). Other organizations in the field emphasize a similar approach to community attempts to tackle problems such as high crime and antisocial behaviour. For example, residents can be effective within their 'circle of control', and their 'circle of influence'. They need to identify which actions they can implement directly, which they can work in partnership with the police and other agencies to implement, and which actions fall outside both their circles of control and influence and need action at a national or global level (Crime Concern 2000).

The partnership approach to the regeneration of disadvantaged neighbourhoods is widely accepted as the most effective model. This model is based on local action and community involvement, but also encompasses transformed public services, economic development, and multi-agency 'joined-up' working (Taylor 1995). Indeed, it is this basic model that has been used in the National Strategy for Neighbourhood Renewal (Social Exclusion Unit 2000).

However, while there is a great deal of overlap and complementarity between these different roles of community groups, it is crucial to distinguish between them and see each on its own merits. Community representation is often ad hoc, and sometimes uninvited by the organizations being lobbied. Community involvement, as the term is typically used, is where representation becomes more structured. Representatives are asked to take on a more engaged and active role contributing their views to structures and services organized and delivered, in the main, by other organizations. Examples of these policies and structures are: the Best Value framework for local authority services; tenant participation compacts; Single Regeneration Budget; New Deal for Communities; local housing companies; Sure Start; and Pathways Partnerships.

The involvement of residents can help to align the work of agencies more closely with the needs of residents and make their task of delivering services easier and more effective. For residents, community involvement can be a means to meet their ends, by tailoring services to meet local conditions, by targeting regeneration efforts on the priorities of local people. Certainly, community self-help by itself is not sufficient to turn neighbourhoods around. The small-scale nature of the groups' direct project activity means that they are very unlikely to create significant, visible, or attributable changes in key indicators such as an area's crime rates or school results. Very small actions like these cannot by themselves transform areas. It is acknowledged that area regeneration works best starting from a base of local action and community involvement, with additional inputs from other agencies and public services (Taylor 1995).

There are many difficult issues in partnership working, such as the inequalities in power between residents and agencies (Hastings *et al.* 1996). Notwithstanding these issues, community involvement in regeneration can potentially contribute to agenda setting, outlining a vision, planning action, and guiding implementation. Communities need service providers, mainstream services, and regeneration agencies to work together to effect significant change in conditions. It can be difficult to see the direct impact of resident involvement on decisions, but it is proven that it increases satisfaction with regeneration schemes (Evans 1998). Examples given later in this chapter show the importance of the lobbying and representative roles of community groups. In the cases we describe, the community groups' role has been to lobby for intervention, provide a liaison point between residents and authorities, and alongside, provide small-scale activities for residents and their families and other hand-to-mouth supports for residents. There are many examples where community action has been part of a wider strategy to effect a significant area impact in this way. Earlier research by LSE Housing, on a fifteen-year experiment on twenty difficult social housing estates, showed that a combination of intensive localized management, physical upgrading, and resident involvement was able to arrest estate decline in terms of reducing vandalism and neglect, and increasing resident satisfaction and area popularity. These actions were also able to mitigate social and economic polarization, although they could not tackle chronic problems such as joblessness (Power and Tunstall 1995). Research (Evans 1998) into the impact of six 'Housing Plus' regeneration initiatives taken by social landlords found that those schemes which consulted residents had a greater impact upon community confidence. Deprived areas need a multiplicity of inputs, some of which are supplied by having many micro-projects and a number of small groups.

Community groups can supply the linkage between 'top down' regeneration and the ground. By what processes does this linkage happen? Figures 12.3, 12.4, and 12.5 illustrate examples of these processes.

These groups have been able to participate as formal partners only after a period of development. Their role in the regeneration plans for their areas has evolved as their experience and confidence has grown. Their general community work and ad hoc lobbying roles have also given them links with the wider resident population and demonstrate their organizational capabilities, which adds to their legitimacy and credibility as representatives. In all three cases, resident pressure helped prompt action by authorities, but the landlords also made independent, 'top down', strategic decisions to regenerate these areas and were met in the middle by the groups. The processes by which community involvement evolved in these cases demonstrate the importance of community groups' general community activity as a basis for community involvement. 'Play groups, environmental schemes, youth activities, and cultural activities may not hit the headlines, but they . . . can be the acorns from which the oak trees of partnership grew [sic]' (Taylor 1996).

Community involvement, as distinct from community self-help, has clear aims that relate to the work of schools, health providers, social landlords, planners, the police, and others. Focusing on formalized community involvement in regeneration schemes means having a narrowly instrumental view of community groups as a means to the ends of the regeneration scheme, or the service providers' delivery structures, for the benefit of both. This means that a focus on community activity solely as community involvement, or on general community activity only as a precursor to community involvement, leads to the view that general community action that does not achieve these specific ends has no intrinsic value. A failure to differentiate and assign significance to each different role for the community, in its own terms, means that those groups who do not develop a role as representatives appear to have limited usefulness. At best, they are representatives in the making. Not all community groups are able or want to take on a role as representatives and partners. General community action that

1993   Set up tenants' and residents' association

1994   Set up youth club, credit union, and food co-op

1995   Started training in tenant management of housing stock

1996   Started regeneration forum

1997   Attended Gatsby Project community training course
        Funding from English Partnerships for resource and information centre

1998   National Lottery funding for food co-op development worker
        Applied for Gatsby Project funding

1999   New resource and information centre finished (3 council houses
           converted)
        Office space to let, landlord and others start outreach surgeries
        Group provides drug-awareness training
        Community café funded through Gatsby Project small grant fund
        European funding for play area, centre manager, crèche, and café workers
        Two of the posts go to local volunteers
        Garden and lunch clubs and crèche start running from centre

2000   Regeneration of 2 streets on the estate to start April/May
        Group a major partner in plans
        Tenant management on hold until regeneration completed

Figure 12.3. *Bushbury Triangle Co-operative Ltd.*

does not lead to wider involvement does have other value. There is a legitimate role for those groups that make a steady ongoing contribution without this development.

A tiny minority of community organizations have developed as organizations of sufficient capacity to be a significant regeneration organization in their own right, with visible and more easily measurable outputs and outcomes. None of the community groups in our Gatsby Project study fell into this category of community-led regeneration organizations that are 'substantial players in [their] localities' (Thake 1995).

1997   A young girl dies of drugs
        Start up of Westfield Residents Action Group

        ↓

1998   Set up committee of 12 people
        Drew up action plan
        Renamed Wheels in Motion

        ↓

1999   Attended Gatsby Project community training course on improving the
        area's image
        Became a Limited Company
        Applied to National Lottery fund for community building—lost the bid
        Got involved in Single Regeneration Budget capital projects
        Renovate wasteland with funding from Gatsby Project small grant fund
        Involve young people in design
        Lobby local authority on empty homes
        Lobby local authority and private landlords on rundown homes

        ↓

2000   Completed action plan
        • private landlords forming new association and agree to voluntary code of conduct
        • local authority agrees to share information on potential tenants with
          private landlords
        • traffic calming and street lighting completed
        • local authority agrees to act on empty homes
        At cross-roads
        • groups' members may move away if demolition goes ahead
        • group trying to set up new committee for project
        • may end here if no new committee

Figure 12.4. *Wheels in Motion: Westfield Residents Action Group*

The Problems of Measurement

So, what value should we put on the community self-help activity? One of the most significant problems in assessing this is how to measure the outputs and outcomes of community activity. Having a framework for measuring these impacts is vital, because 'what is counted, counts'. The concept of social capital does appear to be providing a way forward in the field by giving a framework for measuring the more intangible benefits of community action. As one community activist put it, 'working on the intangibles is the tangible thing we do'. The concept of social capital is a significant leap forward in our ability to assign a value to community activity. It allows us to broaden our view of the instrumental role of community groups, not just as a means to the ends of improving service provision or delivering particular regeneration schemes through representation, but as a means to improving quality of life more generally. However, as we have

Late 1970s	Tenants' association set up to lobby on poor estate conditions

↓

Early 1990s	Local authority produce a watershed report on the need for action Tenants' group lobby for a youth facility, local authority sympathetic but no action

↓

1992	Tenants' association starts small youth group, self-funded by tuck shop

↓

1993/4	Tenants' association, social services, and youth services form working group for youth facility Working group goes too slowly. Disagreements over aims, methods

↓

1995	Youth group still going well—trips, arts group, sport, and concerts Tenants decide to go it alone

↓

1996	Attend several Gatsby Project community training courses

↓

1997	Community safety funding for area agreed Tenants bid for money for a Youth House and get keys to the building

↓

1998	Youth House opens Youth services provide a qualified worker Success means volunteers get exhausted by amount of work Apply for Gatsby Project small grant funding for a paid cleaner, administrator, and youth supervisor Group employs three part-time workers with Gatsby Project funding

↓

1999	Youth House well used—computer class, parent and toddler club, homework club, café, youth drop-in Group involved with two local authority-led partnerships to regenerate area, a Healthy Living Centre bid, the local tenants' group, community association, and police committee

Figure 12.5. *Plas Madoc Youth Partnership*

discussed earlier in this chapter, there are several problems with using this concept. In the context of measuring the value of small-scale community activity, the most relevant problems with the concept of social capital are:

- the close association of the term with direct social contact and social networks rather than informal social controls;
- the focus on the social organization/social system aspects of community at the expense of the services and facilities that also go to make up the community or social infrastructure.

Using the concept of social infrastructure (that is, services and facilities plus social organization) to evaluate community self-help action is an attempt to tackle these issues.

EVIDENCE OF THE CONTRIBUTION OF COMMUNITY GROUPS TO SOCIAL INFRASTRUCTURE

In the rest of this chapter, we use evidence from the community groups linked to the Trafford Hall Gatsby Project to look at the value of community self-help activity in contributing to both wider regeneration, and to social infrastructure. We look at:

- a background description of the groups, their neighbourhoods, and their activities;
- examples of the role of community groups in improving statutory services and facilities;
- examples of additional services and facilities provided directly by groups;
- examples of the contribution of community groups to the social organization of neighbourhoods, such as informal social controls.

Background on the Community Groups

This section draws on in depth research on 40 small community groups around the UK. Three-quarters of the groups work in areas of predominantly social housing. Most of these properties were constructed post-1945, particularly in the 1960s and 1970s. Two-thirds are based in areas that have been subject to special rescue initiatives. The groups represent all areas of England. Half are in metropolitan areas, and half are neighbourhoods of fewer than 1,000 homes.

These groups tackle a wide range of issues, including youth work, the environment, advice, and training/education. Tables 12.1 and 12.2 show the range of the groups' activities. Most are unincorporated associations, and four-fifths have an annual turnover of less than £5,000. They have all been supported to do a specific piece of work through training and small grant programmes run by the Trafford Hall Gatsby Project. Most groups undertake several activities, and a small number perform more than 10 different activities.

Table 12.1. *Range of activities undertaken by*
Gatsby Project groups

Activity	No. of groups
1. Partnership work	33
2. Representation	25
3. Youth	26
4. Training and education	24
5. Environment	20
6. Advice/venue	16
7. Social activities	14
8. Jobs	14
9. Children/play	13
10. Community safety	8
11. Elderly	8
12. Community enterprise	7
13. TMO/Housing management	6
14. Family work	2

Table 12.2. *Span of activities individual*
community groups undertake

No. of activities	No. of groups in range
0	1*
1–4	16
5–9	19
10+	4
Total	40

*Group has closed down.

Examples of the Role of Community Groups in Improving Statutory Services and Facilities

Community groups can represent the views of residents and lobby service-providers in both ad hoc and more formalized ways to achieve improvements and additional statutory services and facilities. In some areas, pressure from residents resulted in improved street cleaning and the purchase of new equipment for the cleaner. In other areas, groups have persuaded the local authority to provide a locally based caretaker and odd-job man which improved the repairs service by allowing small jobs to be done quickly on site (Priority Estates Project 2000). One group persuaded the local authority landlord to change its rent arrears policy so that action was taken more quickly, preventing residents from reaching unmanageable levels of debt before help was offered. Other groups negotiated more accessible bus routes, persuaded a cable TV company to provide installation services on the estate, or the local council to provide dog 'poop' bins. Dog dirt is a priority issue on many estates (Morton 1991). Nineteen of the forty Gatsby groups had successfully worked in this way to improve and create services and facilities.

As we described earlier in this chapter, local services can come under extra pressures in low-income areas. Several of the Gatsby groups helped relieve these pressures by playing an intermediary role between residents and services. For example, two Gatsby groups worked with local social landlords to relet their properties, and helped newly rehoused vulnerable families to settle into the area.

Where joint working between residents and statutory services does happen, what are the impacts? On one estate in Walsall, demand for social housing had fallen in the local authority area as a whole, and this affected the least-desirable estate most. As a consequence of falling demand, homes were allocated to more vulnerable tenants, increasing the pressures on the estate. A spiral developed as existing long-standing residents (more likely to be in work, older and less at risk) started to leave. The estate also suffered from significant youth nuisance, for example, daily incidents of arson. There was a sunken play area in the middle of the estate, which provided a meeting place for gangs. Their behaviour both exacerbated and was facilitated by the population instability in the area. Staff and residents jointly were able to reverse this dynamic through a combination of actions to improve the facilities, reduce the social pressures, and create a new atmosphere. They got rid of the sunken play area and refurbished some of the most run-down flats to a higher than usual standard. They evicted the few individual tenants who were damaging the estate. As well as this, they made a decision to interview new potential tenants to ensure people moving in understood the standards of behaviour required of them. They employed a caretaker to maintain cleanliness and play an active role watching out for residents. This all sent a clear signal to existing and new residents about what staff and the majority of residents would tolerate. This estate is now described by housing staff as 'highly lettable'. Resident pressure contributed to housing staffs' determination to take action. Resident support for the controversial decision to 'vet' prospective tenants was crucial in persuading the local authority to give special dispensation for this to happen. Both staff and residents supported the serious step of evicting tenants who had clearly breached their tenancy agreement as a last ditch measure to tackle an intolerable situation on this particular estate. They acknowledge the potential displacements issues this may raise, and feel good preventive work requires that vulnerable residents need support.

Residents lobbied for problems to be tackled, and the landlord took a lead in initiating the action. The landlord felt sure they could not have achieved this success without support from and action by residents. Residents are now setting up a Tenant Management Organization (resident control of the housing stock) to protect these improvements.

Examples of Additional Services and Facilities Provided Directly by Groups

A significant positive contribution of the community groups to social infra-structure is the development of additional services and facilities through the direct delivery of new provision.

Out of forty Gatsby groups, thirty-five had been able to develop their neigh-bourhoods by delivering and managing new and additional services and facili-ties. Of the other five Gatsby groups, two groups had tried and failed to set up new provision, and the other three played a lobbying role only. The new services and facilities include bread-and-butter projects such as play and youth provi-sion, as well as innovative projects concerned with keeping pace with a chang-ing world. Examples of the types of activities are: play schemes; after-school or homework clubs; cleared and landscaped green spaces; employment-linked projects such as a music recording studio and a 'telematics centre' which will provide accredited software and hardware I.T. training for residents; umbrella projects, such as a community house or centre providing a base for a multiple range of activities. One example of an umbrella project is a group in Yorkshire that developed and manages a community centre. The community centre is the venue for several new community groups on the estate such as the social service-run parents' group. It is also the base for several activities the group runs directly, the crèche, advice centre, youth group. The centre now houses the estate's first locally based housing manager, working to a new service-level agreement which has been recently negotiated with residents. The services and facilities have been judged successful on levels of demand and usage and proven operation.

Examples of the Contribution of Community Groups to the Social Organization of Neighbourhoods

Now we look at the evidence for the impact of community groups in improving social organization. We look at this in relation to the three elements of social organization: friendship networks and informal mutual aid; small voluntary groups, clubs and societies; and informal social controls operated via a set of commonly agreed norms and rules.

Friendship Networks and Informal Mutual Aid

Have the community groups been able to develop social contacts between resi-dents in their neighbourhoods, outside of the groups' own committee?

Twenty out of the forty Gatsby groups have successfully facilitated social events and social contact between residents and mutual-aid networks (other than between the core group of organizers). Eleven of these twenty groups provided opportunities for social contact solely through their youth provision. The other nine facilitated social contact between adults. These include one group which organizes well-attended trips, parties, and bingo, and another group which organizes video and supper evenings for older residents. One group is involved in organizing estate Open Days where residents can socialize, try out yoga, and eat food from around the world.

However, a significant minority of groups who hoped to persuade other residents to socialize found this difficult. Seven of the forty Gatsby groups specifically mentioned their disappointment at the lack of response to their efforts to organize social events. It is difficult to force people to be friends or get on. As we described earlier in this chapter, the existence of friendship networks is closely related to stability of residence (Young and Lemos 1997). Groups can create opportunities for social contact but it may be more difficult to engineer these networks than it is to develop a specific facility, for example. There are positive examples of other agencies facilitating contact between residents. This often happens via their children, with school as the focal point (Forrest and Kearns 1999). One primary school in one of the four 'break-down' neighbourhoods invited parents to come to a family workshop and work alongside their children at literacy and numeracy. This had the added benefit of giving parents a chance to meet each other. One go-ahead social landlord in Bradford, Manningham Housing Association, is experimenting with a 'mutual aid compact' signed by residents in the neighbourhood as part of their tenancy responsibilities.

Figure 12.6. *The multiple benefits of community groups*

Involvement in Informal Voluntary Groups, Clubs, and Societies

Where the groups are active project organizers, they produce multiple benefits. Firstly, the existence of the groups is in itself part of improved social organization. Secondly, half the Gatsby groups have spawned separate small groups in addition to their own, such as a majorettes troupe and a girls' club both run by daughters of the chairpeople of the original community groups. Thirdly, the majority of the groups' 'community' work is structured around specific projects, for example, a group of people running a community allotment producing chemical-free vegetables for sale, or a tool bank run by a small group which loans tools to members to maintain their homes and gardens. Most of the projects organized by the groups also form the additional services and facilities already discussed. Fourthly, developing and delivering these projects can also produce better and more frequent social interaction between the organizers and service-users as additional benefits. Fifthly, the groups are the vehicle for residents' attempts to enforce informal social controls. And finally, the groups can be the start point for linking into wider regeneration. Small voluntary groups are central to the development of the communities' contribution to social infrastructure.

Informal Social Controls, Common Norms, and Standards

Have the groups been able to enforce informal social control and re-establish norms and standards? Twenty-eight of the Gatsby groups have made proactive attempts to do this. These moves include:

- lobbying for action by public agencies on cleanliness and antisocial behaviour;
- performing estate clean-ups;
- developing enhanced facilities to raise the desirability of the area;
- action against rubbish dumping;
- tackling negative images of an area through the media;
- re-educating young people in discipline and social skills;
- providing positive male role models;
- promoting the idea of people taking responsibility for themselves, through things like healthy eating and responsible money management;
- highlighting the idea of collective responsibility for the neighbourhood and the people who live there.

A common theme in the groups' work is the need to care for the young and the old. Twenty-four of the Gatsby groups do work with young people, thirteen work with children, and eight with elderly residents. Youth work and additional supervision of young people is in itself potentially a way to enforce informal social controls over a key 'nuisance'. This can happen through building relationships and/or actual containment for short periods. Several groups described this role as being the 'eyes and ears' of the estate.

All these actions were a response by residents to noticeable changes in an area—both the behaviour of the people who live there, and the lack of care and attention paid to it by insiders and outsiders. They have chosen to try and create cultural change through leading by example, directly challenging unacceptable behaviours and their causes.

It is notoriously difficult for any agency to effect attitudinal and behavioural change. The mechanisms by which this happens are often unclear. We know that six of the twenty-four groups have made a positive impact; the success of the others was less clear. How have the groups managed this? One London group explained that the mechanisms they used were to get people to buy into a vision. They set new norms, and enforced them by rewarding good behaviour, not letting bad behaviour go unchallenged, and through modelling different behaviours for people in practice. They demonstrated examples in everyday life of helping each other, for example, babysitting, carrying people's shopping for them. The rewards included things like giving young people positions of responsibility and small amounts of paid work. In Wolverhampton, one group started negotiations with the police to set up a local office in the neighbourhood. People heard about the plans. Even before the police had agreed to the deal, some residents engaged in criminal activity had already expressed their intention to move out. Other potential new tenants came into the community office to ask if the plans were true as it would make them more likely to move in. In London, excluded pupils learnt how to help others, work in a team, and obey rules through taking part in challenging activities and sports. Another group achieved similar results with young people using outdoor pursuits in Walsall. This meant that the young people were more able to operate socially, an important factor in getting employment (Kleinman, West, and Sparkes 1998).

Several groups have worked to improve the physical fabric of the estates, for example by creating gardens, clearing dumped cars and mattresses, putting up fencing, and rebuilding derelict garages. This has given a strong signal to others that the area is worthy of commitment and things are improving. These groups have provided a series of before and after 'monitoring' photographs which show that rubbish dumping and vandalism has been considerably reduced in those public spaces, although in other areas more direct signals with sanctions are needed. One group successfully created the idea that residents take collective responsibility for each other and be proactive in protecting their community. This was demonstrated when a suspected stalker was spotted in nearby woods. Mothers on the estate then asked the group for help to make other parents aware of the need to supervise their children more closely. The police and housing manager, although sympathetic to the residents' concerns, were unable or unwilling to take action. Residents and professionals maintained a good relationship during the incident.

Sustainability

If the community groups are to play this role in developing the social infrastructure, are they sustainable? The Gatsby groups were on average eight years old, although 20 per cent had existed for over ten years.

These organizations are clearly sustainable on some level. There are two aspects to this: financial sustainability and organizational sustainability.

Community-led organizations with an asset base and clear revenue stream are the most likely to be financially sustainable in the longer term. Other larger community regeneration organizations, such as Community Development Trusts, settlements, and some intermediate labour market organizations have also developed good financial stability via endowments and trading (Thake 1995; Ward and Watson 1997).

Five of the Gatsby groups are tenant-management organizations (TMOs). TMOs do not take over ownership of capital assets and they remain agents of the local authority that owns the homes they manage. But, the formalized responsibilities and budgets that they assume provide them with other kinds of assets. These give TMOs power, legitimacy, and sustainability that most other community organizations do not have. These assets can then act as a base for developing activities beyond housing management. Only a tiny number of TMOs have ever ceased operation, all with the agreement of the residents involved.

Of the remainder of the Gatsby groups, none have either an asset base or substantial income-generating activities. Instead, they all rely on a mix of some discretionary public money (for example, running costs for residents' associations from the local authority or landlord) and on grants from charities. This makes the position of the smaller organizations more financially precarious, but not necessarily unsustainable. Generating income through the private market does not guarantee sustainability, there still has to be sufficient demand for whatever product and service you provide. Being dependent on discretionary grants means these organizations are also operating in a market of a different sort. As long as the groups can continue to sell themselves to funders, they can generate income. The smaller groups all work in this way, for example, out of twenty Gatsby groups which received time-limited revenue funding for specific pieces of work, fifteen had been able to continue their work after the end of the grant. Three of the groups that did not continue their projects felt happy that it had been a one-off piece of work. Of the projects that continued, two groups

Table 12.3. *Length of operation of Gatsby Project groups at the time of application for a Gatsby Project small grant*

Age of group	No. of groups
2 years and under	2
3–5 years	14
6–10 years	15
11–20 years	5
Over 20 years	3
Total	39

received grants of over £70,000 from other funders to continue the work they had piloted with the initial 'at risk' investment of under £5,000.

The other key aspect of the sustainability of community groups is organizational well-being. The majority of residents involved in managing or delivering work are volunteers in the groups studied. Newly created informal associations must build up structures and define roles from scratch. They lack some of the organizational infrastructures that make continuity more likely. The Gatsby groups often identify apathy and difficulties getting other residents engaged in active volunteer roles as key problems. Nearly all the Gatsby groups have seen considerable changes in membership since their inception, and despite failures of specific projects undertaken by the groups, all except one of the groups are still going.

Negative Impacts

Have the actions of the groups had any negative impacts? What are the negative unintended consequences of resident-led actions?

The negative impacts of the community groups' work have sometimes included stress for individuals involved, and antipathy and resentment from other residents. Thirteen of the groups mentioned a backlash from a minority of other residents or from other community organizations as a result of their work. At the extreme end, one group were nicknamed 'grassers' because of their work to tackle crime on the estate, and one member suffered criminal damage to his home as a result. Other groups did not provoke such a strong reaction, but found that other residents felt resentful because it was wrongly presumed that the active volunteers were receiving personal privileges as a result of their involvement. Some groups found that other residents' anger at system/authorities' failures became directed at the group as a result of their lobbying work. Others have found that their work has caused some jealousy or rivalry on the part of other residents or other community groups. Again, most groups were stoical about these reactions, as they anticipate a certain amount of competition or opposition as an understandable response to their work, particularly in disadvantaged areas. Many of the groups mentioned that their volunteer input was having a toll on their personal lives, although they also saw this as part of the 'job', similar to paid employment.

CONCLUSION

What does all this suggest for practitioners and policy-makers interested in regeneration? It suggests that community, in the sense of social infrastructure, is one component of neighbourhood viability. Accessible, good-quality services and facilities combined with social organization, help make places work. When the social infrastructure begins to unravel, as happened in some of the neighbourhoods we studied as they came under extreme social and economic pressures, facilities close, services enter crisis management, and anti-social behaviour escalates.

This is costly, in both human and financial terms. In areas of concentrated poverty, where the social infrastructure comes under greatest pressure, ways must be found to bolster it before it begins to unravel. We have demonstrated that community action can be an important part of such strengthening. Of course, small community groups cannot, by themselves, combat the effects of exclusionary forces like poverty, polarization, and depopulation. A fishing trip is just a fishing trip. But in acknowledging that social infrastructure is a crucial part of neighbourhood viability, we can begin to understand the value of community action.

Community groups can and often do: enable the formal infrastructure to work better by acting as brokers between statutory services and residents; contribute to the formal infrastructure by directly providing additional services and facilities; enhance social organization through their existence as a constituted group, the networks they foster, and the confidence they build to challenge harmful behaviour and strengthen shared norms and values.

In summary:

• Even where problems are too big for community action to tackle alone, community support can help protect other investments (by local and central government for example). Indeed, without it, those investments may be wasted.

• Service-providers, especially in deprived neighbourhoods, should recognize that residents can help them provide stronger management of neighbourhoods and should enforce the controls on behaviour open to them;

• Volunteers and community representatives should be recognized and supported;

• We need to develop new and better ways of measuring the impacts of community activity.

13

Does a Focus on 'Social Exclusion' Change the Policy Response?

JOHN HILLS

The earlier chapters of this book presented new evidence on the extent of social exclusion, the dynamics of incomes and earnings, intergenerational transmission of disadvantage, and area deprivation. Later ones looked in detail at some key policy areas related to this evidence: reducing child poverty; responses to unemployment, disability, and income security in old age; education; and the role of community, or 'social infrastructure'.

Having sliced what the Introduction described as the 'onion' of social exclusion in various ways, this kind of evidence raises a number of questions about policy in general. Does focusing on 'social exclusion' rather than simply on 'poverty' change the policy response? If one concentrates on groups liable to persistent or recurrent poverty, does that change the focus of action, compared to the groups in poverty which would be revealed by a cross-sectional snapshot? Does allowing for dynamics change the content of policy, for instance, through more emphasis on an 'active welfare state'? If so, are the bulk of activities of the welfare state—what one might call 'the day job'—affected? How much do the new insights available from analysis of longitudinal data actually change priorities? What does a focus on inclusion mean for the structure of social programmes, particularly their delivery systems, and for choices between 'universal' and 'targeted' benefits and services? Finally, what has been the impact of using the term been in practice in UK policy-making since 1997?

CONCEPTS OF 'SOCIAL EXCLUSION'

A problem with the first question about the focus of policy is that, as Chapter 1 explains, 'social exclusion' is itself a contested term. Until the late 1990s it was also an unfamiliar one in British political discourse. But that has all now changed, and the term is used frequently. But the new familiarity still leaves the danger of talking at cross-purposes, with the phrase being used in different ways. Different writers have used it to focus on different issues and causes, some stressing individual behaviour and values, some the role of institutions and state systems, and others wider constraints such as discrimination or lack of rights.

To recapitulate part of the earlier discussion, a first implication of using the term is that one should not simply look at cash incomes, but at a much wider range of indicators of deprivation or inability to participate in contemporary society (relating to the many rings of Figure 1.1 in the Introduction). It should be said immediately that by itself this is hardly new: the older phrase 'multiple deprivation' would cover much the same set of problems. Writers such as Townsend (1979) and Veit-Wilson (1998) stress the definition of a poverty line as a level of income below which people cannot fully participate in society in a range of ways as a result of their lack of resources.

In Chapter 3, Tania Burchardt, Julian Le Grand, and David Piachaud present data on four such dimensions: incomes or consumption; productive or socially valued activity; political engagement or involvement in collective decision-making; and social interaction. These, as they show, are related, and low incomes are very clearly important in non-participation in the other dimensions (Table 3.5). However, the different dimensions remain distinct, with the implication that they are better analysed separately, rather than lumped together in order, for instance, to define a single category of 'the socially excluded'.

This already suggests that policy may have to have regard to such dimensions separately, rather than assuming that improving outcomes on one will improve all. Simply being given cash, for instance, does not by itself make someone part of mainstream society. Indeed, completely different policies may be required altogether. For instance, allowing for age, people with lower incomes are less likely to vote than those with higher ones. But there may be much more direct strategies for trying to boost political participation than hoping that raising incomes would achieve this by itself.

Even the idea of participation through consumption activities raises some intriguing questions. In the three 'Breadline Britain' surveys (see Gordon *et al.* 2000, for the most recent) a key activity which the majority of respondents (representative of the whole population) believe no one should be so poor as to be unable to afford is a week's holiday away from home every year. In 1999, 18 per cent of the population said they could not afford one. This was the main item which the majority of adults saw as a necessity for children but which their parents were unable to afford. The conventional way of thinking about this is as a marker of poverty, and the response should thus simply be to raise incomes at the bottom, leaving people's choices undistorted as to what to do with their money. But if this is regarded as such an important aspect of participation in today's society, should we be acting more directly—for instance, by supporting opportunities for children at least to have some kind of time away from home? The balance between strategies is not obvious. In Sen's (1992) terms, should the focus be on ensuring the *capability* of taking a break away from home (which income by itself does not necessarily guarantee will happen) or on the *functioning* of actually taking the break?

Some writers interpret exclusion to mean *extreme* forms of multidimensional deprivation.[1] However, in this book we have not followed this kind of interpretation. Instead we have taken exclusion and inclusion to have two further implications. First, they widen the focus in another way—beyond individuals and households to communities and neighbourhoods (see Ruth Lupton and Anne Power's discussion in Chapter 8). Second, following Berghman (1995), what makes the notion of social exclusion distinct from deprivation is the implication that dynamics are involved, that the time horizon is wider.

Once again, as the Introduction stresses, this is hardly a new idea. Ever since Rowntree (1901), people have been concerned with changes in income over time and over the life cycle. However, as Simon Burgess and Carol Propper discuss in Chapter 4, with the emergence of panel data on the incomes of the same individuals in a sequence of years, poverty analysts have been able to look at income mobility and poverty dynamics in increasing detail. This was possible first in the USA but is now in Britain thanks to the British Household Panel Survey (BHPS) and across Europe thanks to the European Community Household Panel (ECHP).

Amongst other things, this kind of analysis has shown the importance of the duration of low incomes in affecting other measures of deprivation. As Nolan and Whelan (1996) point out, 'incorporating multidimensional measures of disadvantage into poverty measurement. . . . in effect force[s] one to make the shift to a dynamic analysis of processes.' In other words, the multidimensional and dynamic view which we have taken as being embodied by a focus on social exclusion is in their view simply what one should be taking anyway if one is trying to understand poverty properly. In these terms focusing on 'exclusion' would make little difference to policy—we should in any case already have been looking beyond cash and at dynamics.

However, the terminology may help nonetheless. Exclusion and its counterpart inclusion are words that draw attention to *processes*, and to a search for who or what is responsible for the excluding. They imply looking for what may—as John Hobcraft and Kathleen Kiernan's chapters have shown—be complex chains of association and influence or causation. Our chances of developing effective policies will be greater if we can improve our understanding of such processes. As Sen (2000: 44–5) concludes:

If . . . poverty is seen in terms of income deprivation only, then introducing the notion of social exclusion as part of poverty would vastly broaden the domain of poverty analysis. However, if poverty is seen as deprivation of basic capabilities, then there is no real expansion of the domain of coverage, but a very important pointer to a useful investigative focus . . . to the multidimensionality of deprivation and its focus on relational processes.

---

[1] For instance, Room (1999) suggests, 'we are speaking of people who are suffering such a degree of multidimensional disadvantage, of such duration, and reinforced by such material and cultural degradation of the neighbourhoods in which they live, that their relational links with the wider society are ruptured to a degree which is in some considerable degree irreversible.'

DOES ALLOWING FOR DYNAMICS CHANGE THE OBJECTIVES OF POLICY?

As discussed in the Introduction, exclusion and inclusion can reflect a dynamic sequence, in which what are 'outcomes' for an individual (or community) at one period become constraints on (or advantages for) them at the next. Concentrating first on incomes, what does the evidence of the kind reviewed by Simon Burgess and Carol Propper in Chapter 4 on dynamics tell us? Is anything different if we move the focus away from snapshot pictures of incomes at one moment to income over a longer period—perhaps even to look at incomes over people's whole lifetimes?

In some ways it is obvious that it is better to take a dynamic focus. Soon after leaving office, former welfare reform minister Frank Field (1998) described a static approach to analysing incomes as a way of understanding poverty as 'similar to insisting in the age of digital TV that the Brownie [camera] is the most accurate means to recording the actions, say of the contestants for the 100 metres Olympic medal'. But this analogy already hints that we should not get too carried away by new technology: the excitement of a 100 metres race and the way in which the winner emerged are indeed better captured on video; but when it comes to the *result* it is the 'freeze frame' static pictures of the winning moment which tell us most clearly who has won.

One advantage of the new data on income dynamics is that they can allow us to distinguish between the different circumstances in which people find themselves with low incomes and to look at incomes over a longer period. Low income may be a transitory phenomenon—a 'blip' in an otherwise satisfactory trajectory. Or it may be permanent, with someone's income below an acceptable level for year after year. But there is an intermediate and—in Britain, at least— substantial group of people for whom low income is *recurrent*. For instance, only 8 per cent of the BHPS sample were in the poorest fifth for all four of the years 1995–8, but a further 12 per cent were in the poorest fifth for three of the years and the next poorest fifth for the other one (DSS 2000, table 8.5). It is the existence of this group which means that it is a mistake to rush from observations that few people are remorselessly poor year after year to infer that poverty is not a major concern because it is only temporary. This may be true for some, but not for most of those seen as poor at any one moment. By the same token there are those who apparently have reasonable incomes in a snapshot, but this only represents a 'blip out' of a general period of low income. Putting this together, in earlier analysis of the first four years of data from the BHPS, Karen Gardiner and I suggest that the scale of the 'poverty problem' is only reduced slightly by discounting transitory observations of low income (Gardiner and Hills 1999).

Most low-income observations are in fact accounted for by those with low incomes over a longer period. As a corollary, the groups on which anti-poverty policy might focus change only a little if one looks at a longer time period.

Table 13.1 shows what proportion of 'low income' is accounted for by various groups taking either a short or longer-term focus. The picture does change. For instance, couples without children account for a tenth of the poorest 30 per cent at any one time, but only a twentieth of those with 'persistent' low income. A disproportionately large share of persistent low income is accounted for by lone parents and their children, pensioners (particularly single pensioners), social tenants, and people in workless households. However, these are groups on which one might focus anyway, even if one only had the static data shown in the middle column. In some circumstances panel data could transform our priorities. In this case, they improve the evidence available, and show that the problems faced by these groups are even more acute, but they only modify the conclusion slightly.

There is even a danger in putting too much emphasis on duration. If it was intended to focus help only on the 'really poor'—for whom low income is not transitory—one way would be to delay. Cash benefits might be restricted to those who could show that they had been in need over a substantial period. This would reduce the chances of making the 'error' of helping someone who, in these terms, didn't need it. But as most of those poor at one moment do in fact have low incomes measured over a longer period, this would be at the cost of making

Table 13.1. *Characteristics of those with low and persistently low income, 1995–1998*

	% of whole population	% of poorest 30% at any one time	% with persistently low income[1]
By family type			
Couple with children	36	35	33
Couple without children	21	10	5
Single with children	7	13	15
Single without children	16	12	7
Pensioner couple	10	13	17
Single pensioner	10	17	21
By tenure			
Owner-occupied	69	48	43
Social rented	22	41	48
Private rented	8	10	8
By economic status			
Fully employed	29	7	6
Partially employed	25	21	15
Workless	14	34	37
Pensioner	17	27	35
Self-employed	15	11	6

[1] In poorest 30% for at least three out of four years (including first) and in poorest 40% in remaining year.

Source: DSS (2000*b*), table 8.8 (based on BHPS data).

many of a different kind of error—denying help for a time to those who did need it, even on this test. Further, as Burgess and Propper show, *being* poor increases the risk of being *persistently* poor, so even if the major target of policy was persistent poverty, it would still make sense to attack the problems of all those who are poor without waiting.

FOUR KINDS OF INTERVENTION

So understanding income dynamics does not necessarily change much the scale of the problem, or even the identification of the groups which might need help. But in designing welfare institutions it does allow differentiation of the *kind* of intervention for those in particular circumstances. Here it may be helpful to differentiate between policies which are about changing the *risks* of adverse events taking place and those which are about ameliorating their *effects*. This is often thought of as being a contrast between 'prevention' and 'response'— between policies which, for instance, attempt to equalize opportunities *ex ante*, and those which attempt to equalize outcomes *ex post*. In the terms of the framework discussed in the Introduction, prevention can be seen as focusing on the constraints people face, and response on the outcomes at different stages.

Much recent literature stresses a contrast between a 'traditional' welfare state concerned with the latter, and an 'active' welfare state with the former, with a presumption that the active route is superior. Thus, for the Commission on Social Justice, which examined welfare policy while Labour was in opposition,

The intelligent welfare state prevents poverty as well as relieving it, above all through public services which enable people to learn, earn and save.

(Commission on Social Justice 1994: 223).

Reflecting on their analysis of longitudinal data on social assistance recipients in Germany, Lutz Leisering and Stephan Leibfried conclude that,

The time dimension of poverty and Social Assistance . . . suggests the need to reconceptualise anti-poverty policy as *life course policy* [and to focus] on paths out of Social Assistance, rather than just administering care and paying benefits   (1999: 258).

Anthony Giddens puts it more strongly in his description of 'the third way':

We should speak today of *positive welfare* . . . in place of the welfare state we should put the *social investment state* operating in the context of a positive welfare society.

(Giddens 1998: 117)

This theme was picked up by the Labour Government's welfare reform Green Paper, although rather more in terms of adding to existing policies than replacing them:

Where appropriate, the welfare state should be proactive, preventing poverty by ensuring that people have the right education, training and support to make provision for themselves. But where there is poverty, the new welfare system must extend the exits from welfare dependency.   (DSS 1998: 20)

Some caution is needed in making these distinctions. First, there are many circumstances where prevention is better than cure, with vaccination against infectious diseases often given as the archetype. However, without any way of identifying high-risk groups, prevention can be an expensive strategy by comparison with coping with problems as they arise. In retrospect, the British strategy of trying to fix all computer software in advance to pre-empt the 'Millennium Bug' seems to have been quite a costly one, given the lack of major problems in countries which had been less active in prevention (although with a previously unexperienced event this was hard to foresee). As Martin Evans points out in Chapter 10, early high-cost intervention with unemployed people can waste resources on those who would have got jobs quickly in any case.

Second, the 'traditional' welfare state has never been simply a matter of paying out compensation unconditional on behaviour. Unemployment benefits have always had conditions like those of 'actively seeking work', for instance (King 1995), and part of Beveridge's case for assuming that social security would be underpinned by a National Health Service was its role as a 'gigantic service and refuelling station for the nation's labour market' (Harris 1994: 32) to return workers to work as quickly as possible after sickness or injury.

Nonetheless, there is a useful distinction here, and one which can be extended further by drawing on the income dynamics literature to make a distinction between the way in which policy affects those *entering* an undesirable state and those *exiting* from it. Figure 13.1 summarizes this, suggesting that we can differentiate between four kinds of policy:

- *Prevention* of an event or reduction of the risk of entering an undesirable state—for instance, education or training to improve job retention.
- *Promotion* of exit or escape—for instance, 'welfare-to-work' policies.
- *Protection* from the impact of an event, for instance paying benefits to those who become unemployed.
- *Propulsion* away from adverse circumstances by reinforcing the benefits of exit—for instance, the effects of the in-work benefits on the incomes of those leaving unemployment or policies to ensure that the next career move is upwards.

The first two of these are the 'active' parts of the welfare state stressed by the quotations above, affecting the *risks* of adverse or favourable events (something

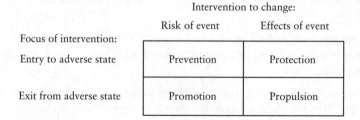

Figure 13.1. *Four forms of intervention*

which may be missed by static analysis). The third and fourth are more about what is sometimes seen as 'passive' redistribution, changing the *consequences* of such events.

Longitudinal data help to highlight which of the four quadrants of Figure 13.1 may be of greatest importance for particular groups. For instance Jenkins and Schluter (2001) use panel data to examine the reasons why child poverty rates (measured in relation to national average incomes) were so much higher in the period 1991 to 1998 in the UK (30 per cent) than in Western Germany (19 per cent). The annual rate of entry into poverty was higher in Britain (11 per cent) than in Germany (7 per cent), but as important a driver was the slower *exit* rate from poverty in the UK (25 compared to 36 per cent in Germany).

Looking at the reasons for this in more detail, they find important differences in whether changes in earnings are associated with exits from poverty. For children in initially poor married-couple households, a year after these gained one or more full-time workers, 63 per cent of the German children but only 52 per cent of the British children were no longer poor (Jenkins and Schluter 2001, table 3). For similar households where the number of workers stayed the same, but earnings rose by a fifth or more, 57 per cent of German children but only 36 per cent of British children were no longer poor. This kind of evidence suggests that policy in the UK does indeed need to focus not just on helping people back into work, but also on the 'propulsion' effect, boosting the incomes of those who get work to ensure that they do actually exit from poverty.

In reality, policies often combine elements of each of the four parts of Figure 13.1, and it may be misleading to concentrate on just one role. For instance, the Working Families Tax Credit (WFTC) is put forward as part of the Government's 'welfare-to-work strategy' with emphasis on its effects in promoting the chances of exits from unemployment. It should achieve this. External analysis based on past labour-supply behaviour suggests that its increased generosity compared to Family Credit may increase aggregate employment by around 30,000 (Blundell and Reed 1999). This is welcome, but small by comparison with the more straightforward 'propulsion' effect of the WFTC, boosting the incomes of those who would have been in work (albeit low-paid) anyway. As David Piachaud and Holly Sutherland showed in Chapter 9, this contributes substantially to the way in which recent tax and benefit changes should lift more than one million children above a poverty line of half average income (see also Hills 2000*a*).

By the same token it can be dangerous to oversell the potential impact of 'active' measures as a complete solution, if this leaves the impression that protective measures or redistribution will no longer be needed. As Hasluck, McKnight, and Elias (2000) show, the voluntary employment advice offered by the New Deal for Lone Parents appears to have had the net effect of reducing the stock of lone parents claiming Income Support by a little over 3 percentage points after 18 months below what it would otherwise have been. For a low cost, voluntary intervention this is not unimpressive and compares well with other schemes of this kind (Gardiner 1997). Even the best-known success story of US welfare-to-work experiments, the compulsory and far more intensive GAIN programme in Riverside, California, only had a net effect of 14 percentage points in numbers employed at any time in the third year after the intervention (Riccio *et al*. 1994, table 2).

Although these are useful effects to build on, they hardly eliminate the need for 'passive' compensation through benefit payments to those who remain without work. What is more plausible is that policies representing all four of the quadrants of Figure 13.1 are required to make a successful assault on poverty, and that it is worth looking for policies to fill the gaps where they are missing. Thus Tania Burchardt's analysis of policies towards disability and the labour market in Chapter 10 identifies a range of strategies aimed at income protection for those who lose their jobs through the onset of disability, such as Incapacity Benefit, but also others aimed at 'propulsion' through reinforcement of living standards of those who gain work, such as the Disability Working Allowance. Action on the prevention-of-entry/promotion-of-exit axis has been more patchy. The Disability Discrimination Act (and the ineffective 'quota system' for employment before it) can be seen as a regulatory attempt to prevent impairments leading to loss of work, and the New Deal for Disabled People is an attempt to promote exit from unemployment, but it is too early to judge their effects. What is clear is that an important contributor to the low-employment rates of disabled people is the rapid rate of exit from employment on onset of disability (Burchardt 2000). More, she argues, needs to be done to find ways to help people who become impaired to retain their jobs—and for employers to retain their workers, in other words a more active prevention strategy.

Dynamic analysis also highlights the complexity of the transitions with which we can be dealing and which policy may affect. Figure 13.1 concentrates on a single move between 'unemployment' and 'employment'. But for working-age couples, there is a much richer set of possibilities, as illustrated in Figure 13.2, as they can move between having no, one, or two earners. The figure illustrates the six possible changes between these states (even this is a simplification, as there may be important differences depending on which partner is the single earner). Thinking about the impact of in-work benefits like the Working Families Tax

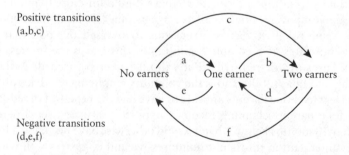

Figure 13.2. *Transitions in number of earners for couples*

Credit, it is the positive incentive towards the transition labelled 'a', from no to one earner, which is often stressed. But its impact on the other five transitions may also be important. For instance, the income 'tapers' used in calculating the credit may act as a disincentive for a second partner to take work, potentially reducing the chances of the transitions to having two earners. This may offset some of its effects in promoting work.

However, analysis of the WFTC's predecessor, Family Credit, suggests that we may also need to examine what is happening to the negative transitions in the lower part of the diagram. Marsh and McKay (1993) suggest that Family Credit had what they called a 'parachute' effect, allowing couples to reduce from two to one earner rather than dropping down immediately to no earners as the incentives in Income Support by itself might have implied (making transition 'd' from two or one earner more likely and transition 'f' down to no earners less so). In turn this made a later move back to having two earners more likely than it would have been if both partners ended up out of work and on Income Support.

This last point is an example of another benefit of dynamic analysis. By focusing attention on trajectories over several periods it can suggest more sophisticated methods of intervention. Much of 'welfare-to-work' policy has focused on the initial transition, from unemployment to work. But the kind of analysis which has shown the extent of the 'low-pay, no-pay cycle' discussed by Abigail McKnight in Chapter 7 suggests that we also need to think much more about *subsequent* transitions, and of ways of trying to help people whose jobs are precarious to move on into better work, rather than to drop back into unemployment. Agencies need to think about the 'aftercare' of their clients, rather than counting them as a finished case once they have a job.

LONGER-TERM STRATEGIES

More generally, a focus on preventive strategies can be helped by identifying factors which have *persistent* effects on the risk of adverse later outcomes. Policies can perhaps be divided into two:

1. Those which change individual *characteristics* in a way which lasts, such as education or training;
2. But also, if there is 'initial state dependence' in the system—that is, if where one starts matters—changing the right elements of people's *initial state* has long-term effects.

In Chapter 11, Jo Sparkes and Howard Glennerster suggested that the links between education and social exclusion are not just associations, but are causal, and have become stronger over time. Poor basic skills in particular, they argue, now have a devastating effect on people's chances of employment or gaining a reasonable income. Further, poor basic skills are linked to poor health, lack of involvement on public life or voting, offending, young parenthood, and mental illness. In other words, remedying poor basic skills both for children and adults has to be a priority in tackling several of the dimensions of exclusion, not just economic ones.

But tackling 'initial state dependence' may be equally important. Gregg (2000) has shown that unemployment early in people's working lives appears to have a 'scarring' effect, increasing the chances of later unemployment, even if other characteristics are the same. Within the cohort born in 1958, and controlling for a range of background characteristics, an extra two months of youth unemployment (before 23) for men was associated with an extra month of unemployment between 24 and 33. Burgess *et al.* (1999), looking at those who left school in the recession of 1981, suggest that this kind of effect can persist for up to 18 years, but in this case for low-skilled individuals only.[2] On this basis it makes sense to put particular efforts into tackling youth unemployment. At the other end of working lives, there is a cycle of low skills leading to early retirement (Campbell 1999), leading in turn to low income in retirement.

John Hobcraft, Kathleen Kiernan, and Abigail McKnight's analyses of birth cohort data in Chapters 5, 6, and 7 offer wider insights into the states or characteristics associated with poorer outcomes later in life. For example, indications of child poverty are associated with a range of poorer adult outcomes, even controlling for the factors like parental education and social class which lead to low parental income in the first place. What may look like a short-term strategy of simply improving the incomes of parents through 'protective' cash benefits may therefore turn out in the longer term to be a 'preventive' strategy for the next generation. As we have stressed above, the outcomes at one time shape the constraints at the next. A focus on the long term may thus *reinforce* the case for action on short-term problems, rather than necessarily changing the nature of the intervention.

Hobcraft and Kiernan's analysis also illustrates the complexity of the relationships between early events and later outcomes. First, none of the associations they show are deterministic: high scores on risk factors in childhood increase the odds of adverse outcomes later in life, but do not make them inevitable. As with what we now know about income dynamics, there is little evidence in the UK for a permanently excluded 'underclass', doomed from childhood, a conclusion reinforced by the evidence presented in Chapter 3. What there is, however, is evidence of groups whose life chances are much less favourable than others. For instance, teenage motherhood substantially increases the chances of the resultant family living in poorer social and economic circumstances even fifteen years later on.

Second, we have to be very careful with which of these links are causal. As Kathleen Kiernan's chapter shows, both experiencing parental separation or divorce as a child and living in a cohabiting rather than married partnership with children are associated with later poorer outcomes on several indicators.

---

[2] In earlier work based on work history data, Gallie, Marsh, and Vogler (1994) similarly showed initially large effects of previous unemployment on current unemployment, but that these decayed over time.

But lone parenthood and cohabitation are themselves associated with other unfavourable earlier characteristics, and controlling for these, some of the associations between parental separation or cohabitation and negative later outcomes become smaller or insignificant.

Similarly, John Hobcraft's analysis (see Figures 5.1 and 5.2) shows strong associations between living in social housing at age 33 and a wide range of adverse outcomes by that age. But this does not tell us is which is cause and which effect (or indeed if there is an unobserved factor driving them all). It could be the result simply of social housing acting as a 'net', catching through its eligibility criteria those most at risk of exclusion in different respects without actually changing those risks. However, there might also be aspects of the way social housing is run, financed, and located (some of which were touched on in Ruth Lupton and Anne Power in Chapter 8) which have made it a trap for some, actually increasing risks of exclusion. Research strategies which differentiated between these two possibilities would be very valuable. Until we have them we have to be a little cautious about rushing to policy conclusions.

WHAT DOES A FOCUS ON INCLUSION MEAN FOR THE STRUCTURE OF SOCIAL PROGRAMMES?

Taking a dynamic perspective may lead to rather more emphasis on some policies than others, even if it does not change them entirely. But does the notion of 'participation' or 'inclusion' lead to any differences in policy? Much of what the welfare state does is about cross-sectional redistribution, and about redistribution across the life cycle (Hills 1997; Falkingham and Hills 1995). It has other aims as well—in particular providing an efficient way of meeting particular needs where the competitive private alternative would be less efficient and more expensive even to the average citizen, let alone poorer ones (Barr 1998; Burchardt and Hills 1997).

If these were the only aims, the *method* of delivery might not matter. For instance, Figure 13.3 (a) shows the stylized effects on income distribution of a 'universal' benefit (such as Child Benefit, or in some senses, the NHS) paid for through a constant tax rate on all gross income. Allowing for the benefit and for tax, net income starts above gross income for the poorest, but ends up below it for the richest. Figure 13.3 (b) shows what is sometimes thought of as the polar opposite of this kind of system: a means-tested benefit paid only to the relatively poor and withdrawn as gross income rises, paid for by tax only on those with too high an income to receive the benefit.

As the diagrams are drawn—with the means-testing withdrawal rate equal to the tax rate—the two systems in fact have an identical distributional effect. In terms purely of cross-sectional inequality there is nothing to choose between them. But in terms of the way people, particularly poor people, are treated—and hence of the 'inclusiveness' of welfare systems or of 'social solidarity' as discussed by Brian Barry in Chapter 2—there may well be very great differences. Systems

John Hills

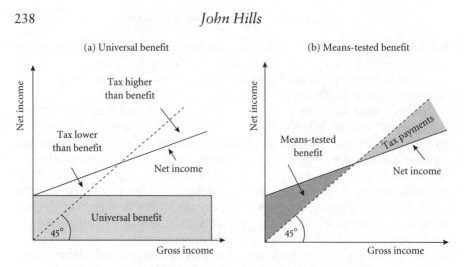

Figure 13.3. *Distributional effects of different social security systems*

designed only for the poor may indeed become 'poor services', while services of no relevance to powerful groups may lose out in the competition for resources.

The figure shows a stylized example, but the lesson that the design of public systems may have effects going beyond the purely distributional is a more general one for the choices made between welfare systems (or more widely for comparisons between countries' welfare 'regimes').

In earlier research, we looked at the way in which the shapes of the boundaries between public and private sectors in welfare activity have developed over time (Burchardt, Hills, and Propper 1999). We found great differences between welfare sectors such as health, education, income maintenance, and housing in the balance of roles which the public and private sectors play in terms of who provides the service, who pays for it, and who decides what services people receive. These differences reflect in part the nature of the service being provided, as well as different ways of achieving similar distributional effects. But the nature of what the private sector does and who uses it also reflects the structure of the public service.

The way people can—or cannot—combine state and private services has implications for the ways in which different parts of society experience the state and decide on what services they receive, including whether those with the highest incomes end up 'socially isolating' themselves in the way Brian Barry discusses in Chapter 2. For services such as the NHS or the basic state pension, everyone is in contact with the state system, even if they add to it privately. In other cases, it is hard to use both at the same time—as with housing or for the core parts of state schooling. In the case of schooling, state provision is extensive enough that only a minority isolate themselves from the majority by 'going private' completely and paying the full cost themselves. But where the level of state provision is restricted, or is well below what people would choose for themselves, it is the other way round: the state provides assistance which may be highly effective in terms of redistribution, but the recipients of those services are put in a very different position from the rest of society. In housing, the majority makes a trade-off between costs and the location or physical quality of what they buy or rent, while the minority is allocated housing of a restricted kind, without any similar choice between cost, location, and physical quality. Particularly where, as in the UK, social housing has been built in large estates, what may look like efficient 'targeting' on distributional grounds may have the side effect of increasing exclusion, both geographically and in terms of the choices people can make about their lives.

As Anne Power and Ruth Lupton showed in Chapter 8 (Figure 8.1), while 3 per cent of electoral wards nationally fall into their classification of 'poverty wards' (with both high worklessness and deprivation indicators in 1991), 87 per cent of wards with over 70 per cent of social housing come into this group. In their chapter they outline some of the potential cumulative impact of area concentrations of poverty, exacerbating the difficulties of those living within them. Again, strategies for coping with these kind of problems can be divided between the quadrants shown in Figure 13.2. 'Protective' strategies in this case would mean additional resources for areas with concentrated problems—the recent proliferation of 'zones', the New Deal for Communities and the SEU's strategy for neighbourhood renewal can be seen as measures of this kind. So would be attempts to improve the 'social infrastructure' of the kind described by Liz Richardson and Katherine Mumford in Chapter 12. Some of these strategies may succeed in promoting exit from neighbourhood problems. But it is also important to think of active 'preventive' policies to avoid neighbourhood polarization—for instance, avoiding allocations policies for social housing which result in only those in greatest need being housed in a particular area—and promotion of a social mix where it has been lost, such as breaking up areas of purely social housing through sales or market renting, while at the same time acquiring or building social housing within less-deprived areas (Hills 2000*b*; 2001).

Looking beyond just the provision of services *to* the residents of deprived areas, another aspect of an emphasis on inclusion is to ask who it is that provides such services. In recent research for the Department of the Environment, Transport and the Regions, Glen Bramley, Martin Evans, and colleagues (1998) showed that it was possible to allocate the benefits of most elements of public spending on a ward-by-ward basis, using the examples of Liverpool, Nottingham, and the London Borough of Brent. This showed that spending for many public services *is* higher for more deprived wards than others, even without any special 'bending' of the programmes. The sheer volume of 'main programme' spending by government on behalf of the inhabitants of even—or perhaps especially—the poorest wards in the country can be considerable: more than £6,000 per head in some wards in 1995–6. The words 'on behalf of' are used advisedly. This spending undoubtedly benefits residents in crucial ways like providing income to live on and access to health care. But what is remarkable is that so little of it shows in terms of spin-off jobs on the ground for the communities who benefit from it. In theory, £6,000 per head could support a part-time job for every household in the ward, in shops, health clinics, schools, housing repairs, and so on. Self-evidently, most of those jobs do not go to local residents. When thinking therefore about the potential for 'bending' main programmes in favour of neighbourhoods with additional problems, it is not just a matter of changing the level of spending. It is also about trying to work out what jobs that spending creates, what skills those jobs require, what is available from the local community, and what needs to be done to bridge the gap between them.

Going further, one of the issues highlighted by the debate around social exclusion has been that of 'agency', that it is not just people's situation, but the extent to which people feel themselves able to realize their objectives as a result of their own decisions (Atkinson 1998). For social programmes this raises the issue touched on in Chapter 12 of who controls budgets—residents or government agencies—and whether 'beneficiaries' have any role in decision-making.

BUT IN PRACTICE . . . ?

All of this suggest that a focus on 'social exclusion' *can*, indeed, change the ways in which we think about policy and hence the responses to poverty, deprivation, and disadvantage. Whether it does so *in practice*, is another question. Here we do, however, have a practical example. As we pointed out at the start of the book, in the UK the Blair Government in its first term from 1997 to 2001 adopted the language of social exclusion, set up a special Social Exclusion Unit, and decided to produce an annual report on poverty and social exclusion. For some, this was at best a meaningless change of language, at worst a potentially damaging one. One can identify three potential reasons for such reservations:

• First, following the example of the European Commission in the 1980s when required to appease the Thatcher Government in Britain and the Kohl Government in Germany, 'social exclusion' was simply being used to allow the development of anti-poverty policies without actually using the word 'poverty'.

• More dangerously, the language was a way of diverting attention towards softer and fuzzier issues and away from more difficult—and more expensive to tackle—issues of straightforward material deprivation, lack of income, and redistribution.

• Alternatively, the word was simply a different kind of code, in this case for bringing in the emphasis on personal responsibility and policy agenda of workfare implied by the US debate on the 'underclass'—what Ruth Levitas (1998) refers to as the 'moral underclass debate' ('MUD'). At its extreme, this discourse condemns the victims of exclusion as deserving of their fate.

At times, and in the mouths of different politicians, there has been some truth in each of these three propositions. But looking at the period as a whole, they would be an unfair characterization of actual policy.

First—and in contrast to pre-1997 governments—the Blair Government has explicitly talked about poverty as well as about social exclusion. Most notably, Tony Blair pledged to eliminate 'child poverty' over twenty years, and the subsequent targets for its reduction by a quarter by 2004 were set in explicitly relative terms. There has been no avoidance of talking about 'poverty' as a problem in Britain.

Second, it is true that the work of the Social Exclusion Unit itself has not been concerned with income poverty per se, but with related issues such as area deprivation, school truancy and exclusions, street homelessness, and teenage pregnancy. If this had been the only focus on poverty, the second criticism would hold. It is also true that there has been no use of the language of 'redistribution', and the repeated pledges to limit rates of income tax have limited the scope for it in practice: there has been little sign of concern about the 'social isolation' of the privileged discussed by Brian Barry in Chapter 2. However, as David Piachaud and Holly Sutherland analysed in Chapter 9, there have been changes in tax and social security policy which will have substantial direct effects on the cash incomes of those at the bottom of the distribution, particularly families with children. Effectively, much of the funding for this has come from the top of the distribution, through changes in pension taxation and the effects of 'fiscal drag'. These changes may not have been introduced as quickly or as transparently as some would have liked, but it is certainly untrue that the official social exclusion agenda has been used to disguise lack of any action on cash poverty.

While there have been times when 'inclusion' has been discussed as if it solely consisted of participation in paid work, government action has clearly not treated social exclusion as the deserved and inevitable fate of an underclass. Through emphasis on the New Deal, the national minimum wage and the introduction of the Working Families Tax Credit, government rhetoric has certainly stressed the work-based aspects of policy. In this, the government has followed public opinion, which favours increases in many social security benefits, but not those for the unemployed, the majority believing instead that the government should guarantee a job for all who want one (Hills and Lelkes 1999). However, behind this pro-work rhetoric—indeed at times using it as a shield—there has been more going on, notably the substantial increases in the rates of Income Support for families with children aged under 11 which drive an important part of the projected reduction in child poverty discussed in Chapter 9. There are, of course, dangers in this, and in the potential failure to build a constituency for what is being done. But again, it is hard to sustain an argument that recent UK policy has been based on the idea of solely personal responsibility for poverty and deprivation and there being no role for the state.

CONCLUSION

Earlier chapters have illustrated the kind of analysis which can be drawn from the rich longitudinal data now available to researchers and policy-makers. This chapter has suggested that this kind of analysis allows more sophisticated policy design than might have been possible in the past. But at the same time it has urged some caution in assuming that this new knowledge will completely transform policy responses.

One of the advantages of focusing on the previously unfamiliar concept of 'social exclusion' is that it draws attention to aspects of deprivation which go beyond cash and material living standards, and in particular to the dynamic processes involved in exclusion and inclusion. It can, of course, be argued that we should already have been focusing on these anyway in terms of anti-poverty policy, but the term helps to emphasize that this is what we should be doing.

Second, new data on income dynamics and mobility do affect the way we understand the incidence of low income, and particularly the differences between those with permanent, recurrent, and transitory low incomes. However, they do not necessarily completely transform either the scale of the problems involved, or our picture of which groups are most at risk. Rather they allow differentiation between people's circumstances and refinement of policy.

Third, alongside a more sophisticated understanding of the dynamics of modern society, policy interest has grown in an 'active' welfare state, intended to change some of those dynamics, as opposed to the previous supposedly 'passive' welfare state, concentrating on income compensation for those who lose out for some reason. But this chapter has argued that these two ideas are not alternatives. The 'old' welfare state was never entirely passive, and there is little evidence that active policies remove the need for old forms of social protection. Nor are 'preventive' strategies automatically superior to responsive ones. Instead, it is helpful to think of policies as straddling two kinds of intervention: those concerned with changing the risk or chances of particular *events*, and those with the *effects* of such events. Further they can be differentiated between those concerned with *entry* to adverse circumstances, and those with *exits* from them. This gives four categories of intervention, described here as prevention, promotion, protection, and propulsion. A possible test of policy is whether it is acting across all four of these categories.

Fourth, an implication of the kind of analysis presented in earlier chapters is that there may be high returns to the identification of key events or characteristics which have long-term adverse effects—outcomes which become later constraints. However, even if this can be done, it does not necessarily change the policy response. The evidence suggests that tackling child poverty is both a protective strategy for the current generation *and* a preventive strategy for the next. This reinforces the case for tackling it now, such as the tax and benefit changes analysed in Chapter 9, rather than suggesting something completely different. In other cases it is hard to disentangle the causalities involved in the associations between early and later life events, and caution is needed before rushing to assume that changing one part of early lives will still have the same association with later outcomes.

Fifth, this chapter has looked at the ways in which an emphasis on inclusion or participation may affect our assessment of policy interventions, singling out the issues around social housing and area polarization as an example of where policies to promote inclusion in one dimension may have had the opposite effect in others. An emphasis on inclusiveness may not change the objectives of policy, but it may well change our view of the instruments which are most appropriate.

Finally, in practice, the emergence of the language of exclusion and inclusion into the UK policy debate since the late 1990s, has, at least, not damaged more traditional concerns. In the most optimistic interpretation, embracing both an anti-poverty and anti-exclusion agenda has led to a much richer policy mix, with a much greater chance of long-run success. In developing such policies—and in identifying where they fall short—we hope that the kind of analysis presented in this book will, through its contribution to improving our understanding of social exclusion, have a useful role to play.

References

Abel-Smith, B. and Townsend, P. (1965), *The Poor and the Poorest*. London: Bell.

Abrahamson, P. and Hansen, F. (1996), *Poverty in the European Union*, Report to the European Parliament. Roskilde, Denmark: Centre for Alternative Social Analysis, Roskilde University.

Arulampamlam, W. and Stewart, M. B. (1995), 'The Determinants of Individual Unemployment Duration in an Era of High Unemployment', *Economic Journal*, 105: 321–32.

Askonas, P. and Stewart, A. (eds.) (2000), *Social Inclusion: Possibilities and Tensions*. Basingstoke: Macmillan.

Atkinson, A. B. (1998), 'Social Exclusion, Poverty and Unemployment', in A. B. Atkinson and J. Hills (eds.), *Exclusion, Employment and Opportunity*, CASEpaper 4. London: London School of Economics.

——and Micklewright, J. (1989), 'Turning the Screw: Benefits for the Unemployed 1979–1988', in A. Dilnot and I. Walker (eds.), *The Economics of Social Security*. Oxford: Oxford University Press.

Bane, M. J. and Ellwood, D. T. (1986), 'Slipping Into and Out of Poverty: The Dynamics of Spells', *Journal of Human Resources*, 21: 1–23.

————(1994), *Welfare Realities: From Rhetoric to Reform*. Cambridge, Mass: Harvard University Press.

Barnes, C., Mercer, G., and Shakespeare, T. (1999), *Exploring Disability: A Sociological Introduction*. Cambridge: Polity Press.

Barr, N. (1998), *The Economics of the Welfare State* (3rd edn.). Oxford: Oxford University Press.

Barry, B. (2001), *Culture and Equality*. Cambridge: Polity Press.

Baumgartner, M. (1988), *The Moral Order of the Suburb*. New York: Oxford University Press.

Berghman, J. (1995), 'Social Exclusion in Europe: Policy Context and Analytical Framework', in G. Room (ed.), *Beyond the Threshold*. Bristol: Policy Press.

Berthoud, R. (1998), *Disability Benefits: A Review of the Issues and Options for Reform*. York: York Publishing Services.

——Lakey, J., and McKay, S. (1993), *The Economic Problems of Disabled People*. London: Policy Studies Institute.

Biehal, N., Claydon, J., Stein, M., and Wade, J. (1992), *Prepared for Living? A Survey of Young People Leaving the Care of Local Authorities*. London: National Children's Bureau.

Blakely, E. J. and Snyder, G. (1997), *Fortress America: Gated Communities in the United States*. Washington: Brookings Institution Press.

Blundell, R. and Reed, H. (1999), *The Employment Effects of the Working Families Tax Credit*, Briefing Note 6/99. London: Institute for Fiscal Studies.

——Duncan, A., McCrae, J., and Meghir, C. (2000), 'The Labour Market Impact of the Working Families Tax Credit', *Fiscal Studies*, 21/1: 75–104.

Bosworth, D. (1994), 'Truancy and Pupil Performance', *Education Economics*, 2/3: 243–63.

Bowman, H., Burden, T., and Konrad, J. (2000), *Attitudes to Adult Education in Disadvantaged Areas*. York: Joseph Rowntree Foundation.

Bradbury, B. and Jantti, M. (1999), *Child Poverty Across Industrialised Nations*, Innocenti Occasional Papers, EPS 1971. Florence: UNICEF.

Bradshaw, J., Kennedy, S., Kilkey, M., Hutton, S., Corden, A., Eardley, T., Holmes, H., and Neale, J. (1996), *The Employment of Lone Parents: A Comparison of Policy in Twenty Countries*. London: Family Policy Studies Centre.

Bramley, G., Evans, M., Atkins, J. *et al.* (1998), *Where Does Public Spending Go? Pilot Study to Analyse the Flows of Public Expenditure into Local Areas*. London: DETR.

Brooks, G., Gorman, T., Harman, J., Hutchinson, D., and Wilkin, A. (1998), *Family Literacy Works*. London: Basic Skills Agency.

Brown, G. (1999), 'A Scar on the Nation's Soul', *Poverty*, 104.

Burchardt, T. (1999), *The Evolution of Disability Benefits in the UK: Re-weighting the Basket*, CASEpaper 26. London: London School of Economics.

——(2000*a*), 'Social Exclusion: Concepts and Evidence', in D. Gordon and P. Townsend (eds.), *Breadline Britain: The Measurement of Poverty*. Bristol: Policy Press.

——(2000*b*), *Enduring Economic Exclusion: Disabled People, Income and Work*. York: York Publishing Services.

——and Hills, J. (1997), *Private Welfare Insurance and Social Security: Pushing the Boundaries*. York: Joseph Rowntree Foundation.

————and Propper, C. (1999), *Private Welfare and Public Policy*. York: Joseph Rowntree Foundation.

——Le Grand, J., and Piachaud, D. (1999), 'Social Exclusion in Britain 1991–1995', *Social Policy and Administration*, 33/3: 227–44.

Burgess, S. M. and Propper, C. (1997), 'Young Americans and Poverty 1979–91', in P. Gregg (ed.), *Jobs, Wages and Poverty: Patterns of Persistence and Mobility in the New Flexible Labour Market*. London: Centre for Economic Performance, London School of Economics.

————(1998), *An Economic Model of Household Income Dynamics, with an Application to Poverty Dynamics among American Women*. CEPR Discussion Paper No. 1830. London: CEPR.

————Rees, H., and Shearer, A. (1999), *The Class of '81: The Effects of Early Career Unemployment on Subsequent Unemployment Experiences*, CASEpaper 32. London: London School of Economics.

Burns, D., and Taylor, M. (1997), 'Mutual Aid, Community Networks and the Informal Economy: Solution, Springboard or Threat?', Paper to the Social Policy Association 31st Annual Conference, University of Lincolnshire and Humberside,15–17 July 1997.

Burtless, G. (1996), *Does Money Matter? The Effect of School Resources on Student Achievement and Adult Success*. Washington: Brookings Institution.

Buss, D. M. (1994), *The Evolution of Desire: Strategies of Human Mating*. New York: Basic Books.

Bynner, J. and Parsons, S. (1997), *It Doesn't Get Any Better: The Impact of Poor Basic Skill Attainment on the Lives of 37-Year-olds*. London: The Basic Skills Agency.

Byrne, D. (1999), *Social Exclusion*. Oxford: Oxford University Press.

Campbell, N. (1999), *The Decline of Employment Among Older People in Britain*, CASEpaper 19. London: London School of Economics.

Card, D. and Krueger, A. (1995), *Myth and Measurement: The New Economics of the Minimum Wage*. Princeton: Princeton University Press.

Card, D. and Krueger, A. (1996), *Labour Market Effects of School Quality*, Working Paper. Princeton: Princeton University Press.

——Kramaz, R., and Lemieux, T. (1996), 'Changes in the Relative Structure of Wages and Employment: A Comparison of the United States, Canada and France', NBER Working Paper No. 5487. Boston: NBER.

Carleen, P., Gleeson, D., and Wardhaugh, J. (1992), *Truancy: The Politics of Compulsory Schooling*. Milton Keynes: Open University Press.

CASE and HM Treasury (1999), *Persistent Poverty and Lifetime Inequality: The Evidence*, CASEreport 5 and HM Treasury Occasional Paper 10. London: LSE and HM Treasury.

Casey, B. and Smith, D. (1995), *Truancy and Youth Transitions*. London: Policy Studies Institute.

Chanan, G., West, A., with Garratt, C., and Humm, J. (1999), *Regeneration and Sustainable Communities*. London: Community Development Foundation.

Chaskin, R. J. (1997), 'Perspectives on Neighbourhood and Community: A Review of the Literature', *Social Service Review* (Dec.).

Cherlin, A., Kiernan, K., and Chase-Lansdale, L. (1995), 'Parental Divorce in Childhood and Demographic Outcomes in Young Adulthood', *Demography* 32/3: 299–318.

Clark, T., Giles, C., and Hall, J. (2000), *Does Council Tax Benefit Work?* London: Institute for Fiscal Studies.

Clasen, J., Gould, A., and Vincent, J. (1997), *Long Term Unemployment and the Threat of Social Exclusion: A Cross-national Analysis of the Position of Long-term Unemployed People in Germany, Sweden and Britain*. Bristol: Policy Press.

Commission on Social Justice (1994), *Social Justice: Strategies for National Renewal*. London: Vintage.

Cook, M. and Johnson, P. (2000), *Saving for Retirement: How Taxes and Charges Affect Choice*. London: Financial Services Authority.

Cousins, C., Jenkins, J., and Laux, R. (1998), 'Disability Data from the Labour Force Survey: Comparing 1997–98 with the Past', *Labour Market Trends* (June), 321–35.

Crime Concern (2000), *Tackling Crime on Estates: Training Manual*. Swindon: Crime Concern.

Crosland, A. (1965), *The Future of Socialism*, (rev. edn.). London: Jonathan Cape.

Cullinford, C. and Morris, J. (1997), 'Peer Group Pressure Within and Outside School', *British Educational Research Journal*, 23/1: 61–80.

Daniel, S. (1995), 'Can Pre-school Education Affect Children's Achievement at Key Stage One?', *Oxford Review of Education*, 21: 163–78.

Danziger, S. and Gottschalk, P. (1995), *America Unequal*. Cambridge, Mass: Harvard University Press.

Darling, A. (1999), 'Rebuilding the Welfare State: The Moral Case for Reform', in G. Kelly (ed.), *Is New Labour Working?* London: Fabian Society.

Dearden, L. (1998), 'Ability, Family, Education and Earnings', IFS Working Paper 98/14. London: Institute of Fiscal Studies.

——Ferrier, J., and Meghir, C. (1997), 'The Effects of School Quality on Educational Attainment and Wages', mimeo. London: Institute of Fiscal Studies.

DEMOS (1997), *The Wealth and Poverty of Networks: Tackling Social Exclusion*. London: DEMOS.

Dennett, D. C. (1995), *Darwin's Dangerous Idea: Evolution and the Meanings of Life*. London: Allen Lane.

DETR (Department of the Environment, Transport and the Regions) (1998), *New Deal for Communities: Guidance for Pathfinder Applicants*. London: DETR.

——(2000*a*), *Towards an Urban Renaissance: The Report of the Urban Task Force*. London: DETR.

——(2000*b*), *Quality and Choice: A Decent Home for All—The Housing Green Paper*. London: DETR.

DfEE (Department for Education and Employment) (1997), *Excellence in schools*, Cm. 3681, London: HMSO.

——(1998*a*), *Permanent Exclusion from School in England 1996/97*, 451/98. London: DfEE.

——(1998*b*), *National Curriculum Assessments of 7, 11 and 14-Year-olds in England, 1997*, Statistical bulletin 4/98. London: TSO.

——(1999), *Statistics of Education: National Curriculum Assessments of 7, 11 and 14-Year-olds in England, 1998*. London: TSO.

——(2000), *National Curriculum Assessments of 7, 11 and 14-Year-olds in England, 1999*, Statistical Bulletin 03/2000. London: TSO.

Diamond, J. (1997), *Why is Sex Fun? The Evolution of Human Sexuality*. London: Weidenfeld and Nicolson.

Dickens, R. (1999), 'Poverty, Low Pay and the National Minimum Wage', in *The National Minimum Wage, Incomes and the Low Paid*, Low Pay Commission Occasional Paper 2. London: Low Pay Commission.

——(2000), 'Poverty and Low Pay', mimeo. Centre for Economic Performance, London School of Economics.

——Machin, S., and Manning, A. (1994), 'Minimum Wages and Employment: A Theoretical Framework with an Application to the Wages Councils', in S. Bazen and G. Benhayoun (eds.), 'Low Pay and Minimum Wages', *International Journal of Manpower*, 15, special issue: 26–48.

——————(1999), 'The Effects of Minimum Wages on Employment: Theory and Evidence from Britain', *Journal of Labour Economics*, 17/1: 1–22.

Disraeli, B. (1845), *Sybil or the Two Nations*. Oxford: Oxford University Press (World's Classics, 1981).

Dolton, P. and O'Neil, D. (1996), 'Unemployment Duration and the Restart Effect', *Economic Journal*, 106: 387–400.

——and Vignoles, A. (1996), *The Impact of School Quality on Labour Market Success in the UK*. Newcastle: University of Newcastle.

Dronkers, J. (1995), 'The Changing Effects of Lone Parent Families on the Educational Attainment of Their Children in a European State', *Sociology*, 28: 171–91.

DSS (Department of Social Security) (1995), *Households Below Average Income, 1979–1992/3*. London: TSO.

——(1997), *Home Responsibilities Protection Statistics 1994/95*. Newcastle: Analytical Services Division.

——(1998*a*), *New Ambitions for Our Country: A New Contract for Welfare*. Cm. 3805. London: HMSO.

——(1998*b*), *Households Below Average Income 1979–1996/7*. London: Corporate Document Services.

DSS (Department of Social Security) (1998c), *A New Contract for Welfare: Partnership in Pensions*, Cm. 4179. London: TSO.

——(1999a), *Opportunity for All: Tackling Poverty and Social Exclusion*, Cm. 4445. London: TSO.

——(1999b), *Social Security Statistics 1998*. London: TSO.

——(1999c), *The Pensioners' Income Series 1996/7*. London: Department of Social Security/Government Statistical Service.

——(2000a), *The Changing Welfare State: Social Security Spending*. London: TSO.

——(2000b), *Households Below Average Income 1994/5–1998/9*. London: Corporate Document Services.

——(2000c), *The Changing Welfare State: Pensioner Incomes*. Leeds: Corporate Document Services.

——(2000d), *Abstract of Statistics for Index of Retail Prices, Average Earnings, Social Security Benefits and Contributions*. London: Department of Social Security.

DTI (Department of Trade and Industry) (1999), *A Detailed Guide to the National Minimum Wage*. London: TSO.

Duffy, K. (1997), *Review of the International Dimension of the Thematic Priority on Social Integration and Exclusion*, Report to the Economic and Social Research Council. Swindon: ESRC.

Duncan, G. (1984), *Years of Poverty, Years of Plenty*. Ann Arbor: University of Michigan Press.

Dunn, J. and Plomin, R. (1990), *Separate Lives: Why Siblings Are So Different*. New York: Basic Books.

Durham, W. H. (1991), *Coevolution: Genes, Culture, and Human Diversity*. Stanford: Stanford University Press.

Dustmann, C., Rajah, N., and Smith, S. (1997), *Teenage Truancy, Part-Time Working and Wages*. London: Institute for Fiscal Studies.

Edwards, P. and Flatley, J. (eds.) (1991), *The Capital Divided: Mapping Poverty and Social Exclusion in London*. London: London Research Centre.

Ekinsmyth, C. and Bynner, J. (1994), *The Basic Skills of Young Adults*. London: Basic Skills Agency.

Elias, P. and Bynner, J. (1997), 'Intermediate Skills and Occupational Mobility', *Policy Studies*, 18.

Elliott, B. J. and Richards, M. P. M. (1991), 'Children and Divorce: Educational Performance, and Behaviour, Before and After Parental Separation', *International Journal of Law and the Family*, 5: 258–76.

EPI (Employment Policy Institute) (1998), *Employment Audit No. 8*. London: Employment Policy Institute.

Ermisch, J. (2001), 'Cohabitation and Childbearing Outside Marriage in Britain', in L. Wu and B. Wolfe (eds.), *Out of Wedlock: Causes and Consequences of Nonmarital Fertility*. New York: Russell Sage Foundation.

ESRC (Economic and Social Research Council) (1997), *Thematic Priorities Update 1997*. Swindon: ESRC.

Etcoff, N. (1999), *Survival of the Prettiest: The Science of Beauty*. New York: Doubleday.

Evans, H. (2001), *Sprouting Seeds: Outcomes from a Community-based Employment Programme*, CASEreport 8. London: London School of Economics.

Evans, M. (1995), *Out for the Count: The Incomes of the Non-household Population and the Effect of Their Exclusion from National Income Profiles*, Welfare State Programme Discussion Paper WSP/111. London: London School of Economics.

—— (1998), 'Behind the Rhetoric: The Institutional Basis of Social Exclusion and Poverty', *IDS Bulletin*, 29/1: 42–9.

—— Piachaud, D., and Sutherland, H. (1994), *Designed for the Poor: Poorer by Design? The Effects of the 1986 Social Security Act on Family Incomes*, Welfare State Programme Discussion Paper WSP/105. London: London School of Economics.

Evans, R. (1998), *Housing Plus and Urban Regeneration: What Works, How, Why and Where?* Liverpool: European Institute for Urban Affairs, Liverpool John Moores University.

Falkingham, J. and Hills, J. (eds.) (1995), *The Dynamic of Welfare: The Welfare State and the Life Cycle*. Hemel Hempstead: Harvester Wheatsheaf.

Featherstone, D. R., Cundick, B. P., and Rodgers, W. (1992), 'Differences in School Behaviour and Achievement Between Children from Intact, Reconstituted and Single Parent Families', *Adolescence*, 27: 1–12.

Feinstein, L. (1998*a*), *Pre-school Educational Inequality?* London: Centre for Economic Performance, London School of Economics.

—— (1998*b*), 'Which Children Succeed and Why?', *New Economy*, 5/2: 104–8.

—— (2000), *The Relative Economic Importance of Academic, Psychological and Behavioural Attributes Developed in Childhood*, CEP Discussion Paper 443. London: London School of Economics.

—— and Symons, J. (1997), *Attainment in Secondary Schools*. London: Centre for Economic Performance, London School of Economics.

Ferguson, R. F. and Dickens, W. T. (eds.) (1999), *Urban Problems and Community Development*. Washington: Brookings Institute Press.

Ferri, E. (ed.) (1993), *Life at 33: The Fifth Follow-up of the National Child Development Study*. London: National Children's Bureau.

Field, F. (1998), '*The Great Divide: The Future of Welfare Reform*', mimeo. Speech to the Social Market Foundation, 6 Aug.

Finn, J. D. and Achilles, C. M. (1990), 'Answers and Questions About Class Size: A State-Wide Experiment', *American Educational Research Journal*, 27/3: 557–77.

Fitz, J. and Gorard, S. (2000), *School Choice and SES Stratification of Schools: New Findings from England and Wales*, Paper presented to American Education Research Association, New Orleans.

—— Halpin, D., and Power, S. (1993), *Grant-Maintained Schools: Education in the Market Place*. London: Koogan Page.

Fletcher-Campbell, F. and Hall, C. (1990), *Changing Schools? Changing People? The Education of Children in Care*. Slough: NFER.

Ford, R. and Millar, J. (eds.) (1998), *Private Lives and Public Responses*. London: Policy Studies Institute.

Forrest, R. and Kearns, A. (1999), *Joined-up Places? Social Cohesion and Neighbourhood Regeneration*. York: Joseph Rowntree Foundation.

Fox, N. (1995), 'Professional Models of School Absence Associated with Home Responsibilities', *British Journal of Sociology of Education*, 16/2: 221–42.

Frank, S. A. (1998), *Foundations of Social Evolution*. Princeton: Princeton University Press.

Freed Taylor, M. (ed.) (2000), *British Household Panel Survey User Manual*, Vol. A. Colchester: Institute of Social and Economic Research, University of Essex.

Gallie, D., Marsh, C., and Vogler, C. (1994), *Social Change and the Experience of Unemployment*. Oxford: Oxford University Press.

Galloway, J. (1985), *Schools and Persistent Absences*. London: Pergamon Press.

Gardiner, K. (1997), *Bridges from Benefit to Work: A Review*. York: Joseph Rowntree Foundation.

——and Hills, J. (1999), 'Policy Implications of New Data on Income Mobility', *Economic Journal*, 109/453: F91–111.

Garnett, L. (1992), *Leaving Care and After*. London: National Children's Bureau.

Geis, K. and Ross, C. (1998), 'A New Look at Urban Alienation: The Effect of Neighbourhood Disorder on Perceived Powerlessness', *Social Psychology Quarterly*, 61/3.

Geronimus, A. T. and Korenman, S. (1992), 'The Socioeconomic Consequences of Teen Childbearing Reconsidered', *Quarterly Journal of Economics*, 107: 1187–214.

Gerwitz, S. (1998), 'Can All Schools be Successful? An Exploration of the Determinants of School Success', *Oxford Review of Education*, 24/4: 11–22.

——Ball, S. J., and Bowe, R. (1995), *Markets, Choice and Equity in Education*. Buckingham: Open University Press.

Gibson, T. (1996), *The Power in Our Hands*. Oxford: Jon Carpenter Publishing.

Giddens, A. (1998), *The Third Way: The Renewal of Social Democracy*. Cambridge: Polity Press.

Gillborn, D. (1996), *Exclusions from School*, Viewpoint no. 5. London: Institute of Education.

Gipps, C. and Gillborn, D. (1996), *Recent Research on the Achievements of Ethnic Minority Pupils*. London: HMSO.

Glenn, N. D. and Kramer, K. B. (1987), 'The Marriages and Divorces of Children who Divorce', *Journal of Marriage and the Family*, 49: 811–25.

Glennerster, H. (2001), United Kingdom Education 1997–2000, CASEpaper 50. London: London School of Economics.

——and Evans, M. (1994), 'Beveridge and his Assumptive Worlds', in J. Hills, J. Ditch, and H. Glennerster (eds.), *Beveridge and Social Security: An International Retrospective*. Oxford: Clarendon Press.

——Hills, J., and Travers, T., with Hendry, R. (2000), *Paying for Health Education and Housing: How does the Centre Pull the Purse Strings?* Oxford: Oxford University Press.

——Lupton, R., Noden, P., and Power, A. (1999), *Poverty, Social Exclusion and Neighbourhood: Studying the Area Bases of Social Exclusion*, CASEpaper 22. London: London School of Economics.

Goodman, A., Johnson, P., and Webb, S. (1997), *Inequality in the UK*. Oxford: Oxford University Press.

Gorad, S. and Fitz, J. (1998), 'The More Things Change... the Missing Impact of Marketisation?', *British Journal of Sociology of Education*, 19/3: 365–76.

Gordon, D., Adelman, L., Ashworth, K., Bradshaw, J., Levitas, R., Middleton, S., Pantazis, C., Patsios, D., Payne, S., Townsend, P., and Williams, J. (2000), *Poverty and Social Exclusion in Britain*. York: Joseph Rowntree Foundation.

Gore, C. and Figueiredo, J. (eds.) (1997), *Social Exclusion and Anti-Poverty Policy: A Debate*. Geneva: ILO.

Gray, G., Smith, A., and Rutter, M. (1980), 'School Attendance and the First Year of Employment', in L. Hersov and I. Berg (eds.), *Out of School*. Chichester: John Wiley.

Green, A. (1996), 'Aspects of the Changing Geography of Poverty and Wealth', in J. Hills (ed.), *New Inequalities: The Changing Distribution of Income and Wealth in the UK*. Cambridge: Cambridge University Press.

——and Owen, D. (1998), *Where are the Jobless? Changing Unemployment and Non-employment in Cities and Regions*. Bristol: Policy Press.

Green, F., Ashton, D., Burchell, B., Bryn, D., and Felstead, A. (1998), 'Are British Workers Getting More Skilled?', in A. B. Atkinson and J. Hills (eds.), *Exclusion, Employment, and Opportunity*, CASEpaper 4. London: London School of Economics.

Greenhough, P. and Hughes, M. (1998), 'Parents' and Teachers' Interventions in Children's Reading', *British Educational Research Journal*, 24/4: 379–98.

Gregg, P. (2000), *The Impact of Youth Unemployment on Adult Unemployment in the NCDS*. Department of Economics Working Paper No. 00/495. Bristol: University of Bristol.

——and Machin, S. (1997), 'Blighted Lives', *Centre Piece*, 2/1, Centre for Economic Performance, LSE: 15–17.

————(1998), *Child Development and Success or Failure in the Youth Labour Market*, CEP Discussion Paper 397. London: London School of Economics.

——Hansen, K., and Wadsworth, J. (1999), 'The Rise of the Workless Household', in P. Gregg and J. Wadsworth (eds.), *The State of Working Britain*. Manchester: Manchester University Press.

——Harkness, S., and Machin, S. (1999), *Child Development and Family Income*. York: Joseph Rowntree Foundation/York Publishing Services.

Gregory, I., Southall, H., and Dorling D. (1999), *A Century of Poverty in Britain 1898–1998: A Geographical Analysis*, mimeo. University of Bristol and Queen Mary's College, London.

Grundy, E., Ahlburg, D., Ali, M., Breeze, E., and Slogett, A. (1999), *Disability in Great Britain: Results from the 1996/97 Disability Follow-Up to the Family Resources Survey*, DSS Research Report No. 94. Leeds: Corporate Document Services.

Hales, J. and Collins, D. (1999), *New Deal for Young People: Leavers with Unknown Destinations*, Employment Service Research and Development Report, ESR21. Sheffield: The Employment Service.

Hall, P. A. (1997), 'Social Capital: A Fragile Asset', *Demos Collection*, Issue 12.

Halsey, A. H., Lauder, H., Brown, P., and Wells A. (eds.) (1997), *Education, Culture, Economy, and Society*. Oxford: Oxford University Press.

Hannah, L. (1986), *Inventing Retirement: The Development of Occupational Pensions in Britain*. Cambridge: Cambridge University Press.

Hannon, P. (1987), 'A Study of the Effects of Parental Involvement in the Teaching of Reading-Test Performance', *British Journal of Educational Psychology*, 57/1: 56–72.

Hanock, P. (1997), 'Building Home-School Liaison into Classroom Practice: A Need to Understand the Nature of the Teacher's Day', *British Educational Research Journal*, 24/4: 399–414.

Hanushek, E. (1986), 'The Economics of Schooling, Production and Efficiency in Public Schools', *Journal of Economic Literature*, 24: 114–117.

Harris, A. (1971), *Handicapped and Impaired in Great Britain*, Pt. I. Office for Population Censuses and Surveys. London: HMSO.

Harris, J. (1994), 'Beveridge's Social and Political Thought' in J. Hills, J. Ditch, and H. Glennerster (eds.), *Beveridge and Social Security*.

Harris, J. R. (1998), *The Nurture Assumption: Why Children Turn Out the Way They Do*. New York: Free Press.

Hasluck, C., McKnight, A., and Elias, P. (2000), *Evaluation of the New Deal for Lone Parents: Early Lessons from the Phase One Prototype—Cost Benefit and Econometric Analyses*, DSS Research Report 110. Leeds: Corporate Document Services.

Hastings, A., McArthur, A., and McGregor, A. (1996). *Less than Equal? Community Organisations and Estate Regeneration Partnerships*. Bristol: Policy Press.

Haveman, R. and Wolfe, B. (1994), *Succeeding Generations*. New York: Russell Sage.

Hedges, B., and Clemens, S. (1994), *Housing Attitudes Survey*. London: Department of the Environment.

Hedges, L. V., Laine. R. D., and Greenwald, R. (1994), 'Does Money Matter? A Meta-analysis of Studies of the Effects of Differential School Inputs on Student Outcomes', *Educational Researcher*, 23/3: 5–14.

Hendry, L., Roberts, W., Glendining, A., and Coleman, J. C. (1992), 'Adolescents' Perceptions of Significant Individuals in Their Lives', *Journal of Adolescence*, 15: 225–70.

Hibbert, A. and Fogelman, K. (1990), 'Future Lives of Truants: Family Formation and Health-related Behaviour', *British Journal of Educational Psychology*, 60/2: 171–9.

——Fogelman, K., and Maoner, O. (1990), 'Occupational Outcomes of Truancy', *British Journal of Educational Psychology*, 60/1: 23–36.

Hills, J. (1995), *Inquiry into Income and Wealth*, ii. York: Joseph Rowntree Foundation.

——(1997), *The Future of Welfare* (rev. edn.). York: Joseph Rowntree Foundation.

——(1998*a*), 'Does Income Mobility Mean that We Do Not Need to Worry About Poverty?', in A. B. Atkinson and J. Hills (eds.), *Exclusion, Employment and Opportunity*.

——(1998*b*), *Income and Wealth: The Latest Evidence*. York: Joseph Rowntree Foundation.

——(2000*a*), 'Taxation for the Enabling State', in *Public Policy for the 21st Century: Social and Economic Essays in Memory of Henry Neuburger*. Bristol: Policy Press.

——(2000*b*), *Reinventing Social Housing Finance*. London: Institute for Public Policy Research.

——(2001), 'Inclusion or Exclusion? The Role of Housing Subsidies and Benefits', *Urban Studies*, 38/11: 1,887–1,902.

——and Lelkes, O. (1999), Social Security, Selective Universalism and Patchwork Redistribution', in R. Jowell, J. Curtice, A. Park, and K. Thomson (eds.), *British Social Attitudes: The 16th Report*. Aldershot: Ashgate.

HM Government (1999), *Supporting Families* (Green Paper). London: TSO.

HM Treasury (1999*a*), *Access to Financial Services (Report of Policy Action Team 14)*. London: HM Treasury.

——(1999*b*), *The Modernisation of Britain's Tax and Benefit System (Tackling Poverty and Extending Opportunity)*. London: HM Treasury.

——(2000*a*), *Tackling Poverty and Making Work Pay: Tax Credits for the 21st Century (The Modernisation of Britain's Tax and Benefit System)*, No. 6. London: HM Treasury.

——(2000*b*), *The Pre-Budget Report*. London: HM Treasury.

——(2000*c*), *Comprehensive Spending Review*, Cm. 4807. London: TSO.

——(2001), *The Budget Report*. London: HM Treasury.

Hobcraft, J. (1998), *Intergenerational and Life-course Transmission of Social Exclusion: Influences of Childhood Poverty, Family Disruption, and Contact with the Police*, CASEpaper 15. London: London School of Economics.

——(2000), *The Roles of Schooling and Educational Qualifications in the Emergence of Adult Social Exclusion*, CASEpaper 43. London: London School of Economics.

——and Kiernan, K. (1999), *Childhood Poverty, Early Motherhood and Adult Social Exclusion*, CASEpaper 28. London: London School of Economics.

Horowitz, D. L. (1997), 'Self-Determination: Politics, Philosophy and Law', in I. Shapiro and W. Kymlicka (eds.), *Ethnicity and Group Rights*. New York: New York University Press, NOMOS, 39: 421–63.

House of Commons Select Committee on Education and Employment (2000), *Fourth Report*, HC (99–00). 60. London: TSO.

Howarth, C., Kenway, P., Palmer, G., and Street, C. (1998), *Monitoring Poverty and Social Exclusion: Labour's Inheritance*. York: York Publishing Services.

Huff Stevens, A. (1994), 'Persistence in Poverty and Welfare: The Dynamics of Poverty Spells: Updating Bane and Ellwood', *American Economic Review Papers and Proceedings*, 84: 34–7.

——(1999), 'Climbing Out of Poverty, Falling Back In: Measuring the Persistence of Poverty Over Multiple Spells', *Journal of Human Resources*, 34/3: 557–88.

Humphries, S. and Gordon, P. (1992), *Out of Sight: The Experience of Disability 1900–1950*. Plymouth: Northcote House.

Hyde, M. (1996), 'Fifty Years of Failure: Employment Services for Disabled People in the UK', *Work, Employment and Society*, 10/4: 683–700.

Industry in Education (1996), *Towards Employability: Addressing the Gap Between Young People's Qualities and Employer's Recruitment Needs*. London: Industry in Education.

Jarvis, S. and Jenkins, S. (1996), *Changing Places: Income Mobility and Poverty Dynamics in Britain*, Working Paper 96-19, ESRC Centre on Micro-Social Change. Colchester: University of Essex.

————(1997), *Marital Splits and Income Changes: Evidence for Britain*, ESRC Research Centre on Micro-Social Change Working Paper 97-4. Colchester: University of Essex.

————(1998), 'How Much Income Mobility is There in Britain?', *Economic Journal*, 108: 428–43.

————(1999), 'Marital Splits and Income Changes: Evidence for Britain', *Population Studies*, 53/2: 237–54.

Jenkins, S. (1999), 'Income Dynamics in Britain 1991–6', in *Persistent Poverty and Lifetime Inequality: The Evidence*, CASEreport 5/HM Treasury Occasional Paper No. 10. London: LSE and HM Treasury.

——(2000), 'Modelling Household Income Dynamics', *Journal of Population Economics*, 13/4.

——and Schluter, C. (2001), *Why Are Child Poverty Rates Higher in Britain Than in Germany? A Longitudinal Perspective*, Working Papers of the Institute for Social and Economic Research, 2001–16, University of Essex.

Jones Finer, C. and Nellis, M. (eds.) (1998), *Crime and Social Exclusion*. Oxford: Blackwell.

Jonsson, J. and Gahler, M. (1997), 'Family Dissolution, Family Reconstitution and Children's Educational Careers: Recent Evidence from Sweden', *Demography*, 34/2: 277–93.

Jordan, B. (1996), *A Theory of Poverty and Social Exclusion*. Cambridge: Polity Press.

Joshi, H. and Verropoulou, G. (1999), *Maternal Employment and Child Outcomes*, Paper presented at Equality in Action Seminar, 11 Downing Street. London: Centre for Longitudinal Studies.

Keese, M., Puymoyen, A., and Swaim, P. (1998), 'The Incidence and Dynamics of Low Paid Employment in OECD Countries', in R. Asplund, P. J. Sloane, and I. Theodossiou (eds.), *Low Pay and Earnings Mobility in Europe*. Northampton, Mass.: Edward Elgar.

Kestenbaum, A. (1997), *Disability-Related Costs and Charges for Community Care.* London: Disablement Income Group.

Keys, W., Harris, S., and Fernandez, C. (1996), *Third International Mathematics and Science Study (First National Report, Pt. I).* Slough: National Foundation for Education Research.

Kiernan, K. (1980), 'Teenage Motherhood: Associated Factors and Consequences', *Journal of Biosocial Science*, 12/4: 393–405.

——(1986), 'Teenage Marriage and Marital Breakdown: A Longitudinal Study', *Population Studies*, 40/1: 35–54.

——(1992), 'The Impact of Family Disruption in Childhood on Transitions Made in Young Adult Life', *Population Studies*, 46/2: 213–34.

——(1995), *Transition to Parenthood: Young Mothers, Young Fathers: Associated Factors and Later Life Experiences*, Welfare State Programme Discussion Paper No. 113. London: London School of Economics.

——(1996), 'Family Change: Parenthood, Partnership and Policy', in D. Halpern, S. Wood, S. White, and G. Cameron (eds.), *Options for Britain*. Aldershot: Dartmouth.

——(1997a), *The Legacy of Parental Divorce: Social, Economic and Demographic Experiences in Adulthood*, CASEpaper 1. London: London School of Economics.

——(1997b), 'Becoming a Young Parent: A Longitudinal Study of Associated Factors', *British Journal of Sociology*, 48/3: 406–28.

——(1999), 'Childbearing Outside Marriage in Western Europe', *Population Trends*, 98: 11–20.

——and Cherlin, A. (1999), 'Parental Divorce and Partnership Dissolution in Adulthood: Evidence from a British Cohort Study', *Population Studies*, 53/2: 39–48.

——and Estaugh, V. (1993), *Cohabitation, Extra-marital Childbearing and Social Policy*. London: Family Policy Studies Centre.

——and Hobcraft, J. N. (1997), 'Parental Divorce During Childhood: Age at First Intercourse, Partnership and Parenthood', *Population Studies*, 51/1: 41–55.

——and Mueller, G. (1999), 'Who Divorces?', in S. McRae (ed.), *Changing Britain: Families and Households in the 1990s*. Oxford: Oxford University Press.

——Land, H., and Lewis, J. (1998), *Lone Motherhood in the Twentieth Century: From Footnote to Frontpage*. Oxford: Oxford University Press.

Kinder, K., Wakefield, A., and Wilkin, A. (1996), *Talking Back: Pupils' Views on Disaffectional*. Slough: NFER.

King, D. (1995), *Actively Seeking Work? The Politics of Unemployment and Welfare Policy in the United States and Great Britain*. Chicago: University of Chicago Press.

Kleinman, M. (1998), *Include Me Out? The New Politics of Place and Poverty*, CASEpaper 11. London: London School of Economics.

——West, A., and Sparkes, J. (1998), *Investing in Employability: The Role of Business and Government in the Transition to Work*. London: BT/LSE .

Kumar, A. (1999), *Pension Reform in the UK: From Contribution to Participation*, Paper presented at Workshop in Tokyo, July.

Lareau, A. (1997), 'Social Class Differences in Family–School Relationships: The Importance of Cultural Capital', in A. H. Halsey, H. Lauder, P. Brown, and A. Wells (eds.) (1997), *Education, Culture, Economy, and Society*.

Lawless, P., Martin, R., and Hardy, S. (eds.) (1998), *Unemployment and Social Exclusion: Landscapes of Labour Inequality*. London: Jessica Kingsley.

Layte, R., Nolan, B., and Whelan C. (2000), 'Targeting Poverty: Lessons from Monitoring Ireland's National Anti-Poverty Strategy', *Journal of Social Policy* 29/4: 553–75.

Le Grand, J. (1991), *Equity and Choice*. London: HarperCollins.

——(1995), 'The Market, the State and the Distribution of Life Cycle Income', in J. Falkingham and J. Hills (eds.), *The Dynamic of Welfare: The Welfare State and the Life Cycle*. Hemel Hempstead: Prentice Hall.

Lee, P. and Murie, A. (1997), *Poverty, Housing Tenure and Social Exclusion*. York: Joseph Rowntree Foundation.

Leisering, L. and Leibfried, S. (1999), *Time and Poverty in Western Welfare States: United Germany in Perspective*. Cambridge: Cambridge University Press.

Lenoir, R. (1974), *Les Exclus*. Paris: Seuil.

Leslie, D. (1997), *Unemployment, Ethnic Minorities and Discrimination*. Florence: European University Institute.

Levacic, R. and Hardman, J. (1999), 'The Performance of Grant-Maintained Schools in England: An Experiment in Autonomy', *Journal of Education Policy*, 14/2: 185–210.

Levitas, R. (1996), 'The Concept of Social Exclusion and the New Durkheimian Hegemony', *Critical Social Policy*, 46: 5–20.

——(1997), 'Unemployment and Social Exclusion', mimeo. Paper presented at CASE seminar, Nov.

——(1998), *The Inclusive Society? Social Exclusion and New Labour*. Basingstoke: Macmillan.

LPC (Low Pay Commission) (1998), *The National Minimum Wage (First Report of the Low Pay Commission)*. London: TSO.

——(2000), *The National Minimum Wage: The Story So Far (Second Report of the Low Pay Commission)*. London: TSO.

Lumsden, C. J. and Wilson, E. O. (1981), *Genes, Mind, and Culture: The Coevolutionary Process*. Cambridge, Mass: Harvard University Press.

Macaskill, M. (2000), 'Black Market Takes Over in Slum Towns', *Sunday Times*, 30 April.

Maccoby, E. E. and Martin J. A. (1983), 'Socialization in the Context of the Family: Parent-Child Interaction', in P. H. Mussen (general ed.) and E. M. Hetherington (series ed.), *Handbook of Child Psychology, iv., Socialization, Personality and Social Development*. New York: John Wiley.

Mack, J. and Lansley, S. (1985), *Poor Britain*. London: Allen and Unwin.

Maclean, M. and Wadsworth, M. E. J. (1988), 'The Interests of Children after Parental Divorce: A Long-term Perspective', *International Journal of Law and the Family*, 2: 155–66.

Macnicol, J. (1998), *The Politics of Retirement in Britain 1878–1948*. Cambridge: Cambridge University Press.

Mansbridge, J. J. (1980), *Beyond Adversary Democracy*. New York: Basic Books.

Marsh, A. (2001), *Earnings Top-up Evaluation: The Synthesis Report*, Department of Social Security Research Report No. 135. Leeds: Corporate Document Services.

——and McKay, S. (1993), *Families, Work and Benefits*. London: Policy Studies Institute.

Martin, J. and White, A. (1988), *The Financial Circumstances of Disabled Adults Living in Private Households*. London: HMSO.

Marx, I. and Verbist, B. (1997), 'Low-paid Work, the Household Income Package and Poverty: A Cross-country Analysis', Paper presented at the LoWER conference, London, Dec.

Maughan, B. and Lindelow, M. (1997), 'Secular Change in Psychosocial Risks: The Case of Teenage Motherhood', *Psychological Medicine*, 27: 1129–44.

McInnes, C. and Toft, M. (1998), *Healthier Schools Partnership Project (Monitoring Report)*. London: Lewisham Education and Community Services.

McKenna, F. (2000), 'Who'll Benefit from the Cash in Hand Economy?', *New Start*, 14 April.

McKnight, A. (2000), *Trends in Earnings Inequality and Earnings Mobility, 1977–1997: The Impact of Mobility on Long-Term Inequality*, Employment Relations Research Report Series 8. London: Department of Trade and Industry.

——(2001*a*), 'A Widening Gulf between the Prospects of Rich and Poor Kids', mimeo. CASE, London School of Economics.

——(2001*b*), 'From Childhood Poverty to Labour Market Disadvantage', in J. Bynner, P. Elias, A. McKnight, H. Pan, and G. Pierre (eds.), *Changing Pathways to Employment and Independence*. York: Joseph Rowntree Foundation (forthcoming).

——Elias, P., and Wilson, R. (1998), *Low Pay and the National Insurance System: A Statistical Picture*. Manchester: Equal Opportunities Commission.

McLanahan, S. and Sandefur, G. (1994), *Growing Up with a Single Parent*. Cambridge, Mass: Harvard University Press.

Mead, L. (1997) (ed.), *The New Paternalism: Supervisory Approaches to Poverty*. Washington: Brookings Institution Press.

Meadows, S. and Dawson, M. (1999), *Teenage Mothers and Their Children: Factors Affecting Their Health and Development*. London: Department of Health.

Middleton, S. and Ashworth, K. (1997), *Small Fortunes: Spending on Children, Poverty and Parental Sacrifice*. York: Joseph Rowntree Foundation.

Millar, J. (2000), *Keeping Track of Welfare Reform: The New Deal Programme*. York: Joseph Rowntree Foundation.

——Webb, S., and Kemp, M. (1997), *Combining Work and Welfare*. York: Joseph Rowntree Foundation.

Miller, D. (1997), 'What Kind of Equality Should the Left Pursue?', in J. Franklin (ed.), *Equality*. London: IPPR.

Moore, M. H. (1999), 'Security and Community Development', in R. F. Ferguson and W. T. Dickens (eds.), *Urban Problems and Community Development*. Washington: Brookings Institution Press.

Mortimore, P. and Mortimore, J. (1983), 'Education and Social Class', in R. Rogers (ed.) (1986), *Education and Social Class*. East Sussex: Falmer Press.

——and Whitty, G. (1997), *Can School Improvement Overcome the Effect of Disadvantage?* London: Institute of Education.

——Sammons, P., Stoll, L., Lewis, D., and Ecob, R. (1988), *School Matters: The Junior Years*. London: Open Books.

Morton, T. (1991), *Dogs on the Lead: Good Practice for Dogs on Housing Estates*. London: Priority Estates Project.

Moser, C. (1999), *Improving Literacy and Numeracy: A Fresh Start*. London: DfEE.

Moss, P. and Tiley, C. (1995), *Soft Skills and Race: An Investigation of Black Men's Employment Problems*. New York: Russell Sage Foundation.

Moustaki, I. (1996), 'A Latent Trait and a Latent Class Model for Mixed Observed Variables', *British Journal of Mathematical and Statistical Psychology*, 49: 313–34.

Mueller, C. W. and Pope, H. (1977), 'Marital Instability: A Study of Its Transmission Between Generations', *Journal of Marriage and the Family*, 39: 83–93.

Murphy, M. (1984), 'The Influence of Fertility on Early Housing Career and Socio-economic Factors on Tenure Determination in Contemporary Britain', *Environment and Planning, A*, 16: 1303–18.

Murray, C. (1990), *The Emerging British Underclass*. London: Institute for Economic Affairs.

——(1999), *The Underclass Revisited*. Washington: AEI Press.

National Commission on Education (1996), *Success Against the Odds: Effective Schools in Disadvantaged Areas*. London: Routledge.

Neighbourhood Initiatives Foundation (1999), *Practical Tools for Community Action: Training Manual*. Telford: Neighbourhood Initiative Foundation.

Nickell, S. (1999), 'Unemployment in Britain', in P. Gregg and J. Wadsworth (eds.), *The State of Working Britain*. Manchester: Manchester University Press.

Noble, M. and Smith, G, (1996), 'Two Nations? Changing Patterns of Income and Wealth in Two Contrasting Areas', in J. Hills (ed.), *New Inequalities: The Changing Distribution of Income and Wealth in the UK*. Cambridge: Cambridge University Press.

Noden, P., West, A., David, M., and Edge, A. (1998), 'Choices and Destinations at Secondary Schools in London', *Journal of Educational Policy*, 13/2: 221–36.

Nolan, B. and Whelan, C. (1996), *Resources, Deprivation and Poverty*. Oxford: Oxford University Press.

O'Brien, M. and Jones, D. (1999), 'Children, Parental Employment and Educational Attainment: An English Case Study', *Cambridge Journal of Economics*, 23: 599–621.

OECD (Organisation for Economic Co-operation and Development) (1996), *Employment Outlook*. Paris: OECD.

——(1998), *Employment Outlook*. Paris: OECD.

——(2000), *Education At a Glance* (OECD indicators). Paris: OECD, London: TSO.

——(2001), *Knowledge and Skills for Life: First results from PISA 2000*. Paris: OECD.

OFSTED (Office for Standards in Education) (1993), *Access and Achievement in Urban Education*. London: HMSO.

——(1995), *Pupil Referral Units: The First Twelve Inspections*. London: HMSO.

——(1996), *Exclusion From Secondary Schools 1995/6*. London: HMSO.

O'Keefe, D. (1993), *Truancy in English Secondary Schools: A Report Prepared for the DfEE*. London: HMSO.

ONS (Office for National Statistics) (1999), *Birth Statistics 1998*, Series FM1 27.

Orchard, T. and Sefton, R. (1996), 'Earnings Data from the Labour Force Survey and the New Earnings Survey', *Labour Market Trends* (April): 161–74.

Osbourne, A. and St Claire, L. (1987), 'The Ability of Children Who Have Been in Care or Separated From Their Parents', *Early Child Development*, 28/3: 187–354.

Oxley, H. (1999), 'Poverty Dynamics in Four OECD Countries', in *Persistent Poverty and Lifetime Inequality: The Evidence*, CASEreport 5/HM Treasury Occasional paper No. 10. London: LSE and HM Treasury.

——Dang, T.-T., and Anton, P. (2000), *Poverty Dynamics in Six OECD Countries*. Paris: OECD.

Page, D. (2000), *Communities in the Balance: The Reality of Social Exclusion on Housing Estates*. York: Joseph Rowntree Foundation.

Parkin, M. (1979), *Marxism and Class Theory: A Bourgeois Critique*. London: Tavistock.

Parkinson, C. E. (1982), 'Rating the Home Environment of School Age Children: A Comparison With Cognitive Index and School Progress', *Journal of Child Psychology*, 23: 329–33.

Parsons, C. (1995), *National Survey of LEAs, Policies and Procedures for the Identification of and Provision for Children Who Are Out of School by Reason of Exclusion or Otherwise*. London: DfEE.

—— (1996), *Exclusions From School: The Public Cost*. London: Commission on Racial Equality.

—— (1998), 'Trends in Exclusion from school', *FORUM*, 40/1: 11–14.

Paugam, S. (1996), 'Poverty and Social Disqualification: A Comparative Analysis of Cumulative Social Disadvantage in Europe', *Journal of European Social Policy*, 6/4: 287–303.

—— (1998), 'La Dynamique de la disqualification sociale', *Science Humanities* (May).

Pearce, N. and Hillman, J. (1998), *Wasted Youth: Raising Attainment and Tackling Social Exclusion*. London: Institute for Public Policy Research.

Peters, M. (1996), ' "Social Exclusion" in Contemporary European Social Policy: Some Critical Comments', in G. Lavery, J. Pender, and M. Peters (eds.), *Exclusion and Inclusion: Minorities in Europe*. Leeds: International Social Policy Research Unit, Leeds Metropolitan University.

Piachaud, D. and Sutherland, H. (2000), 'How Effective is the British Government's Attempt to Reduce Child Poverty?', CASEpaper 38. London: London School of Economics.

———— (2001), 'Child Poverty in Britain and the New Labour Government', *Journal of Social Policy*, 30/1: 95–118.

Plomin, R. (1994), *Genetics and Experience: The Interplay Between Nature and Nurture*. Thousand Oaks: Sage.

—— DeFries, J. C., McClearn, G. E., and Rutter, M. (1997), *Behavioral Genetics* (3rd edn.). New York: W. H. Freeman.

Power, A. (1996), 'Area-based Poverty and Resident Empowerment', *Urban Studies*, 33/9.

—— and Mumford, K. (1999), *The Slow Death of Great Cities? Urban Abandonment or Urban Renaissance*. York: Joseph Rowntree Foundation.

—— and Tunstall, R. (1995), *Swimming Against the Tide: Polarization or Progress on 20 Unpopular Council Estates, 1980–1995*. York: Joseph Rowntree Foundation.

Priority Estates Project (2000), *The Caretaking Plus Guide*. London: Priority Estates Project.

Putnam, R. (1993), 'The Prosperous Community: Social Capital and Community Life', *American Prospect* (Winter).

Rahman, M., Palmer, G., Kenway, P., and Howarth, C. (2000), *Monitoring Poverty and Social Exclusion 2000*, New Policy Institute, 3rd Annual Report. York: York Publishing Services.

Reynolds, D., Sammons, P., Stoll, P., Barber, M., and Hillman, J. (1996), 'School Effectiveness and School Improvement in the United Kingdom', *School Effectiveness and School Improvement*, 7: 133–58.

Riccio, J., Friedlander, D., and Freedman, S. (1994), *GAIN: Benefits, Costs, and Impacts of a Welfare-to-Work Program (Executive Summary)*. New York: Manpower Demonstration Research Corporation.

Ridley, M. (1996), *The Origins of Virtue*. London: Viking.

Robertson, D. and Symons, J. (1996), *Do Peer Groups Matter? Peer Group Versus Schooling Effects on Academic Attainment*. London: Centre for Economic Performance.

Robinson, P. and Oppenheim, C. (1998), *Social Exclusion Indicators: A Submission to the Social Exclusion Unit*. London: Institute for Public Policy Research.

Rogers, R. and Power, A. (2000), *Cities for a Small Country*. London: Faber and Faber.

Room, G. (1995), *Beyond the Threshold: The Measurement and Analysis of Social Exclusion*. Bristol: Policy Press.

——(1999), *Social Exclusion, Solidarity and the Challenge of Globalisation*, Social Policy Papers, No. 27. Bath: University of Bath.

Rowntree, B. S. (1901), *Poverty: A Study of Town Life*. London: Macmillan.

Rutter, M. and Madge, N. (1976), *Cycles of Disadvantage*. London: Heinemann.

——Pickles, A., Murray, R., and Eaves, L. (2000), 'Testing Hypotheses on Specific Environmental Causal Effects on Behaviour', *Psychological Bulletin*, 127/3: 291–324.

Sammons, P. (1998), 'A note to the DfEE', Centre for Educational Research, LSE, mimeo.

——and Smees, R. (1998), 'Measuring Pupil Progress at Key Stage One: Using Baseline Assessment to Investigate Value Added', *School Leadership and Management*, 18/3: 389–407.

——Kysel, F., and Mortimore, P. (1981), *Education Priority Indices: A New Perspective*. London: Inner London Education Authority.

——West, A., and Hind, A. (1997), 'Accounting for Variations in Pupil Attainment at the End of Key Stage One', *British Educational Research Association Journal*, 23/4: 486–511.

Sampson, J. R. (1999), 'What "Community" Supplies', in R. F. Ferguson and W. T. Dickens (eds.), *Urban Problems and Community Development*. Washington: Brookings Institution Press.

Sayce, L. (2000), *From Psychiatric Patient to Citizen: Overcoming Discrimination and Social Exclusion*. Basingstoke: Macmillan.

Schluter, C. (1998), *Income-Dynamics in Germany, the USA and the UK: Evidence from Panel Data*, CASEpaper 8. London: London School of Economics.

Sen, A. (1992), *Inequality Re-examined*. Oxford: Clarendon Press.

——(2000), *Social Exclusion: Concept, Application and Scrutiny*, Social Development Paper No. 1. Manila: Asian Development Bank.

SEU (Social Exclusion Unit) (1997), *Social Exclusion Unit*, brochure. London: Cabinet Office.

——(1998a), *Rough Sleeping*. London: TSO.

——(1998b), *Bringing Britain Together: A National Strategy for Neighbourhood Renewal*. London: Cabinet Office.

——(1998c), *Truancy and School Exclusion*. London: TSO.

——(1999a), *Teenage Pregnancy*. Cm. 4342. London: TSO.

——(1999b), *Bridging the Gap: New Opportunities for 16–18-year-olds Not in Education, Employment or Training*. London: TSO.

——(2000), *National Strategy for Neighbourhood Renewal: A Framework for Consultation*. London: TSO.

Shepard, J. P. and Farrington, D. P. (1995), 'Preventing Crime and Violence: Pre-school Education, Early Family Support and Situational Crime Prevention Can Be Effective', *British Medical Journal*, 310/4: 271–2.

Shepherd, P. (1985), *The National Child Development Study: An Introduction to the Background to the Study and Methods of Data Collection*, NCDS User Support Group, Working Paper No. 1. London: City University.

Silver, H. (1995), 'Reconceptualising Social Disadvantage: Three Paradigms of Social Exclusion', in G. Rodgers, C. Gore, and J. B. Figueiredo (eds.), *Social Exclusion: Rhetoric, Reality, Responses*. Geneva: ILO.

Smart, C. and Stevens, P. (2000), *Cohabitation Breakdown*. London: Family Policy Studies Centre.

Smith, D. and Macnicol, J. (1999), *Social Insecurity and the Informal Economy*, Paper presented at the Annual Conference of the Social Policy Association.

Smith, G. (1999), *Area-based Initiatives: The Rationale For and Options For Area Targeting*, CASEpaper 25. London: London School of Economics.

Snow, C., Barnes. W., Chandler, J. Goodman, I. and Hemphill, L. (1991), *Unfulfilled Expectations: Home and School Influences on Literacy*. London: Harvard University Press.

Sparkes, J. and West, A. (2000), *An Evaluation of the Learning for Life Project*. London: Centre for Educational Research.

Stewart, M. B. (1998), 'The Dynamics of the Relationship between Low Pay and Poverty in Britain', mimeo. University of Warwick.

——(1999), *The Dynamics of Low Pay and Low Incomes*, Low Pay Commission, Occasional Paper 2. London: Low Pay Commission.

——and Swaffield, J. K. (1998), 'The Dynamics of Low Pay in Britain', in P. Gregg (ed.), *Jobs, Wages and Poverty*. London: Centre for Economic Performance, London School of Economics.

Stirling, M. (1992), 'Absent with Leave', *Special Children*, 52.

Sutherland, H. (2001), 'Five Labour Budgets (1997–2001): Impacts on the Distribution of Household Incomes and on Child Poverty', Microsimulation Unit Research Note MU/RN/41. www.econ.cam.ac.uk/dae/mu/mupubsrn.htm.

Sylva, K. (1994), 'School Influences on Children's Development', *Journal of Child Psychology*, 35: 135–70.

——and Hurry, J. (1995), *The Effectiveness of Reading Recovery and Phonological Training for Children with Reading Problems*. London: Institute of Education.

Tabberer, R. (1998), 'Poverty and Education: Evidence for Education's Role in Combating the Transmission of Poverty', in *Persistent Poverty and Lifetime Inequality: The Evidence*, CASEreport 5 and HM Treasury Occasional Paper No. 10. London: LSE/HM Treasury.

Taylor, M. (1995), *Unleashing the Potential: Bringing Residents to the Centre of Regeneration*. York: Joseph Rowntree Foundation.

——(1996), 'Community Organisations in Urban Regeneration: Does Empowerment Work?', Paper to 25th Annual Conference of ARNOVA, New York, 7–9 November.

Thake, S. (1995), *Staying the Course: The Roles and Structures of Community Regeneration Organisations*. York: Joseph Rowntree Foundation.

Therborn, G. (1986), *Why Some People Are More Unemployed Than Others*. London: Verso.

Thomas, S. and Mortimore, P. (1996), 'Comparison of Value Added Models for Secondary School Effectiveness', *Research Papers in Education*, 11/1: 279–95.

Thomas, S. and Smees, R. (1997), 'Dimensions of School Effectiveness: Comparative Analyses Across Regions', Paper presented at the 10th International Congress for School Effectiveness.

Thrupp, M. (1999), *School Making a Difference: Let's be Realistic*. Buckingham: Open University Press.

Tizard, B., Mortimore, J., and Burchell, B. (1981), *Involving Parents in Nursery and Infant Schools*. London, Grant McIntyre.

Tizard, J., Schofield, W., and Hewison, J. (1982), 'Collaboration Between Teachers and Parents in Assisting Children's Reading', *British Journal of Educational Psychology*, 52: 1–15.

Touraine, A. (1991), *'Face à l'exclusion'*, *Esprit*, 169: 7–13.

Townsend, P. (1979), *Poverty in the United Kingdom*. Harmondsworth: Penguin.

—— (1981), 'Employment and Disability: The Development of a Conflict Between State and People', in A. Walker and P. Townsend (eds.), *Disability in Britain: A Manifesto of Rights*. Oxford: Martin Robertson.

Turok, I. and Edge, N. (1999), *The Jobs Gap in Britain's Cities: Employment Loss and Labour Market Consequences*. Bristol: Policy Press and Joseph Rowntree Foundation.

UNICEF (2000), *Child Poverty in Rich Nations*. Florence: Innocenti Research Centre.

Utting, D. (ed.) (1999), *Communities that Care: A Guide to Promising Approaches*. London: Communities that Care.

Veit-Wilson, J. (1998), *Setting Adequacy Standards: How Governments Define Minimum Incomes*. Bristol: Policy Press.

Waldfogel, J. (1998), 'Early Childhood Intervention and Outcomes', in *Persistent Poverty and Lifetime Inequality: The Evidence*, CASEreport 5 and HM Treasury Occasional Paper No. 10. London: LSE/HM Treasury.

Walker, R. (1998), *Unpicking Poverty*, Paper prepared for Institute for Public Policy Research seminar 16/17 Feb. Loughborough: Centre for Research in Social Policy.

—— (ed.) (1999), *Ending Child Poverty*. London: Policy Press.

Ward, M. and Watson, S. (1997), *Here to Stay: A Public Policy Framework for Community-based Regeneration*. London: Development Trusts Association.

Warnock, M. (1978), *Report of the Committee of Enquiry into the Education of Handicapped Children and Young People*. London: HMSO.

Wedge, P. and Prosser, N. (1973), *Born to Fail*. London: Arrow Books.

Weinberg, A. and Ruano-Borbalan, J-C. (1993), 'Comprendre l'exclusion', *Sciences Humaines*, 28: 12–15.

Wellings, K., Wadsworth, J., Johnson, A., Field, J. *et al.* (1996), *Teenage Sexuality, Fertility and Life Chances (A Report Prepared for the Department of Health Using Data From the National Survey of Sexual Attitudes and Lifestyles)*. London: DoH.

West, A. (1995), 'How London Gets Smaller Classes', *Parliamentary Brief* (May) 52.

—— and Pennell, H. (1997), 'Educational Reform and School Choice in England and Wales', *Education Economics*, 5/3: 285–304.

—— —— (1998), 'School Admissions: Increasing Equity, Accountability and Transparency', *British Journal of Educational Studies*, 46/2: 188–200.

—— —— (2000), 'Publishing School Examination Results in England: Incentives and Consequences', *Education Statistics*, 26/4: 423–36.

—— Noden, P., Edge, A., and David, M. (1997), 'Parental Involvement in Education in and Out of School', *British Educational Research Journal*, 24/4: 461–84.

—— Pennell, H., West, R., and Travers, T. (1999), *The Financing of School-Based Education (End of Award Report to the ESRC: Main Findings)*. London: Centre for Educational Research, London School of Economics.

Whitty, G., Power, S., Gamarnikow, E., Aggleton, P. J., Tyrer, P., and Youdell, D. (1999), 'Health, Housing and Education', in A. Hayton (ed.), *Tackling Disaffection and Social Exclusion*. London: Koogan Page.

Wilkinson, D. (1998), 'Towards Reconciliation of NES and LFS Earnings Data', *Labour Market Trends* (May) 223–31.

Wilson, E. O. (1998), *Consilience: The Unity of Knowledge*. New York: A. A. Knopf.

Wilson, W. (1987), *The Truly Disadvantaged: The Inner City, the Underclass and Public Policy*. Chicago: University of Chicago Press.

Woolcock, S. (1998), 'Social Capital and Economic Development', *Theory and Society*, 27.

World Bank (1994), *Averting the Old Age Crisis*. Oxford: Oxford University Press.

Wright, L. (1997), *Twins: Genes, Environment and the Mystery of Identity*. London: Weidenfeld and Nicolson.

Young, M. and Lemos, G. (1997), *The Communities We Have Lost and Can Regain*. London: Lemos & Crane.

Index

Note: Page numbers for chapters are in **bold**. Most references are to **Britain**, except where otherwise indicated.

Index